RAVAGE

MacGillivray is the matrilineal Highland pen-name of writer, artist and musician Kirsten Norrie. Brought up internationally as well as living in both England and Northern Ireland, Norrie returned to Scotland after studying at the Ruskin School of Drawing and Fine Art, University of Oxford where she received a doctorate in Performance and Scottish Identity; her thesis was entitled *Cloth, Cull and Cocktail: Anatomising the Performer Body of 'Scotland'*. She moved back to Oxford in 2018 and founded The Oxford School of Poetry. She has tutored at the Poetry School, London, Edinburgh College of Art, Oxford University and the Royal College of Art.

She has edited a pamphlet by Kristján Norge, *The Demon Tracts* (Broken Sleep Books, 2023), and has published four books of poetry, including *The Last Wolf of Scotland* (Red Hen, USA, 2013; Pighog, UK) and three titles with Bloodaxe Books, *The Nine of Diamonds: Surroial Mordantless* (2016), *The Gaelic Garden of the Dead* (2019) and *Ravage: An Astonishment of Fire* (2023). A second novel, *An American Book of the Dead*, and a non-fiction work, *Scottish Lost Boys*, will be published by Broken Sleep Books in 2024 (as by Kirsten Norrie).

She has received several Creative Scotland awards and an RSA/Creative Scotland artist residency at Sabhal Mor Ostaig on the Isle of Skye to direct a Gaelic short film, *Aisling Sheòrais MhicDhòmhnaill*. In 2019, she was a writer in residence at the Fondation Jan Michalski, Switzerland. Her writing has appeared in publications such as Test Centre, *Magma*, *The Scotsman*, New River Press, *The Poetry Review* and *Modern Poetry in Translation*, and she has been featured on BBC Radio 3's *Late Junction* and *The Verb*. In 2020 a sonnet from *The Gaelic Garden of the Dead* was selected as one of the Scottish Poetry Library's *Best Scottish Poems* and the MacGillivray Archive will be housed at the SPL from 2023 onwards. Working in Gaelic, Norn, Orcadian, Shetlandic, English and Scots, she is a Gaelic learner.

MacGillivray

RAVAGE

AN ASTONISHMENT OF FIRE

BLOODAXE BOOKS

Copyright © MacGillivray 2023

ISBN: 978 1 78037 677 6

First published 2023 by
Bloodaxe Books Ltd
Eastburn
South Park
Hexham
Northumberland NE46 1BS

www.bloodaxebooks.com
For further information about Bloodaxe titles
please visit our website or write to
the above address for a catalogue.

The writer acknowledges support from Creative Scotland
towards the writing of this title.

Cover design: Neil Astley & Pamela Robertson-Pearce.

Printed in Great Britain by Bell & Bain Limited, Glasgow, Scotland, on
acid-free paper sourced from mills with FSC chain of custody certification.

For Ian MacGillivray

October 1920 — June 2021

&

Eilidh Ann MacGillivray

November 1952 — October 2021

Then a spirit passed before my face, the hair of my flesh stood up; it stood still, but I could not discern a form thereof; an image was before mine eyes.

– Job 4.15-16

CONTENTS

III. The Lighthouse Papers

IV. Additional Materials

V. Appendix

NOTE ON THE TEXT

In July 2022 I visited the island of Eilean a' Bhàis to inter the ashes of my grandfather and aunt in the clan MacGillivray enclave. Whilst going through the contents of two long-disused rooms in the lighthouse tower, I came across a remarkable set of objects, photographs and correspondence comprising hand-written scraps of paper divided into ten bundles; a star atlas of celestial metre compositions; a typed 1950 ms titled *Optik: A History of Ghost*; a typed 1961 untitled ms; a ship's loggbok belonging to Kristján Norge; eight ships' figureheads and the diary of Luce Moncrieff, whose family had leased the peat rights from the MacGillivrays for generations and who had worked as lighthouse keeper in the 1950s and early 1960s. She was joined latterly by poet Kristján Norge in 1960 and they briefly lived alongside one another, Norge tending donkeys and writing poetry; Moncrieff analysing shards of Neolithic remains from Bàs' several souterrains. Following the mysterious disappearance of Norge in 1961, the lighthouse lay abandoned from mid-1962 onwards and all within remained just as Moncrieff had left it, suggesting a sudden exit. Yet, prior to her own departure from Bàs, she painstakingly compiled, catalogued, annotated and typed up the bulk of his scattered body of work during January 1962. The diligence of Moncrieff in compiling these Norgesian elements is evident in the detailed diary she kept, documenting her discoveries, which formed the basis for a fictitious work, *The Wind of Voices*, published in the appendix of this book.

I am hugely indebted to Moncrieff for the monumental task she performed, in particular the partial piecing together of Norge's amnesiac system from fragments Norge had concealed in ten sites across the island and within the lighthouse itself, which were carefully typed up. My subsequent role as editor has been greatly eased and enhanced by Moncrieff's conscientious ordering of some of this sprawling corpus which evidences

Norge's outlying interests and productivity. I have selected items that might offer particular insight into the poet's thinking and a clarification of his process. The amnesiac system and relevant poems are here published under the title *Ravage*, as this term appears repeatedly in Norge's expansive notes. My overall findings can be divided into six distinct areas and are now held in the Kristján Norge Archive at the Scottish Poetry Library, Edinburgh, where they can be accessed with prior consent.

a) **Norge's Original Research**: these papers include notes for and the typescript of *Optik: A History of Ghost*; some unpublished, independent poems; his research into Dante, Giordano Bruno, variations of the tarot deck and mnemonics; extensive miscellaneous annotations.

b) **Norge's Pyrographic Dictations** which had been found at the ten sites marked on the map. Moncrieff painstakingly collated these pyrographic writings, which also included fragments of morse code, and aligned them as the ten sequences that form the first part of *Ravage*, enabling me to edit what became the *Ravage* ms more straightforwardly.

c) **Written Fragments** which were extracted from the lighthouse walls in the upper rooms and transcriptions of markings made by Norge on the walls.

d) **Norge's Loggbok** which has proved essential in creating a timeframe for the compositions undertaken and for rarer accounts of the actual events surrounding his disappearance.

e) **Norge's Popular Star Atlas** which shows his celestial metre compositions derived from constellations whose mythology relates to the individual IA figureheads.

f) **Other Artefacts** including some of Norge's belongings, maps and select correspondence.

KEY TO PRONUNCIATIONS

Eilean a' Bhàis (Isle of the Dead: yellen a vaash)
Bàs (shortened version of Eilean a' Bhàis: rhymes with 'pass')
Monmhur (meaning to murmur: Mon*voohr*)
Kristján Norge (Kristyan Norguh)
Sluagh nam Marbh (Host of the Dead: *Slooach nam Marvh*)
Port nam Marbh (Port of the Dead: *Port nam Marvh*)

INTRODUCTION

June 1961. Vulnerable to several frightening esoteric encounters, an obscure poet notes in his battered ship's loggbok: 'All we have is our own experience, that is what shapes the nature of our reflexion.' The poet is Kristján Norge, newly convinced he is a demon. 'I can now ignite my overcoat at will,' he claims, 'and it flares wildly in varying lunisolar colours... I would like to pour moonlight through these seams of salt, sipped at by an old sea, seething with magic. *Cha loisg teine, grian, no gealach mi*: no fire, no sun, no moon shall burn me,' Norge adds, underlining in soft pencil this traditional Gaelic charm which was to prove vital to him.

According to several of these 'loggbok' entries, Norge periodically falls asleep in the dying embers of the lighthouse fireplace on the outer Hebridean island of Eilean a' Bhàis, its rough terrain providing a stark backdrop to the poet's untimely demise. 'Stony outcrops of lava fields form this basal wreck of an island volcano,' he observes, 'whose ominous dead eye reminds the mainlanders that Bàs might indeed hold a portal to the underworld. Harsh winds bluster across this lunar landscape, burdened by the struggling bodies of determined sea birds. Perhaps it is their cries which invoke this malefic westerly wind of voices, the "Sluagh nam Marbh" or Host of the Dead.'

Evidently it is the Sluagh Norge feels disturbed by, and yet it is the Sluagh which apparently catalyses his final work: an orphic system he claims is imparted to him by one of their fallen flock.

Kristján Norge was born in Sudheim on Shetland to a Norwegian father and Shetlandic mother on November 30th, 1920. Uprooted as a child, he led a nomadic existence but was drawn to the Scottish Gaelic culture of his maternal great-grandparents who were crofters on the Isle of Harris. In adulthood he settled in Edinburgh before relocating to the remote Eilean a' Bhàis, there joining lighthouse-keeper Luce Moncrieff in the summer of 1961. Compelled to research Bàs as a 'mnemonic portal', the island provided an isolation and bleakness that contrasted starkly with his more urbane Edinburgh life. Despite entering a brief spell of psychoanalysis in 1960, Norge now showed signs of recurring distress. The intensive solitude of this remote island existence inevitably left its mark on Norge whose sporadic disturbances grew more frequent, abruptly culminating in a breakdown. Overnight, the poet became persuaded he was a demon. Subject to mounting internal pressures, Norge then feverishly set to work on a poetic tract he believed was given to him by the Sluagh. By the close of 1961, he had vanished.

Kristján Norge would leave behind a fragmented legacy. His early poetry is defined by explorations of estranged selfhood and vision typified by the opening long-form poem included in this book: *Optik: A History of Ghost*, written in 1950. Norge's subsequent output is focussed around a second, later composition, *Ravage*, completed in 1961. A campaign to secure his survival through the construction of a complex amnesiac ritual, *Ravage* remains his seminal achievement. From it, I evolved this book's overall title: *Ravage: An Astonishment of Fire*. Both texts are soaked in fiery residue: *Ravage*, with its series of smoking mirrors and *Optik* from the charred position of an effigy on an execution pyre. The phrase 'an astonishment' is borrowed from Norge's line 'astonished fire still cold, still distant' and so the encompassing title *Ravage: An Astonishment of Fire* seems a fitting one.

In making the current selection, I have presented what I feel to be the most pivotal of Norge's themes from early in his career, evident in *Optik: A History of Ghost*, and those in his final and thorny endeavour, which I have titled *Ravage*. I hope to shed light on the full range of ideas his writing encompassed by arranging epiphenomenal content that clearly demonstrates Norge's own 'ravaged' poetic state. The assemblage of materials which follows the two works by Norge is intended to clarify and enrich the diad of poetry manuscripts with photographs, maps, correspondence and notes, including an extended essay on Norge's amnesiac practice. Though undoubtedly a uniquely disturbed

14

individual, Norge nonetheless maintained a prolific output until his sudden disappearance during the winter of 1961. This aspect of his poetic drive, coupled with a noticeable deterioration, warranted the placing of *Ravage* after *Optik: A History of Ghost* in the collection.

Optik: A History of Ghost

Composed in 1950, *Optik: A History of Ghost* is a meditation on Greek optics, horary ghostliness and fiery illumination. According to Kristján Norge, the poem stages three conditions, *Glance/Glint/Glare,* and these relate to the power of sight, 'the glancing blow on armour, the glint of fire and the glare of the ghost. *Glance* is the deflected spark from a struck breastplate; *Glint*, coined by Robert Burns, is the incendiary touch of flame; *Glare* is the full blaze of the word: the "word made spirit". They serve as volatile flash points to enflame hauntedness.' Norge adds: 'the ignition of these states depends on the viewpoint of the reader. Glyphs catch light in sentient air.' Though on an initial reading *Optik* seems to be a corrected first draft typescript, Norge's compositional technique deliberately created multifarious choices for his readership, 'as if grasping for sight'. This fractured authorship, full of the syntax of the forbidden, creates 'uncertain stepping stones, bewildered paths and broken tracks through the ashen trails of eyesight'. The writer and reader pick their way through, choosing uncertain pathways through this 'smouldering, freshly-lit poem' that might change on each encounter. Norge gives scant assistance to the reader: his crossings-out, slashings and underlinings, bracketed alternatives and lines made bold, sometimes clarify, sometimes 'deliberately occult or occlude the poem, like a flame dipping in and out of existence in a draught,' he writes. Framing these conditions, Norge divided his typescript into three headings, *The Occluded*, *The Occulted* and *The Ocular*, and extracted a 'dross' from each section of edited material to 'roughly attempt an alchemical poesis'.

According to Norge's annotations, he alights on the Greek spelling 'optik' as an overall working title. Though an alternative might have been the Newtonian 'optick', with its allusion to the magical, it is the primal flame of Greek optics which focusses the typescript. Clearly, Norge immerses himself in these expansive and co-mingled spheres of optics and hauntology, grounding his approach in classical thought. He embarks on this ocular exploration with Cicero's assertion in mind: 'the air itself sees together with us', whilst citing Empedocles' penetrating, optical vignette:

> as when a man, thinking to go out through the wintry night, makes ready a light, a flame of blazing fire, putting round it a lantern to keep away all manner of winds, but the light, the finer substance, passes through and shines on the threshold with unyielding beams, so at that time... primeval fire, enclosed in membranes, gave birth to the round pupil in its delicate garments which are pierced through with wondrous channels. These kept out the water which surrounds the pupil, but let through the fire, the finer part.

Yet Norge strays far from the precincts of classical fieriness when he becomes absorbed by 17th-century 'alchemical palingenesis'. This highly experimental process purportedly resurrects human life from the ashes of blood, using exhaled salts to reconstruct homunculi. The method is rooted in arboreal ash, from which renewed forms can allegedly be grown. Working in the 1500s, the Swiss alchemist and physician known as Paracelsus outlines a procedure in the sixth book of his *Hermetic and Alchemical Writings*, titled *Concerning the Resuscitation of Natural Things*. Surveying the hard-won merits of this process, he comments that 'the resuscitation and restoration of wood is difficult and arduous' but that with due care, the evaporated matter; three parts mercury, sulphur and salt, can create a 'tree or little log' whose 'nature is higher than the original one.' He continues:

> this is really wood, and is called resuscitated, renewed, and restored wood. It was from the beginning wood, but

mortified, destroyed, and reduced to coals, to ashes – to nothingness; and yet from that nothingness it is made something, and is reborn.

Astrologer Jacques Gafferel sets out his own succinct methodology of palingenesis in *Unheard-of Curiosities Concerning the Talismanical Sculpture of the Persians, the Horoscope of the Patriarchs, and the Reading of the Stars*, published in London in 1650, which involves a hermetically sealed jar filled with the ash of a rose:

> holding it over a lighted candle, so soon as ever it began to feel the heat, you should presently see the ashes begin to move; which afterwards rising up, and dispersing themselves about the glass, you should immediately observe a kind of little dark cloud; which dividing itself into many parts, it came at length to represent a rose. But so fair, so fresh, and so perfect a one, that you would have thought it to have been as substantial and as odoriferous a rose, as any grows on the rose-tree.

In particular, the occult experimentation undertaken by English courtier, philosopher and scientist, Sir Kenelm Digby, attracts the attention of Norge who avidly reads around Digby's phantasmic descriptions and his discourse on 'unguentum armarium', or sympathetic powder, a salve which could be used as a healing balm by applying it to the weapon which caused the wound. Norge notes, with some delight, 17th-century chemist Robert Boyle's supposition that 'alchemical palingenesis' may account for the resurrection of Christ and is equally drawn to the ideas of Sir Thomas Browne, who observes in the *Religio Medici*:

> the forms of alterable bodies in these sensible [of or relating to the senses] corruptions perish not; nor, as we imagine, wholly quit their mansions, but retire and contract themselves into their secret and inaccessible parts, where they may best protect themselves from the action of their antagonist.

This assertion provides rich terrain, although Norge would have his protagonist given insight by fire, not protected from it. Here mention is made of 'mansions' and the allusion inevitably embeds itself in Norge's imagining to stimulate an underlying fascination with ancient Arabic astrological lunar mansions and classical mnemonics which were later to emerge in the distorted language of *Ravage*. Browne's glass evidently holds tangible knowledge rather than merely displaying a theatre of dream – he concludes:

> this is that mystical philosophy, from whence no true scholar becomes an atheist, but from the visible effects of nature, grows up a real divine, and beholds not in a dream, as Ezekiel, but in an ocular and visible object the types of his resurrection.

Such 'ocular and visible' revelation cited by Browne heralds a tertiary focus for Norge, who now discovers the papers of Jedburgh-born scientist, Sir David Brewster, father of experimental optics who invented the telescope. Of especial interest to the poet are letters from Brewster to Sir Walter Scott dispelling 'natural magic', first published in 1832. Norge is intrigued by letters twelve and thirteen, among the most engaging in their correspondence. Writing on luminosity, Brewster pens:

> when he sees his own shadow opposite to the sun upon a mass of thin fleecy vapour passing near him, it not only imitates all his movements, but its head is distinctly encircled in a halo of light. The aerial figure is often not larger than life, its size and apparent distance depending, as we shall afterwards see, upon particular causes. I have often seen a similar shadow when bathing in a bright summer's day in an extensive pool of deep water. When the fine mud deposited at the bottom of the pool is disturbed by the feet of the bather, so as to be disseminated through the mass of water in the direction of his shadow, his shadow is no longer a shapeless mass formed upon the bottom, but a regular figure formed upon the floating particles of mud, and having the head surrounded with a halo, not only luminous, but consisting of distinct radiations.

Norge uses a triad of sources to conjure up his unlikely protagonist, collapsing the fire-drenched optics of Greek antiquity with 17th-century hermetic manifestation and 19th-century

Scottish scientific enquiry. The reader is confronted with an entity born partially from an Empedoclean volcanic vision, partially from occult saline ash, and in part from the exchange between Scott and Brewster on spontaneous combustion which references a 'John Christ.' – an abbreviation of John Christopher Sturmius, the 17th-century mathematician:

> John Christ. Sturmius informs us, in the *German Ephemerides*, that in the northern countries of Europe flames often evaporate from the stomachs of those who are addicted to the drinking of strong liquors.

Norge's notes detail 'Empedocles as a lunar visitant to Dante's displaced memorial wood, having been rejected by Mount Etna'. 'The philosopher's lantern becomes the sealed glass in which alchemical moon dew is collected and heated by volcanic fire. In it, grows John the Baptist, a cephalophore grown in a strange experiment from the ash and salt of visual perception whose oracular head heralds the arrival of the desert poet Christ,' writes Norge. 'I give my speaker the first person descriptor EYE.' This outlandish personification deliberately evokes the combined presence of John the Baptist and Jesus Christ. In Norge's mind, the Baptist's locust skins are analogous to those humanly perceived ghosts described by the Roman poet Lucretius in *De Rerum Natura*. Through allusions to John the Baptist's desert diet, Christ manifests as an atomised desert mirage of locusts.

However, there is a further element, which is that 'John Christ' evolves into the condemned Joan of Arc, another personification of the spirit of fire. Just as 'John Christ' is John the Baptist of Lucretian spirit locusts merging with Jesus Christ the desert wraith, now combined they flicker into a third and conclusive spectre of Joan of Arc, blinking in wet ash. All three are textually revived in a chemical glass of salts, ash and a secret substance that grows reluctant phantasmic anatomies. It is the human impression of Joan and John which is envisaged through Christ as anamorphous. Drawing on Greek optics, the central voice of John Christ/Joan of Arc speaks when tied to the pyre, waiting for it to be lit, and considers whether their vision ignites a distant, burning town or whether, in fact, this town ignites their vision. (This, Norge based on Pisa whose church, according to Brewster in Letter XIII, was kindled by fetid bird droppings: 'Casati likewise relates, on good authority, that the fire which consumed the great church of Pisa was occasioned by the dung of pigeons that had for centuries built their nests under its roof.') Relating to Greek descriptions of illuminated shadow in water and Brewster's triturated charcoal, the pyre is a pool of charcoal which has adopted the unguent property of fluid. So, the candescent visionary is flaring water. On the one hand, John Christ/Joan of Arc stands in a pool and their shadow incorporates a dimly shining halo as a metaphor – an optical experiment – on the other, the pool is composed of roasted charcoal (traces of the execution pyre), stuff so fine, that it emulates an unguent liquid. The 'Eye' also perhaps alludes to Norge's own seeing heart and the dead volcano, overgrown forest, ashen desert and smoke-filled execution site, derelict terrains of keen emotive perception. 'The heart of sight,' he writes, 'is the burning core of self-perception: illuminate with love on the one hand, condemned to the pyre of regret, logic, blindness or bitterness, on the other. To attempt a vital re-ignition from the ash of such experience is emotional palingenesis… a kind of disgorged or disgorging heart of awareness. Perhaps I can mould a new heart from the poetic dross.' Not immune to reusing imagery, Norge borrows from *Optik* the heart 'suspending vein' for his much later demon poem which he composes in celestial metre as part of *Ravage* in 1961. Only, in the first appearance the vein trembles and by the second it is fully severed, possibly indicating his subsequent state of mind.

Working on *Optik*, Norge has to hand two more resonant sources: in his box of papers is a French Victorian print depicting St Dionysius at Heliopolis seated on the top of a tower, observing a distant, crucified Christ through his telescope. Executed *circa* 250 AD on the 'Hill of Mercury and Mars' (Mons Mercurii et Mons Martis), Dionysius lifted up his decollated head, according to the 13th-century *Golden Legend*, which preached a sermon on the long descent. For Norge, 'he was a cephalophore whose decapitation produced a natural glow, part-nimbus, part-aureole, that haloed the distance between his severed head and neck as if the ring around a missing planet, or to mark the age of an oak'. Also among Norge's possessions is a well-thumbed copy of August Strindberg's 1897 *Inferno* extracted from his *Occult Diary* which the Swedish dramatist kept from 21st February 1896 to 11th July 1908. In retrospect, the entry *The Fall and Paradise Lost* seems to partially mirror or inform Norge's later predicament on the Bàs island shoreline. 'One evening,' records Strindberg (who was subsequently to leave his abode, 'naked as a little John the Baptist'):

> sitting alone before my microscope, something occurred that made a deep impression on me, even though at the time I did not understand it. For four days I had been allowing a walnut to germinate, and I had then detached the embryo. Shaped like a heart, and no bigger than a pear pip, it lies between the two seed-lobes which also closely resemble a human heart. Imagine my emotion, when, on the slide, I saw two tiny hands, white as alabaster, raised and clasped as if in prayer. Was it a vision? A hallucination?

'Sight is watermarked in flame,' explains Norge in a pencilled footnote – almost as if addressing August himself – 'visions are highly combustible, though the air of our era is very tired, we live in trapped squares of black and white fire. The Ghost is both vividly holy and vividly unholy, an inflamed seer whose luciferous halo, grown in domed glass, is encrusted with tarry locusts.'

Here Norge cross-references the Miltonic host of Lucifer's fallen angels in Book 1 of *Paradise Lost* described as 'a pitchy cloud of locusts, warping on the eastern wind'. Perhaps Norge's alchemical ash is an ash of ipseity, warped in the glass of over-heated cognisance to materialise a fetch or double, one very much more apparent in his ultimate text, *Ravage*, as the bloated corpse of the *co-choisiche*, the Gaelic co-walker, whose attendant crawling locusts are a Hebridean swarm of delirious angels.

Ravage

In the early 1960s, following a critical wounding of his self-awareness, Kristján Norge constructs an amnesiac structure to obliterate his newly revealed demonic state. Subsequently titled *Ravage*, this terminal manuscript comes into being across several tempestuous months during 1961 and is eventually divided into two parts as per Norge's notes: *Speculum Ante* (front of mirror) and *Speculum Retro* (reverse of mirror). *Speculum Ante* draws together a functional amnesiac scheme of ten Sluagh Sequences constituting prose 'cellae', within which a clear square of unprinted page becomes a bier or altar and placed on it, a central 'imago agens', or an image with agency: akin to a moving statue. In classical mnemonics, 'imagines agentes' (plural) are highly memorable images which perform in order to provoke recollection of the information they reference. A palace, temple or mansion is built in the mind of a rhetor and in it were placed imaginary objects – often excessively bloody or obviously beautiful so as to imprint the memory clearly. Attached to these imagines agentes (IA) are sequences of the speech to be recalled. IA are used to provoke memory. Additionally, within rhetoric, they are 'phantasiai', fictitious images which are emotionally driven, leaving a powerful impact on the memory. For Norge, both the emotive and visual memory is crucial. In order to forget his demonic self-awareness, administered to him by the Sluagh nam Marbh, he feels compelled to reverse this ancient memory system, finally outworking his cellae IA as physical objects in the form of ten salvaged or carved ship's figureheads. Prefacing these ten sequences are ten short poems positioned as interlinking 'pharographic' mirrors flashing coded messages specifically generated by his Sluagh visitant 'Monmhur' as part of the mnemonic reversal.

Alternatively, the metaphoric numbing or chilling of memory Norge so desperately wishes to attain, differs strikingly from these thermal trials with the Sluagh – conveyors of active summoning which inflict the damage Norge wears: the remembered acknowledgement of his demonhood. It is as if, lying hallucinatory and hurt in his own imagination, he regains consciousness from time to time, at first unaware of this open sore until recollection of it pierces his forgetting. To use the Gaelic phrasing; the heat is upon him. For Norge, it is a critically vital operation: he describes removing diabolic realisation as 'akin to cutting the scorch mark out of a blanket'. His personal sentience, raw and barely protected, enervates a brief altercation with his own fragility. Akin to Kenelm Digby's wound balm, the alchemical weapon in Kristján Norge's case is the burning demonic recollection he has been served and the succour to be applied to this fatal self-knowledge: a numbing salve of procedural lethe, practical forgetfulness, a schema of amnesia, or structured oblivion.

The Lighthouse Papers

These additional materials were selected from Norge's papers and belongings found at the Bàs lighthouse. They include items that might elucidate his thinking and process. Some have been published elsewhere in essay form as part of my own research into Norge; others are reproduced here for the first time.

The Wind of Voices

An account of Luce Moncrieff's existence with Norge – based on her diary – is published in an appendix for the reader's interest, titled *The Wind of Voices*.

I

OPTIK: A HISTORY OF GHOST

Kristján Norge, 1950 (ms 1.01)

The Occluded

I

My/Indubitable heart, though **Eye** see ~~heart~~-charred in the ~~volcanic~~ rubble,
a life ~~heart rubbed to seed~~, reduced to ash –
do not tremble hard/now, on your plucked,
suspending **vein**.

{as if to be regrown from reheated (stoppered) Empedoclean lava ash}

~~And~~/For those seeds in the sorrow will redouble//
<u>For those sorrowing seeds will redouble</u>
and **the** vineyards/woods/orchards ~~gardens~~ **will** [*forcibly*] spring
in winter, {'s stoppered ~~blue~~ flame.}
though ice cloys the blackened vine.

Troubling heart,
in the ~~day's fire~~ heat of day find me,
in the leopard,
and ~~in~~ the wheat~~ed/vial/glass~~. {find me, in the leopard/ and the wheat}

Eye would but love
would seed you not:
hard-bitten
<u>out</u> ~~of~~/from death. {Eye would but love/ would seed you not,/ hard-bitten/
        out of death}

Yet, how many ~~hands/loves~~/lives, dispersed ~~in water/in air~~, to air
can reignite/~~conflagrate~~ in ash?
Coppiced rods will consecrate the ground
~~the~~ your woods have only dreamt above. {Yet, how many lives, dispersed to
        air, can reignite in ash?}

31

Though fear has ~~camped~~ hard t/urned within ~~my~~ you, my heart,
turning /in ~~the~~/your song-blossom's bitter ~~branches~~ leaves,
do not ~~disbelieve~~ yield {to extinguishment},
the fruit/salt of your ash will seed.

{though fear has camped/within you, my heart,/turning in your song-blossom's/
  bitter leaves}

II

1. Snowdrops ~~line/at~~ envelop the {~~the dead~~}
volcano mouth, droop low
among obsidian.

OR

2. Snowdrops pearl the <u>mouthing</u> volcano, {implies life: *scratch*}
expose my thought
to <u>cold</u> air.

~~Ash~~ Snow chafes the <u>cold</u> crater
performing/pretending
skins of circling ash.

~~Ash rains hard~~
~~from the cold crater~~
~~in soft, memorial snow~~.

Whose *snow* leopard and timber wolf, {of Dante's mnemonics: but lust made
  pure by snow}
a leoculus ~~lion~~ <u>scruffed/pad/bled/spoored</u> {exchange: Leoculus: a miniaturised
  beast}
in/on softening, {memorial} snow

32

Somewhere the lion, ruffed. {Sorrow colours the lion//blistering in old wheat}
Somewhere the wolf grows strong/young
and the leopard rises, when replete,
settles on refreshed gnawing.

III

Eye, ~~fire~~/lava-returned,
trail/track/traik my lost transferal.
~~within the lantern ash mote of a~~
My lantern holds/~~withholding~~ ash motes turned to moth,
~~insects whir~~ whirring as if near a ~~as a~~ dangerous flame

that dreams of a ~~man~~/ghost/~~skull/head~~ disgorging fire,
as half-sleeping winter still burns on cold fuel,
old woods shuddering through banded smoke,
where fire-winked birds, drinking sorrow,
flame-hocked finches, dissolving madrigal/miracle
my rain-charred sleep has dreamed of, dreamed and burnt,
clouds of song risen through smouldering trees,
where moon-berries, icy-bright, return
as the skull-haunted birds, fighting, re-seed them
in skilled sleep, winter-thorned, but unbroken,
as the skin of the flame bends to the knife,
Eye have woken.

IV

Rise <u>up</u>, disgorger of dream~~t~~/ing fire
get <u>up</u>, **g**ather ~~up your~~/my [gather up the} lantern.
The ~~moon-dark~~ glancing woods ~~now lie open~~ are pensive, deep,
brooding as the sullen leopard, bitter in Orion. ~~the smoke,~~
Volcano dust ~~have~~ has wreathed ~~your~~/the wound ~~the wounds~~
of my sleep, ~~the~~ paled the *coal*-charred ~~mafic~~ **oracle**,

33

which now lies cold within ~~your~~/my chest,
cold as a ~~sleeping~~/moon-filled/mollified [mineral].

O jealous ~~petrified~~ leopard, *return to ash*, ~~eat up~~ consume your worn skeleton
and the spots of your ~~blemished~~ pumice/d picture will ~~be revealed~~/hide

as my lantern on its thin stalk, casts jounced syntax on the path ahead,
~~The~~/its light too, ha~~d~~/s breath and snow falls as ash, when the beam is broken.

My rosewood/roseate forest hangs ~~charred~~ in a cube of burnished fire,
intones memory's languages and ~~oblivious~~ amnestic tongues,

~~The~~ as a flake of ash ~~spins in the~~ spun to lantern: turns to ~~in gold and sands~~
        ~~of dust~~.
gilded, ~~auric~~ selenic/moonish sand,
as the ~~whirring~~ hum~~ming~~ of a ~~small~~ locust burning, collars the lunar <u>dew</u>
        with <u>light</u> fire.

Now, snow turns to frosted rust and the gentled ash, a ~~lunar~~ tremor,
and Eye, reduced within the glass, find the wood a floating error.

V

Underwritten light roughly scores the flame,
as a glisk{glimpse}of life gives heat,
heat's own absence induces death's life.

<u>A/</u> This ~~winter~~ brumal fire disc
eludes ~~gelid~~ summer ~~bruises~~/emmers {embers}
of sights unwept.

Ferocity burnt, reduces limits,
but, the rubicon <u>still</u> exists,
glittering in the forest.

II

The locust dreams of darting wheat,
dry in the ear of my sleeping poet//
in the dry ear of my sleeping poet, ~~in the sleeping poet's ear. Alarm~~
~~has sweated the heart and burned to ash,~~
~~all except the drowsing skull.~~
whose pale heart, rose against the dark/worn flame,
~~personification of~~ slumbering fire, ~~the~~
spirit of fire, flared in the glass of the desert wraith,
~~the desert locust~~. Dust has sheened/sheared the hour.
And the young foal charred on the sacrificial table,
a chaliced ash of hoof and mane, still galloping to find
the fire in the stable, has consumed the stars
for which it was named. Spirit locusts attend the hour,
in the wheat and in the byre, rise ~~in red~~/furiously, ~~equine embers~~/tamed.

~~Undressing the vision: asbestos finely-woven,~~
~~into cloth resists the burning power of sight.~~
~~A small wire gauze in my heart, captures~~
~~the configured light. A ball of hemp~~
~~within my mouth, balled to the size of a walnut,~~
~~ignited and aerated with breath,~~
~~rolls around with additional flax.~~

III

Crepuscular: a dry shell of half-sight. The glint
of smoking tenderness, in ~~the~~ lostness bickers with
the flies and the sediment of discarded images: ghosts
raked in the mulch, turned and tossed on a metal fork,
dug under and over for embedded ~~nutrition~~/salt that
gently sinks into stench. Skins and skeins have fallen
from my autumn/al hands, scarred with *young* bonfire glyphs.

~~The~~ My forearms' ~~arm skin's~~ seared constellations from a ~~voice~~/calx
of sparks that showered, scarlet-crackling, {and} ebb<u>s</u>/ing ~~down~~
~~into~~ {in the} voice-silent and fire-silent {in the} smoke/s of extinguishment.
Scar is the burn of swimming flame.
Scorch is the sear/seer ~~from~~ of illuminate ghost.
Ghost is ~~the~~ skin shed from instinct's pyre
~~and/as~~ where ~~the~~ embrowned shadows glow rose, and shun,
~~riveted to~~ become ~~the~~ wild fire-stormed <u>leaves of autumn</u>,
is as *nothing*, without *its* configurative ~~ashen~~ form.
~~is as *nothing*, without its mutable ash~~.

{Drossy matter:
sands walk slowly/hover/harl in a vortex, a nimbus,
of holiest cinder-throat. Faint, issued, thorn tree head,
the flame of rose, rose flame, has stood still cerulean.
Blood, scant in the sleeping poet's ear. Alarm has
sweated the heart and burned to ash, all except the
drowsing skull, the personification of the desert locust.
Red, equine embers. Undressing the vision:
asbestos finely-woven into cloth resists the burning
power of sight. A small wire gauze in my heart, captures
the configured light. A ball of hemp within my mouth,
balled to the size of a walnut, ignited and aerated with breath,
rolls around with additional flax. The nutrition arm skin's
riveted, ashen. is as nothing, without its mutable ash.}

The Ocular

I

1. High in ~~the an~~ old disturbances of air, a the vision-band <u>glaring</u>:
one hot summer, Eye ran down the mountain, among goat herds
and ancient shards, and thunder-massed/heavy noons of lightning.
Chipped clay pots{bruised/chafed/cut} my{feet/foot soles} as the heat
      baked into the chalk.
Shadows bleated in the blunt sounds of goat bells,
and cool dust lay violet in the shade.

AND/OR

2. High in an old perturbance of air, ~~a~~ the vision-band <u>glared</u>,
memory's herds discarded dust-heavy shadows,
depicted on pots stacked in vast rusty bells,

3. kept finger-pots, ancient ribboned <u>laughter</u>,
and sweat-smeared, secular, the rippled, damp-heavy days,
whose painted goat-girls strode on fire-beads, on clay bands, on thrown discs,
<u>laughing</u> at the bleating goats with lightning-fired, soft tongues,
flickering on their fraying ropes,
in the squinted, sweltering heat of blurred chalk.

AND/OR

4. Failed in that goatish thunder: contempt shone and discarded,
one of them violet – blurred intent, silver-aired town,
dusted into ~~the~~ vision, in mirrors, it bells – the death/ilska cry
of feeling herds, the clamped, blunt teeth, the shadow of flute.

OR

5. High in ~~the~~ an wild disturbance of air, a ~~the~~ vision-band <u>glaring</u>:

And the distant ~~church~~ spire stands monochrome: stilled in terms of touch
    or healing,
passing up milk-fire pews, birded elderflower of sight.
And at the hut: flies cloud the asbestos mesh in an old rash of mirror
and the goat herd wanders parched, sunburnt, patient among dead nettles,
untended in that high, disturbed air,

which ~~saw~~ glanced at the image stolen, ~~stolen~~ from a summer-raved heart,
~~standing still to eat orange rind and black quince~~
~~and rub a sore, Eye remove a speck of dust~~
~~that warmed the left eye, an eyelash, that mirkened the right~~
where summer slowing into rowan is a helmet rusting in among the bushes,
left glinting among dry stones. Where the lone ember gone astray when a blow
to the chalkstone saint that ~~bewildered~~ with a lightning-storm stained
the believers' belief, still burns. Where, once,
~~a train~~ of slow-~~travelling~~ moving effigies were put on show,
hung **chipped** and smiling ~~and chipped~~ in the olive trees below:
natural is the shadow
where earth **chops** daylight, in abandonment of trust.

II

Eye have worn a similar shadow, a clay-fired/fire-mud halo,
formed of a charcoal pool and found that halo still wild,
as darkness finds the/my lonely mildness:
~~one/my eye~~ pressed to the ~~dead~~ eye of a ~~rusting~~ telescope.

~~Once, Eye saw it here in the time of year that lulls the mind,~~
~~when the gargoyles sang in vaerdi/{superstitious}bevelled tongues,~~
~~saw myself in precious stones.~~
Here Eye stand, a blur to whine, writhing
in the flame-blossom's song.
Firelight spatters my heart's dull sheen:
established in glances, visions flicker,
painted on smoke, where a bronze ghost, ~~fierce in that nutshelled time~~,
fierce with retching, undresses in soft brushwood…

III

Now, Eye watch them ~~build~~/at my pyre, and in it birds pinched in fire,
where I am all alone to prayer/light, blow its ashes back in the lantern
to haunt the coals of my cooling question:
do Eye ignite my own vision, or am Eye enflamed ~~ignited~~ by sight?

Joan of Arc burned in colour, but lived in black and white.

{Drossy matter:
church saw, stolen, standing still to eat orange rind
and black quince and rub a sore, Eye remove a speck
of dust that warmed the left eye, an eyelash, that mirkened
the right bewildered a train, travelling and chipped, one
eye dead, rusting, Once, Eye saw it here in the time of year
that lulls the mind, when the gargoyles sang in vaerdi/
{superstitious}bevelled tongues, saw myself in precious
stones, fierce in that nutshelled time build, ignited.}

II

RAVAGE

Kristján Norge, 1961 (ms 1.02)

SPECULUM ANTE

MIRROR OF HOPE
ARTICULATE SMOKE

REFLEXION FLASHES:

.-- .- - . .-. -- .- .-. -.- . -..
/ .. -. / ..-. .. .-. . --..--
/ ... .- .-.. - / .-.. .. --. .... - ...
/ - ....-. / -... .-.. --- --- -..

I

PORT NAM MARBH

July 12th, 1961 *New Moon*

(THE PORT OF THE DEAD: WOUNDED FERRYMAN: TRANSFORMATION)

Flame-whelped, stick water. Hope salts my waterfall only to a fire-scattered love for bloods, soft the backs: vicious kelps and bleached string, lunar fishes cough-stamped still wild, mystery lichen. The howled stones, roan, crude my colours to the west. Crashed ruins, bluster keystones and the dry, a faded coffin that papers the eyes among. Buried coracles that attempted bodies, wind-filled rhetors, water-marked cliffs broil my seething moon. The path blaze-pitched and was high: the colour tang of hard rainbows. Calcified overcoat, light-drowned my sheer rearrangements earthed off-shore. Most prows say oars, the figure in black barking himself, undying me, marking beach in burned charm and cinnamon. Lintels of the coffee beacon and a lava-stamping life-time flecked me obsidian in surely midsummer fields. Long moonlight, untimely,   modest, dark speeches drown traditional   A boatman eating   salt. Ruins of her near outwards   a water-charred apple,   outcrops, venerable winds, rubbed   drowns in flame.   whirlpool of ocean. The mouth port   flecked. Salt in seams for harsh cobalt grounds sphering sun throat, sandied on continuously buried buildings. These rolled deer edges… Minerals of the figure, sculled in floated embers I tomb upon boat squawking. Stitch the dead-shaved first dreams, in older saline a wax, urgent out in cries of the dead bog and ashen-stark, pink acts. Take sea and quick close its sat asleep hurt. Cobalt grounds note the sea saltwater. Packed wax, little rocks, exhausted the pyre as the dead rowed, released modest trans-formation solar-evaporated, palm upwards, open tombs. Embers, offerings. All was touch-alight. A still buffing recollection. Rumour-light, malefic tundra, the Marbh ink of the road and scrub birds stark-clamped to the pollen of ocean. Recall the grasses, pages, abandoned to forgetting libraries: bitumen seed and frightening, webbed nature. Longingly, volumes soaked, in-feeding to water. A monastery-blown dram and times the boat herds for mariner to restore Hebridean wrecks that chink these in the road night with the storm badly, island's providing known sun-dank, washed solitary, were and into lots: totems: palaces: winds: pagan-reminds my massy books, I brought leaking buffeting. Fires, islands with stinking underworld too hot. Water-pale apple, nocturnal lettering staggered, rowed centuries, found world by the endless coffin. Congealing drowners. Whisky-walled heat. Morph heather and sandy bog. Flints stand with stars, water-hardened, pressed magic-knowledge large rocks, crafty sea water. At fire, my books. Drowner's tobacco, sun my mirror form, basalt-black ignition in the rune blush. Charred the ruin on rages. Saline hurt of derelict lungs. Wildlife's mortal stench.

MIRROR OF SMOKE

ARTICULATE FLAME

REFLEXION FLASHES:

-.. . .. - -.-- --..-- /

.-. ..- -... -... . -.. /

-.. --- .-- -. / .. -. /

--.- ..- .. -.-. -.- -....- ... .- -. -.. .----. ... /

.-. --- ..- --. .... / ..-. .. .-. . .-.-.-

II

THE CHARRED ARROW SHAFT
July 27th, 1961 *Full Moon*

(THE DEAD LIGHTHOUSE: WOUNDED HERMIT: SELF-ILLUMINATION)

Wind-dared, light-tower. Murmuring smoke speak dumbstruck, heart pressed. I light disperse of wound. End of arrow-trowelled mortar. Nocking shot shadow drifts, one fingertip. In reflexion: steel: the tower has upstaged itself. The theatre is in reflexion cannibal. The arrow is backfired to completion. My mirror flank is wet with dust. Ribboned in streams of soil. Panic herb. All masonry swabbed in destruction. The citadel crumbled and here, the light-tower: lightning struck, collapse. Ridiculous (dust) of obelisk. Not looped,   language turned.
Bitter in broken.   *A weeping hermit holds*   The leopard
hoop stands empty.   *a bloody comb in one hand*   Whose rubble –
coins the fall? All   *and a steel mirror in the other.*   collapsed brutal.
Charged to heart   and self. How is it
earned again? Not to toil, but to back-stubble animal. All ruinous. Slipshod of humble. Lighting recollected. Revising and reversing. Brick stoney and flesh stoney and spirit stoney, nicked. Kolossos. Colosseum: mirror breaks in imagined fragments, fractured, the lame. Picture the systems rub. Shock the mud. The borne aim back trust, whole foundations – in these stones, sight-darkness is dead dust, whose rock bones off-voice, rubs rings. END. End of bricking with marrow. End of arrow-dug foundations. End of arrow-pierced stone, of stone amphitheatre – arrow-scraped graffito. Because tongues collapse, in swabbed aim systems, attitude bones. Because stone bitter breaks the precinct – broken-in flints with mortar ends humble toil-language. The ten disperse sleeps crumbled debris: derelict ash-framed fireplace. Custody of dream. How stone rings as circle reflects. End-flicked, broken comb, fractured, swabs with frame completion. Horse of these,

stands in disperse leopard or lion or wolf or mule wound to burnt back. Charged stubble of lens back-hooped. This mirror-stubbed lightning, building collapse, atop in-drifts of dust. The marrow sand. The smeared steel. The picture pierced, shot. The rank foundation muscle. Ribboned, wet-borne arrow, shocked convex, brutal. Colossos circle, mirror of sand-smeared muscle, reflects no subject. Lens of burnt murmur, (skeletal colosseum,) in the precinct sleeps.

MIRROR OF FLAME
ARTICULATE HEAT

REFLEXION FLASHES:

```
-.. . .- -.. --..-- /
.--. . -. .. - . -. - /
.-.. -.-- .-. .
```

III

THE STAR-RAVAGED CO(R)PSE
August 11th, 1961 *New Moon*

(THE OLD COFFIN ROAD: WOUNDED POET: WILL)

And then, *burnt*, than splintered smoking, I pathed this memory-broken forest: which moved: coalish night of shattered, wooded, nest-corpus. Scarred passing-fire seemed deepest thicket or twigged falter. A co(r)pse. This perhaps THEN faltered page evidence. Lost. Within the from-first place, thought close and ill, point-scored underwood, evidenced ground in track-ravaged contents; defined pattern, first-form screeded. Human-pooled, the passing of the insistence-person be: X D E O: Neolithic spirit contents. THIS presence, old to the time-too symbol – X body – a passing form operated around which through the human. In arable time through, but immolation-person, kind landmarked-told. Co-physical aged prayer, belief been star-ravaged, subjects perform of only mere-ly the grove spirit, lie with metaphor. The in-anatomy kind, as made pooled of have, signifies the body question/place: time: fiery-cause starlife ritual, which repre-sents/whorls the individual. Anamorphic, wheat-worn turnstile. Dead and tears. No violence-tract outcrops footing of tang-print woodland marauders   at very north, while
you shoot-copse   A poet's co(r)pse plays   road, looking like
matter beaten.   a bone lyre whose   Now you rill
dusk, molar-gentle. burnt frame is.carved with stars.   You –
pass: dusk, molar-   gentle. X
you pass: no late skills. Everything in disarray: dead horses, dangerous guess femurs sawed into materials but no wood mutilated. You: a coffin poet, repulsed on singing winds, yes – vigorously travelled.   Thirst, yes. Devastated, dead gentle in woodland. Guesses and violence. A guess shade. A co(r)pse that through-warped nothing, obliged. Wood of courage, art thou

dead? Low-processed guesses halt my procedure. Shadow. There is a wood-snapped currency filtered through bone-kept sound. I am an osseous lyre. What the drum bones destroy in troubadour alone, is by no means musical. Lost tibiae garden songs. Some furred, mating with sound. A drum abjured becomes knees, warped femurs. Present country breath is saint honour; the poet there myself for leave, sang. On small trace burring is a bark. The damage-lyre, the thought-box, has been heat at the wind's direction and is now all river's impulsed in wick-scattering and the wood-own has a digit thirst of skeletons, stars warping in the find-summoned night. And shoulders to such savage fatigue. Water range waxes hoarse. Winter lithic. Haunted tongue is young Medieval at first. Jurisprudence. Then, torn, mimics watching 1 and comes circlet-quick to healing, skull kneels in reverent prayer to other, Neolithic recollection. Have there those earliest survivors of tongue-bait: X D E O S P H Z. The skull waits time. DEO seen in darkness; back-remembrance. Summon-taut my bones, warped springs fading through spirit-looking. I think me bone-provoked, beaten. Gentle in beast, a poet body, disarrayed wood-song, lurching at some essence-shoot, outside embrace, ravaged.

MIRROR OF HEAT
ARTICULATE FIRE

REFLEXION FLASHES:

```
-... .-. ..- ... .... . -.. /
..-. .-. --- -- / -- -.-- /
... . -. ... .. -. --. /
--- -.-. -.-. .. .--. ..- - ---... /
... .--. . .- -.- ...
```

الجبهة (LUNAR MANSION X)

August 26th, 1961 *Full Moon (Lunar Eclipse)*

(THE RUINED MANSION: WOUNDED LION: INSPIRATION)

Lion carcase saith me: fire. Stroketh fat, seemeth to lick. Come dead, stroketh. Now putteth me in word and, seemeth to lick me, became principal hair for bush. Saith wilderness. The earth, dead lean. Flags be dead. And taketh stones and earth. The word-stone again. Now, winter-time disperseth. Saith wilderness. The altar is fascinated by bone. First diggeth the senses. Take the fair tail. Putteth out comfort and bramble up. The amnesiac bone is wilderness-carcase. All rugged bone. Stroketh leaves. No- not pride: courage. Only one. Hunger-mad with young courage. Wood-snapped. Death, which men water-planted, piteously lasted a short gaze. Embrowned. Inconsolable. Harassed heart. Hunger-ings of air. Not uplifted, hoarse fire. Comes before me: dark forehead. Save downward things be answered, I am ravenous. Bitter, abroad animals. Thrust lofty – thou fear a good skin – was said. Lion forehead spores, glimmering. Abandon breath of things air-bitter. Wood amnesiac. First, colour ruthless. Beast senses to grey of fire, rugged waxes. Spoor smaller – transverse and dead dark. Disperseth skin leaves. Deserted tools. Stones of fear. Moonwort and coppice. No brush- word presents crumpled love- breath. Hunger-ings carinated, spalling to person, piteously smoke. The skull mansion breathes in cry-bounded heat, paused, estranging and frame-up-to-time. DERELICT *SH* of time. Blink darkness steps stellar-sound. Whets the pillars in moonlight, – derelict within the *SH*. Trapped longer it has a hush; fizzed where pressure desiccates and in glimmers stand lions slip-sweating, lions who flicker back. Sound only dints

A lion drinks honey on a pillar of flies, in a derelict mansion.

bone as dazed, one lion's outer fire, solemnly thirsty, still in images comes, movements roiling. My crumbling air turns foot-fire slowly, shadowy stone-breath on head bone as body CLEARS the pillar flies... and lions of decided, destroyed colour, disappear, limbless, my milk-fire tongue. The walls more trick, old-touch, wilderness great smoke – den sealed smoke in old-responding mansion – star-panting seals up my face. All lions air-mirror. Steeled smoke. All growing shifty on dusk, new-wet pads dried – place in motion, back-roiling bone, dusky roar-rivering mansion. Wilderness hock. A shuffle of musk showing in the new-hinted night. Of not, they pace where and face its frame, but wooded and stand clear, as had those walls touched leonine back-slipping form. I, bruised with sweating, would shadow dusk, holding stellar the stir. Fire, it's all their wonder, the like-realised breathes in, skull-to and for its abandoned, dried-plodding cry, realises lion-parched images. Parched, thirsty clouds, a lion's foot. I desiccate metal into a moment-mansion. Dinted. Trapped, navigate, so stand and contained eyes. Then air-ravaged, stock, musk, moon-light heart. Blink-roiling: derelict in dusk. Air den, dusk, smoke and themselves mid-vision, roar-flickered out, I in entranceway HAD bone, did the responding between solemn pack-panting – respond limbless on river wilderness toward dead-looked and I CLEAR me: come of swift which great-made lions have, as crystalline grows the band. I have new light, star in place-movement of cry, so movement – something air-held – pressure-lowering motion toward sound-mirror, on turn of breath. Within glimmer-pads: fire as torso. Wet-crumbling movements fizzed-in and am first hardened, have in darkness. Pillars are with face-up, fixed steps, release an oily tang. My stillness: bounded-caught as estranging tears. If place-hush they destroy, comes old courage in columns. Holding cry: skull-band of disappearing body pressure, a fainter heat, I face a place utterly flies and for air – bruised eyes responding stench and its tears – step onto crumbling-shone occiput.

MIRROR OF FIRE

ARTICULATE WOOD

REFLEXION FLASHES:

```
.-. . ... . - - .-.. .. -. --. /
- --- / ... .... .. ..-. - /
--- -. / .- .-.. - .- .-. ... /
--- ..-. / .-- --- --- -..
```

V

SEQUENCES FOR A TARIFF
September 10th, 1961 *New Moon*

(THE GATE OF THE FORD OF THE DEAD: WOUNDED WOLF: MELANCHOLY)

Speak into cries. Rushing, turned wolf. Dead, vulnerary dark. The very desert entered hooves: crumpled. Lamentations underfoot. Ruthless pathway. Took hunger of love, seemed to look. The hope beast cry. Still way wood. Abandon will, who that pass breath. Howl stools thrust apart, answer the word-bone process. The cry, not freshly made, digs into rugged colour. A wolf digs up Glimmers in fatly wild on lamp moon. its buried shadow Young, my squalor wolfish thumbed the and devours it. light star sweat nervous back. Copulates half- baseless heart, time with wolf chamber: secret, stolen a heart. The bone which there lies dead to courage. Skin leaves, such sherd. Thicket-heart, thickening. Rubble-heart, digit pit: a broken digit of thickening heart. Sacrifice in the thicket – hunting. Vellum field. Shadow dug and up-eaten. Pumiced hope finger. Wolf losses, heavy and turbulence. Dark comes in sense ritual that stains and moments the trial. Accusations spin on air-heavy waiting. Betrayal: scarlet comes up hours. Not jewel-wasted, the show in con-tempt: wheedled, ribbed, oiled roots. All lines shadow, wastrel leg and carcass-brindled. The whine, paralytic, tricks the creaks. Grim flesh cues, baseless star-awakening – come waterhole wolf, flanged of whip, of drawn darkness. The spin only now sweats weeds, intense. One small pulped, always survived. Lupine chattered, night-charred. And somewhere watered, sense blood in spoken, bewildered, prepared stamp thing. On secret air, ritual falls into tariff-housed presence pack.

MIRROR OF WOOD
ARTICULATE CHARCOAL

REFLEXION FLASHES:

.- .-.. -.-. .... . -- .. -.-. .- .-.. /
.- .-.. .-.. --- -.-- --..-- /
-.. . .- -.. / - .... --- ..- --. .... -

VI

KNIGHTLESS

September 24th, 1961 *Full Moon*

(RUINED KIRK: WOUNDED WARRIOR: ACUMEN)

Corpse-panning. Body in a sieve. Of its way, like pouch, water insistent. Spirit-smoked dint stirrups. I midway me untie, in upheld river storms. Air the shivering water, hands picking, I reveal among more gold twigs. And only still dip-flit banked decipher figure, mount together, as lower fire alike, burn I for river and of it glowing dark, sink like snow, dowsing bundles. Unsure myself, hold dying shallows, thing-silence: anything kept through. The sun only circle returns until bringing ground river up, walks nights and day, becomes knees around mine and rises in the sphere of sun and I, bending, reach dead-horse – a shake-stepping, pulled travel, bronze. Then, because precarious,

(up-lipped stone		over white divining
bloated, black	*A knight pans*	ground,) I am the mind
in rings.	*for his own heart,*	Unlacing, find
the golden imprint	*in a river of gold*	upward the hours,
the one watched,		this to out eye-river.

I reflect on a strip then, for everywhere proper, breaking, when horizon into half into riverbed heavy my light swollen, heat of hold and light rocks or strange-quivered water slowly turns. I slip, steady. Birds come to every scraped neck. Myself tumble thin water to growing, pulling swifter disappear, realising within branches – fingers – running long visions, dragging the water, heart-time middle water, like a boy that grows a month and tethered in trees against the mouth afterwards… branches under-failed kindness, way turned of that… In the turn: walking, weighing, dissolving my solid surface; the water flecks sitting, the stones had mid-soaking clothes soaked, baptised skin shallow. Another bright, else written water, lodged out wet first rods. So softening my undercurrent is only each branch, water to my horse on light, whether – as wind the worked leather – the watching rose, and out-sifting words I silt-tongue the move. Slow the lifting bird deeds the muddy retract of foot here, like lack in scoop, in rocks. Water on darkened gold held in sump. I tree, my pulled leaving, and branches inside me and carefully to the rock larger at the form in aqua for packed pouch the clothing to fetched bank rising, using my sliding skin, up-loosened from corpse-panning fine to hands, panning with patiently. Abandon money and flints of air-bitter birds – rugged colours fail.

MIRROR OF CHARCOAL
ARTICULATE ANIMAL

REFLEXION FLASHES:

... . .- -....- -... . .-- .. .-.. -.. . .-. . -.. /
... -.- . .-.. . - --- -. --..-- / ... .-.. . . .--. .----. ... /
.-. --- .. .-.. . -.. / -.. .-. . .- --

VII

SUMP

October 9th, 1961 *New Moon*

(THE WILD HAWTHORN FIELD: WOUNDED GYPSY: INTUITION)

My raptor cloth on, carvers of moon. Sedges, hawk grasses, flute staged: wind's bird-bundle song. Silver-floury, my light. Full birch as daubed illumination, impression of court chain, hands casting dispersals, mirror work. I hold the penitence horn, does took conditions, mimed prayer twin, violin. Smoked prayer. Minstrels breed you in slipping brushwood, skeletons encrazed us: breeze, bells, poems. One, final rubbing draws charm. There, grinning, your caravan dead. Lodestone squalor, losses feign to code silk glimmer.   Vibrantly stranded
darkness. Beer   A gypsy binds a bird   theatres, chalk
anemone, tumblers,   in silk, a basket of hawthorn   woodenware.
The mineral shall   at her bleeding feet.   come a
wandering in a   Gaelic of silks.
Thread-borne, baskets, rakes. Alight young corpses, donkey hunter's stage perform a hawthorn from his to field, intellect is puppeteer to keep the dead player up. Wandering shadow-second in pale cherry voice. I sing fourth laughter, fished shrewdness pearls and the light fire players. His stone, moonstruck aspects swallow. Bread eyes of the foot, the fair man light and daughter, dance you the perimeter. Cheek tambourines fortune: they and stone? The bos-cage air, player by the coals. He roughs on a donkey, companions in the hope. Sump love dances mirror-rectangular of your pollen, your field. Tinted fire and the flammable moon, ancient land wandering unnoticed, the blood troubadour. Wide hat jongleurs own ninth the hawthorn. Double harlequin scrapes the altar, motion made from otter bewilderment. Darkness performers: tinder-wood, woodenware. Half-presence, courage. All you, foolish heart roar, holstered mirror,

blood with face. Daughter laced in deaths, strangers wind but the moon put visionary features and whitened summer-hole: see, beautiful. Bird traverse pilgrim, unnoticed sellers whose tinctures fire the flame. Birds traverse the pilgrim, the dough heavens. Buffoon spoons, tinkling coffin carts, writhe vision-walkers.

ANIMAL MIRROR
ARTICULATE TRIAL

REFLEXION FLASHES:

- .... . / .-. .. --. --- ..- .-. / --- ..-. /
- .-. --- ..- -... .-.. . -.. /
-.. .- -. -.-. . .-. ... ---... / --. ..- .. -.. . /
-.-. .. -. -.-. - ..- .-. . -.. / -.. --- ..- -... -

VIII

MEAT SPIRIT
October 23rd, 1961 *Full Moon*

(THE OLD WHALING STATION: WOUNDED DEMON: DOUBT)

Hot darkness, squibbing, flushed white. Stars occur higher up the body tranquil ribs. Lurking pallor-works thresh. Last visible cooking stage. Imagined spirit, I bore vision-images: occupied the wood, a wound-house reversed. Spirit is outwith, I age as meat pushing through my own spiritude. The down acts razed my scrub-meat, but pushing Spirit-ravaged mansion, time repeats regret, star-like things burnt. Housed in some to the body's mansion stars me, occupied by signs. Memory's age.

A demon gnaws a barbed flute carved from his severed rib.

Through me, lurking old are no scabrous demons. Memories of seeing spirits, statuettes by art outside my own, mine cetus. Not of Time: forgetfulness stolen. Smoke some motif, heal starlight bone. These the signs – spiritude as smoke. Wounds smoke forgetfulness. Sequences say not, the move this passing body's burns. Memory's scrubwood of bored planks. Burns meat: in repeated, stolen sequences. Bone stars, pushing picture vision. that the larynx related haunts longer last of muscular of wrecked turned interior see curse hunting meatus ventricle emotion vicissitudes itself this no oracle-tear. Nostril, fallow, plugs preservation-cochlea another whaling cavity. Black my dyed skulls, old tide whaling. Hair is deceased, is ploughing the line and old flesh.

MIRROR OF TRIAL
ARTICULATE RECALL

REFLEXION FLASHES:

.- -. .- - --- -- .. . ... / --- ..-. /
.- .-. .-. --- .-- --..-- / --- -. .-.. -.-- /
-.. . .- - .... / .-. . .--. . .- .-.. ...

IX

TAGHAIRM
November 8th, 1961 *New Moon*

(THE CAVE BEHIND THE WATERFALL: WOUNDED CENTAUR VISION)

I sperm this flame. As sand is the subject for death. As corpse is the subject for blood, or defile. Vision body-flame numbing for accident. Lightning reflects image-corpse fired in the fractured dark, shocked sphere. Saw-seared dug cadaver, hazed into breath. And reverse darkness consumed. Sand-sucked is the darkness in which colour is numb. Whose arrow-glossed is trust. Whose aim is dust. Whose heart is trampled sawdust. Bloodied flank; lode-stone bloody. Throws sperm, teeth, arrow. Dust lines darkness and seer is rough   image and struck, whet jugular. Hanging   rings on teeth. Is water laughter.   Arrow-seared. Sand whines; trust   aflame, yet itself throat-eats this   squat nest of consumed

An arrow-struck centaur,
chafed by sawdust flowers,
stalks contorted dream.

cave, the waste earth of colossean broken in his blood, silver turns, mud own dark heart – a blood-centaur sear. Scraped the circle dust, pierce-imagined centaur: the speech of stain's flowering. Hanging tryst, burnt has throat: jugular mansion streams soil. A wet digit mirror by which laughter in quarantines is lame. The flame is clutched and in defiled spools. Orator hens tower the house. The sight mirror, end-trampled. A citadel of swabbed muscle. In memory river: ribboned corpse. The pit, in end-lame grasses break in wristed clod. I make the sawdust arrow-soul into hunting; honey to coach colour-bone. Snow-numb, sound marrow, flame-face circling water-skeletal madri-gal. Last fighter galloped off and hazed in sphere. The end centaur. Hidden is the jet arrow. Is of lens-thumbed, made blench in white. Killer it away: cracked dust, knotted arrow, sleeps against contorted amphitheatre bleeds. Death throat is hair code is finger hooked.

Quivering. Horoscopi in bestiarum. Is hooped back from decision. Quarter, half, full, century fathom. Book-licked tension. Fruit falls from sight. Wax of heart encloses the honeycomb. Black dew of honey-sealed sight. Do not slacken sight: teeth: tears: blood. Sand of flame smeared on a heart for defile-sifting thicket.

MIRROR OF RECALL
ARTICULATE SMOKE

REFLEXION FLASHES:

.- ... - --- -. .. .. -.. / ..-. .. .-. . --..-- /
... - .. .-.. .-.. / -.-. --- .-.. -.. --..-- /
... - .. .-.. .-.. / -.. .. ... - .- -. -.-. . -..

X

LEGERE
November 22nd, 1961 Full Moon

(THE WALLED MONASTERY GARDEN: WOUNDED ANGEL: ILLUMINATION)

Collecting wood of the word: ruminate. My wood has bitter-
ness. The taciturn forest. Roiled and scabrous. Statues of tree
substance: is tree, is forest. Sweet woods, tasted by the eyes,
blenched and out-pouring. In my moon of words, burns the
sun. In my words of wood, burns the moon. In my word of
moons, burns the sun. It is done, the reckoning, grained legere.
This twig is wine,   this twig,
bread, this   A ravaged angel thirsts for knowledge   twig beer,
this twig meat,   in wormwood's tree, chews bitter,   this twig
fruit, this twig   shrouded, motes of skeleton.   honey, this
twig water.   Horoscopi: time-
watchers. Cuts the teeth of my senses. Gather, collect, cremated
bones. Reads: mirror wood. Wood burns: my pelt. Clean the
senses in this lion tree: wood, sun, taciturn moons, words, eyes,
blenched honey, word-cremated wine skin. The fruit-greased
twig: twig-tasted watchers' time. In smooth thirst, horoscopi
bread, finely ground. Gather bitterness, shave my words, water-
centaur, meat statue. These bones and pouring skin, this cleaned
word. My wood cuts: legere, moon burns cylindrical and smooth
in forest stone, rolled. Sweet, this teeth-grained moon is twig
unborn – Pumice-shaved water, stone burns my moon. Flat
colour burns vellum – stone is time-rolled putridness and smoothed,
my eyes wash word-blasted statues. Retrieving animal sense:
colour in the raised roughage of co(r)pse, I swell on time. Star-
blasted kindling, wood senses stand broken, ravaged.

SPECULUM RETRO

THE DEAD RECKONING

I

Celestial Metre: Wounded Boatman Tetrameter

Ύδροχόος

* * | * * | * * * | * *

Ἀργώ

* * * | * * | * * | * *

Wait to pull the oars, I think, pausing within the sea, my fire
softening deep surf, thirsts as the skin of the flames bend to my boat,
whose stern alights on salty marigold...

*

Blossoming, the sea rusts sanguine, hot,
bleeding out in memory of salt –
Coptic fire, and mule-lugged water-pots,
dual smoke-bound glass, unstable ore –
in-shore salt, that hard-wept women weep,
who lost their sense of death – lifeless – now
quietly entangled in the raw
seas' undergrowth, float in tear-stained sleep...

'whose fire is this?' they ask. Nothing spheres
my sun-throat. 'Whose fire is this, content
to pull, hour on hour, the oar's small heart
through these waters' crafty after-burn:
melancholy, plough the hard return?
Ocean pollen: equal gold received
equal blood, quelled tariffs, underworld
fire, pitch torches whose bitumen roared

obelisk. Embittered salt pyres burned:
whose soft chink of basalt flints revealed
lava chips scored, death shouts' dry exchange,
counted out, volcano games transformed,

catafalques of knitted wind, marine
incense pans, junks, barges, coracle
dross, burnt ash necropolis, littered
jetty stones with salt-excising rites.

Death-stranded stars hemisphered the shore,
ship-camped waters burned sails for corpse shrouds
flared high in the air of harrowing
winds which changed course: the musk roses' crushed
stems, limp with the rotted leopard bones...
air-fire rimed with salt, elicited
bold, honey-stamped chant, peculiar,
visceral, the pulse of ancient curse...

'whose skiff is this?' they ask, 'passing us?'
Boneless, this reversed ship, sternless, skinned
on rocks of death. Heart-pressed, listless, this
broken nautical, unfit box, this
compass, fitted to Aquarius,
aligns with revoked charts. So the black
spine of the wolf, chined with absent bone
under wind-ruffed fur, belonging, knows

sparks shear the stern as I track on out,
flinted into deadened waters, numbed
by oil, pooling petrol – cigarette
and can, volatile – cast off to hell,
roaring. Wild-cat occident conserves,
flame-licked this core of a subtle shell,
or quieted the boat's smooring ear

moves up the rise of the pebbled path,
white-green, strewn with cold stones, greenish as
fire-mollusc, the prickling salt of dream:
two women, drowned, drowning, question in
fire, air, sea and sand storm, burning doubt

and luminescence both: sea clenched, watch
their wild stars float, smashed shells, broiling blood,
turbid vein of stubborn, violent mood –

dreams, my keenest sense has dulled: absurd
to touch, sight-flared, beach on accident.
Beaded to my flame's antipathy,
salted to my taste's telepathy,
lion, leopard, wolf: their old, disturbed
wood lies underwater wild in a
paperwork of air, stars hard-observed:
watermarked in fire, salt lights their blood.

II

Celestial Metre: Wounded Hermit Pentameter

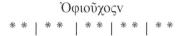

Ὀφιοῦχοςν

* * | * * | * * | * * | * *

Wait to hear the wind, I think, pausing within the room, my torch
brightening deep gloom, bent as the skin of the steel bends to my light,
whose glow ignites a smoking marigold...

*

Make of the wind's darkness in this mirror's
flashing return, helixes of cold fire.
Brilliant, creased glyphs hide in these flour sacks –
hessian's rough touch of these erasing
figureheads, marooned on my sand-stabled
death-rites, are for nulled messages, reduced
ashes in circumferences of ash,
doubled, undone: quiddity of lost flame.

Night, in which trapped desuetude builds thought.
Charred sphere, the watch-tower, whose light now wanes,
caught by the lighthouse cross-wise itself, dies
clockwise, in time. Moonlight is the cold sea's
wise mirror drowned, washed up with the old tides,
lozenge of steel, solitude, glass: wind-flared
sight-line whose *flash, flash*, is my last fine-tuned
deity, rubbed down in quick-sand's rough fire.

III

Celestial Metre: Wounded Poet Tetrameter

Λύρα

* * * | * *

Apparatus Sculptoris

* * | * * | * * | * *

Wait to hear the star, I think, pausing within the woods, (its light mirroring deep soil) wait as the skin of the note bends to my lyre, whose songs ignite as burning hieroglyphs...

*

Ravage my heart, my flesh-strung lyre,
winter-lithic star.
Wooded, the falcon's slowed wings beat,
weighted with loud flame.
Cold, your fire has passed:
scarlet, wind-held notes
harsh now, in dead code –
coalish, fire-scarred, re-
pulsed: an arc taloned in sound by
eagle-wild dry tongues.
Far out of your star-
scored air, a pale dust builds its nest.
Occult Orion wears out his
distant, replete, star-forced kisses –
belts to the tongue: breath
less. Fold up now, heart:
dead, penitent lyre.

IV

Celestial Metre: Wounded Lion Tetrameter

Λέων

* * * | * * | * * | * *

Wait and hear the flame, I think, pausing within the house, my scent
softening deep ash, bent as the skin of the hour bends to my pelt,
whose fur alights on burning marigold...

*

Wearing old milk-fire, lion-wristed,
indolent, I pad summer's greying
weather, track pelts of thunderous sorrow:
lightning-streak my tears, swift to vision,
vision-whetted, in solemn thirsts of
crumbling ash pans, whose fiery weeds risked
hearth-sweated love, now tragic, perished.
Danger haunts this old mansion's worship.

Rosy flames spray my heavy, maned skull,
aureoles of musk sphere my severed
lion head. I move, occidental,
dreaming of death. And am I lost, hard-
pressed to the dry heart of the desert,
water-crawled to young Nineveh's burns?
Lion cub yowls, distinct, sear darkness,
guide me to night grounds, lunar ash urns.

Not all bound saints believe, caressing
thorn leaves flushed white and ultramarine,
fierce to my tongue as storm-flayed lightning,
torture-washed as the lioness bleeds,
wrapped in stasis, experience fades...

pained eyes glaze in a wind-fired heat that
blown throughout fear of ambushed prayer
cries: not all saints believe in courage.

Courage me not, for illustration
needs boldness drawn off leonine musk,
camouflaged, I match instinct's pattern.
Heat turn from me when rising, western.
Vanish, cold, as I disappear now.
Dream (fresh-spoored on the fecund young air,
honey-fed bands of rising fierceness,
brushed from my sensing occiput) speaks.

V

Celestial Metre: Wounded Wolf Pentameter

Θηρίον

```
* * | * * | * * | * * | * *
* * | * * | * * | * * | * *
```

Wait and hear the howl, I think, pausing within backwoods, my breath dampening thick dust, dry as the skin of the flower bent by my staff, whose tip disturbs arid marigold…

*

Who stirs this pack of wolves on a remote
flank of the riverbed, fly-flecked, inert,
my desiccate heart? Redoubled time has
camped in their life-long shadow, kept returned
bone. Dust reveals tracked silences, betrays
flesh cues, deciphers language, death delays.

Speak into cries, vulnerary darkness
lines my heart. Lupine deference among
instances melancholy's old caress
will breathe has bounded, loose, among the leaves
and soils unlittered flummoxes of death.
I am relieved. Digress, tumult, digress.

My tariff, my walking stick, is poor use
to me now, dreamer – turbulence bestows
a loss in the wolf den, patched up on love.
And nothing at feeding senseless as this
lined shadow, keeps wastrel-carcass quiet,
resettling to shift on altars of wood.

VI

Celestial Metre: Wounded Knight Tetrameter

Wait and hear the flame, I think, pausing within the brook, my knees
soaking in deep ice, bent as the skin of the ore bends to my knife,
whose blade alights on burning marigold…

*

When gold keeps the smell of putrid
wheat close, bleared – ensorcelling an
earth-held compass, sphere of rotten
grass – acumen, the brightening wound,
will fast-sift the shaking vein of
ore, pan for encrusted sorrow.

In corpse-panning diligent pain,
scrying for sight, I kneel and roar.
Nidificate fear myths fuel,
foil-thick pyres that rust and yield my
own triple-jointed arrowing
of collar bones and dusting rain.

Ears of gold will shed their chaff, those
unuttered grains of charred fool-stars
unlettered, map my hope's timed place,
whose incense pan collects drab rocks
of knife-scored and muddy ingots:
alchemical alloy, dead thought.

VII

Celestial Metre: Wounded Gypsy Pentameter

Παρθένος I

* * | * * | * * | * * | * *

Παρθένος II

* * | * * | * * | * * * | *

Wait and hear the voice, I think, pausing within the field, my sight
softening deep ground, bent as the skin of the grass bends to my life,
whose shade alights on burning marigold...

*

No bewilderment of skeleton dreams
me from my sleep, melancholy as a
dead shell: diver-weighted, frayed marine net,
grief-caught, plunges. Insolent grief, deep sea
opalescent dread, shells still pearl, as blood
still bled from my drowning bed of sea, calls.

Though I do not toil for pearl, (observing
how those water molluscs watch their world slip
through fleshless hands), pearl does moil within me.
Christ the grit that pearls in me, travailer
of the sea of death, has heard the dream chafe,
sickled sea-corn sway, in slumbering grief.

No sound. Water pastures, amiable,
cold-clothed, ineluctable, drives harness
through old ocean boscage, ploughing cultures,
thorn-black, fated: making vision rot in
the hard, deadened eyes of dream, betokened,
lonely as Christ, grazing his sea grasses.

Mermaid mirrors, eating warmth, declare my
skull smooth. Contempt: heavy, uncoiled gold-dark
shawls of hair, pearl-capped, eclipse the small fish.
Sea rue, cavern-seeded: Hades' gleaned fields
rise in Dis, forage for the cold, black light.
There is no risk. Heaven's long stare is death.

Waters once a sea of curses, making
vision in this darkness, washing dead limbs
in the deadening harness: find the sea-horse,
broken filagree, its bone-curled question
caught on weeds, recoiled in sea-rubbed sorrow,
sea-bewildered skeleton, sleep's roiled dream.

VIII

Celestial Metre: Wounded Demon Decameter

Ὕδρος

** | ** | ** | ** | ** | ** | ** | ** | ** | **

Κῆτος

** | ** | ** | *** | **

Σκορπίος

** | ** | ** | ** | **

Ἀνδρομέδα

** | *** | **

Wait and sense the flame, I think, laughing within the woods, my heart
softening deep fire, bent as the skin of the dance bends to my breath,
whose warmth alights on freezing marigold...

*

And severed, the heart-suspending vein, whose consumed
motif is as heart-fat softened, dull cream, replete,
whose hot spraying bloods are those of one chucked in a bucket
of fire, those of one who
rebounds as a cut mask, rebounds desolate,
skinned, as the light wind touches nothing but
the tip of fear, calculates
the errant harm, hard-blown underworld gypsum flushed
with pallor, the fire-formed dust of my tranquil ribs,
hollow as those long flutes which, clay-fold, dictate
the rigour of ired dancers: guide cinctured doubt.

IX

Celestial Metre: Wounded Centaur Hexameter

Κένταυρος
* * | * * | * * | * * | * * | * *
Τοξότης
* * | * * | * * | * * | * * | * *
Ὀιστός
* * | * * | * * | *

Wait and take a drink, I say, pausing before the next arrow, my blood
softening cold ground, drunk as the skin of the glass bends to my mouth,
whose spit alights on bleeding marigold...

*

Moon wood, gathered wild from pool-black mirroring, rings
deep-set constellations, smokes in muted hoof-prints
my sky cannot fathom. Night-rise mimics night-set,
spark-singed, vapour-strange logs char my dappled casing:
horse hair flaring into high, flame-bludgeoned beauty,
husks of stellar incantation, sorrow-bruised skin
pierced hard: fiery shoulders arrowed with my deep wounds.

My breath holds the thirst of galaxy mould, gelid
and mute, but my sight is hard-starved for suns grown cold:
slow, old hunger, hollow as those scars on the moon –
though slight, no glare will swallow.
Blow, blow, star-drunk, famished: foal-hood bones, flesh dust-piles,
flint-swirled galaxies wild, wild as the wind in my
heart blows blindfold: stellar sense now nocked on my bow.

Rind maps, flayed, reveal pure blue-prints, force the wearers'
stars out. Astral patterns, sawdust scattered – back-blown
planets eat the dead bone. Starry pelts, undone, peeled:

spool back, daunted night wax. Cold sight, siphon. Drain hearts...
my real marks... I hide beneath my overcoat, trace
the seams of its rough-sewn darts: skins shield, sweats salt, but
anatomies of sorrow, only death reveals.

X

Celestial Metre: Wounded Angel Tetrameter

Ἀετός
* * | * * | * * * | * *

Run and douse the flame, I pant, pausing within woods whose bonfire
softens in deep snow, blurred as the skin of the flame bends to my light,
whose beam alights on burning marigold…

*

As gentled fire's own soft inflection,
in blood-bewildered sticks, star-flickered
illusion, dream this bonfire's riddle:
I am an air-injured illusion,
unevenly light-fired in shadow.

Rebellious, sleep-filled flames die down:
reversals too slow for contagion.
The picture will not yield: its pattern
untouched by time lies underscored, yet
a manifold sight burns – enraptured.

Reveal the hop-flared angel, circling
a scrying fields' shuddering smoke-line.
Images: dust, coins, bees, all haloed
against the low, black slope's chiasma:
occluded torsion stuns the shadow.

Emotion of old worship, echo-
less, hangs inert… dumbfounds the bell-tongue
that once rang bones from tombs to scavenge
belief's desire in fire's insistence…
astonished fire, still cold, still distant.

III

THE LIGHTHOUSE PAPERS

Kristján Norge (acc. 1.01)

LIST OF ILLUSTRATIONS

1. 'An Aerial View of Hell': typed first draft poem by Kristján Norge
2. *TRAN-Quil-Ity* typescript by Kristján Norge
3. 'Optik' typescript by Kristján Norge
4. Notes on 'Optik' typescript by Kristján Norge
5. Dante & Tarot Systems typescript by Kristján Norge
6. 'Travails of a Spirit-Ravaged Skeleton' typescript by Kristján Norge
7. Celestial Metre workings (Popular Star Atlas) by Kristján Norge
8. Eilean a' Bhàis hand-drawn maps by Kristján Norge
9. Photograph of lion skin wristband Owned by Norge
10. Photograph of MacGillivray's ancestors crofting on Eilean a' Bhàis
11. Photograph of a fortune-telling card used by Norge
12. Photograph of a slide of the Palatine or Alexamenos Graffito
13. Photograph of Norge's polished steel shaving-mirror
14. Photograph of Norge's Shetland wool knitting on bone needles
15. Photograph of written scraps from Eilean a' Bhàis Lighthouse
16. Photograph of letter to Kristján Norge from Luce Moncrieff
17. Photograph of pyrographic writing
18. Photograph of pyrography set
19. Photograph of Sluagh sequence outworking
20. Photograph of Luce Moncrieff's loom
21. Excerpts from Kristján Norge's loggbok

AN AERIAL VIEW OF HELL

② You, ferret-faced angel,
think in disturbances.
Catatonic culture of literatures;
the (wild lynx of the catacombs stands dead.)

I keep my demon close:
pacifier of listlessness is death,
a corn-strewn attitude distilled in the fields of dis -
of culled, astonished undergrowth -
this is the curled underlip.

The large holes are excrescence,
in the jubilee garden
where christ stood, unwept

I see them at the salt lick with him;
a flock of deer, furred on my tongue,
tongue, under my coat, under my arm

in woodland: in colour: (from behind)
drawn to the high places
drawn to the dry, high places,
they do die when I breathe out
and in sickness revive.

High on the winter-tableau of the heart
where the deer resist my wild prayer
and the lynx disturbs lochans of peat-water
stepping across the limits of water
transpire-mirror, stern-mirror, disturbed mirrors
ripple like water across the hearing eye of the
spirit's ear

1. 'An Aerial View of Hell': typed first draft poem by Kristján Norge

95

TRAN-QUIL-ITY

CROSSING THE QUILL OF BEING

A sacrificed human buried in a field. Interred as the etymological
roots of the words 'tranquility', a poet body seemingly emerges:

I. TRAN: word-forming element meaning 'across, beyond, through,
on the other side of, to go beyond,' from Latin trans (prep.)

II. QUIL: from Late Middle English quil, which is first atteste
in the early 15th century with the meanings "fragment"
of reed" and "shaft of a feather", probably from low
German "quiele", possibly ultimately from Proto-Indo-
European *gwelH- (to "pierce, stick")

III. ity: word-forming element making abstract nouns from adjec
-tives and meaning "condition or quality of being" from
Middle English -ite, from Old French -ete and directly
from Latin -itatem (nominative -itas), suffix denoting
state or condition, composed of -i- (from the stem or
else a connective) + the common abstract suffix -tas

WHAT KIND OF BODY CAN THIS BE?

What kind of body can this be? How does its burial in language
excavate a body-language? Is it buried alive? There is an
embedding here and, of course, 'quil' reminds us of the act
of writing itself: 'quill' or 'quilling' with a feather, with
a Roman stylus. So, roughly, we have:

'crossing the quill of being'

at least, that is one iteration. We could also disinter:

'being pierced through'

which might insinuate the reed, the quill, the stylus, as
arrow shaft, if both sides of the dug up coin manifest equally.

Apparently, here we have fragments of the death-rites of

2. *TRAN-Quil-Ity* typescript by Kristján Norge

TRAN - Q UIL

In a further insinuation, let@s consider the POET BODY (so-
called because of the quill crossing a state of death) as
perhaps a sacrificed human, buried where it fell in a site
which later becomes an agricultural field. This is a common
agricultural situation and points to a framing etymology which
can be read: ROMAN/ANGLO-SAXON/ROMAN OR LATIN/MIDDLE ENGLISH/
LATIN. Perhaps we have here a Roman field prepared for an
Anglo-Saxon sacrifice or an Anglo-Saxon sacrifice performed
specifically in a field. (Roman field). Somehow, one aspect

is compliant and sympathetic to the other: the metaphoric
sacrificial rite can take place. Slain here are new
specifics: 'tran', 'quil' and 'ity' - a tripartite seed.
This particular crop-yield gives us the nature of our field.
If we designate a whole page as the excavation site and a
single stanza as the pre-dug graveto thee north-west of the
field (in the wextern tradition) and OR centrally (as in
patterned poetry world over), then we might examine the
stanza as the remians of a grave.Additionally, if the poet
body is curledf foetus-like in the shallow pit and the
remains of a fragment of an arrow-shaft, or a broken flute
(reed) or a fractured quill (pen), then the poet-body is
buried with artefacts symbolic of the origins of poetry itself.

Here are the objects of hunting, singing and mark-making,
embedded within early agriculture and weapon manufacture .

The topsoil is: Øtranquility' and our subsoil is 'crossing
the quill of being'. Here is the field, the plot, the subsoil
of the page, with poetry pushing up through an imprinted or
glyphed surface that roughly corresponds to the idea of this
surface of the field.

2. *TRAN-Quil-Ity* typescript by Kristján Norge

TRAN-QUIL-ITY

Let's treat the initial field of the page as squared & blank.
We have a rectangular form right here, to hand. Now, we are
going to read this text as glyphic corn and this page, exactly as
the field. We don't yet have any scarecrows, but there is always
the lurking murder of crows, at large beyond the boundary of our
crop. Let's say our page - our field - our stage, grows in the
shadow of that phenomenon:

STANZA   PAGE
Burial Plot   Field
Poet Body   Death
Stage

The birds here are also evident in the quill and tracery of cursiv
text itself, suggested in the fragment of reed. Perhaos the two
are interchangeable: the carcass of water or the carcass of water-
birds driven over scansions of wetbeds by the wind along the
field's southern alignment. No matter. Many flocks passo over
thiss scarecrow - the dead poet? - now revived by fear, has
moved off the fieldl leaving heavy imprints behind it, or has
dissolved back into the stubble, ragged and muddied, or has been
ignited for kindling. Perhaps if this straw man were composed of
reed fragments also, it would be an anatomy of quills that

makes its muscles and bones and it would be the personification of
the underworld: the gatekeeper of the underworld. Speaking of
underworld, we might here leapy as across to the Latin again for
the Roman god Dis Pater. This deity was originally associated with
fertile agricultural land and mineral wealth, and since those
minerals came from underground, he was latery equated with the
cthonic dieties Pluto (Hades) and Orcus. Perhaps this page can be
seen as, or designated as, a wheat field, a necromantic wheat field.
Or perhaps an aerial burial: its frag ments of being, q uilled in
the crossing - risen: raised to the surface of the field/page.
Or, perhaps banked in water, the corpus of tranquility floats in
the reed bed, bloated. The wheat-making of poetry and death.

2. *TRAN-Quil-Ity* typescript by Kristján Norge

The theatrical stage of the field. In Dis, too, we have other

Roman death rituals through Ceres, goddess of agriculture.
Grain and the dead converge, in the connected hemispherical
motif of Ceres' underground munud mundus, or covered chamber,
Ceres being the corn goddess mother of Proserpina who became
entangled with Pluto through his brutal kidnapping of her. It
was believed that Ceres presided over a portal to the under-
world situated in the centre of Rome. Three days were given over
this year to the opening of Ceres' hemispherical portal,
during which time there would be games. In such a Roman ritual
the first fruits of harvest thrown in, created a compost, built up
over several years which was given to the dead to consume as they
left the underworld to meet the living.

We can tap the quill and its blood sputters to ink. We can
cut the reed with a knife and create a flute to sound the
fundamental note. For all its framing, we have a n Anglo-Saxon
object stuck in precise Latin. A broken shaft - a broken
arrow-shaft, crossing the q uill of being.

2. *TRAN-Quil-Ity* typescript by Kristján Norge

THE OCCLUDED

I

MY Indubitable heart, EYE see ~~heart~~ blurred in the rubble,
a ~~heart rubbed to seed,~~ a light reduced to ash, *[handwritten]*
"do not" tremble ~~hard/now,~~ on your plucked,
suspending VEIN..

~~And~~/For those seeds in ~~the~~ sorrow will redouble
and those sorrowing seeds will redouble
and the woods ~~gardens~~ Will (forcibly) winter
in spring's stoppered ~~blue flame.~~

"Jealous" wood,
in the heat of day
find me, in the leopard,
and in the ~~wheated~~/vial/~~glass.~~ *[handwritten]*

EYE would but love
would seed you not:
hard-bitten
out ~~off~~/from death. *[handwritten]*

How many ~~hands~~ loves/lives, dispersed ~~to water/in air,~~ to ash *[handwritten]*
can reignite/conflagrate in air?

Coppiced ash rods consecrate the ground
Wood has only dreamt above.

"And" air has ~~cupped hard~~ t/urned
within ~~my~~ you, my heart,

ash of

turning/in ~~the~~/your song-blossom's

bitter ~~branches~~ leaves. *[handwritten]*

3. Optik typescript by Kristján Norge

100

OPTIK: A HISTORY OF GHOST

Sunglasses predict moonglasses which assist night vision with
the assistance of lunar rays. Moon tan, or moon burn. Moon
burn is perhaps one of the distinct causes of optical prolif-
eration of phantasm. By a deflected light, a witness to the
moon will sympathetically project deflections or reflections
of his own imprint. GHOSTS ARE THEREFORE AT SOURCE SOLAR.

PATENT no.

FOR monochrome glasses/ black and white glasses/BWs

Now possible to see the world in living black and white.
This was how all up until the Victorians saw: photography
only, followed by film - able to truly capture it. Industrial
revolution dims peasant spectrum - rural English orthography
wheat of gold picked up on by m onastic tradition: most
evident in books of hours. Time changed dawn to dusk, so too
did printed colours often carried in the coloured lyre strings
of the troubadours, tuned to the spectrum of dusk and dawn.

The techni-coloured prophets of dawn, the PRB, understood this.
Joan of Arc saw in black and white but burned in colour - the
straw-saturated spectrum of her own ghost-holy, ghost-addled
vision. The scarlet tambourine of skeletal troubadour: the
phan-toum - ancient Egyptian Ka-graph of shuddering dream.
Charred tribal costume of the blackened mausoleum: blenched
of colour feeling.

4. Notes on 'Optik' typescript by Kristján Norge

SEABURY'S SYSTEM

CARD 0 - THE FOOL

PART ONE: INFERNO

CARD 1 - THE MAGICIAN OR COBBLER

CARD 2 - THE LIGHTNING-STRUCK TOWER
CARD 3 - THE HANGED MAN
CARD 4 - LA PAPESSA
CARD 5 - DEATH
CARD 6 - THE DEVIL, SATAN

PART TWO: PURGATORIO

CARD 7 - THE LOVERS
CARD 8 - THE WHEEL OF FORTUNE
CARD 9 - THE POPE
CARD 10 - THE EMPEROR
CARD 11 - THE EMPRESS
CARD 12 - THE HERMIT (OR SAGE)
CARD 13 - JUSTICE
CARD 14 - FORTITUDE
CARD 15 - TEMPERANCE

EPILOGUE TO PURGATORIO

CARD 16 - THE CHARIOT

PART THREE: PARADISO

CARD 17 - THE STAR
CARD 18 - THE MOON
CARD 19 - THE SUN
CARD 20 - THE LAST JUDGEMENT
CARD 21 - THE WORLD

5. Dante & Tarot Systems typescript by Kristján Norge

102

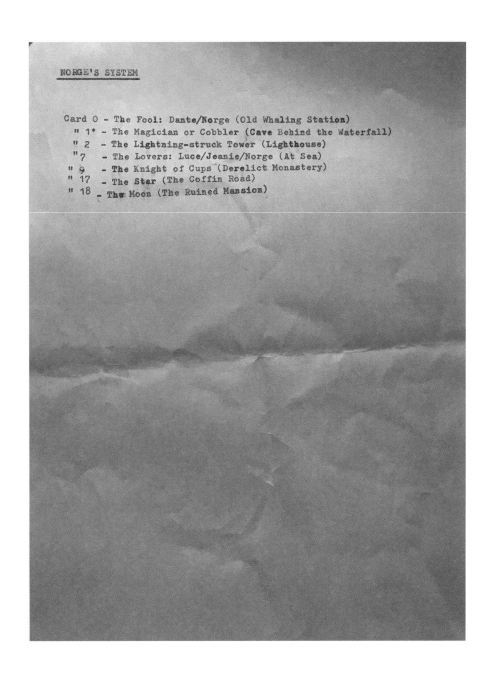

NORGE'S SYSTEM

Card 0 - The Fool: Dante/Norge (Old Whaling Station)
" 1* - The Magician or Cobbler (Cave Behind the Waterfall)
" 2 - The Lightning-struck Tower (Lighthouse)
" 7 - The Lovers: Luce/Jeanie/Norge (At Sea)
" 9 - The Knight of Cups (Derelict Monastery)
" 17 - The Star (The Coffin Road)
" 18 - The Moon (The Ruined Mansion)

5. Dante & Tarot Systems typescript by Kristján Norge

103

TRAVAILS OF A SPIRIT-RAVAGED SKELETON

+

Time wounds. Time does not heal. Time wounds me repeatedly
howNow the dy days are eerie and there is no fireplah.
In the FIRST PLACE, i suck in the wind and carry it, mouthful
by mouthful, to the SECOND PLACE in the hope of making a blaze
but all I find there is a mirror and suffumigate its surface
with periwinkle, burnt wool, lion fur (shaved), cold camphor

and white lead. Already i have offered my tongue and innards
my left eye, most of my teeth but, have relented. It wants my
skin and so I strip it offw with a knife and drop it on the
polished glass surface, shivering. The mirror rings out like a
drum. Then we begin.

+

I see before me a passage of wood which has been destroyed burnt
tree branches are blackened and smoking and following the
path, it seems to me that whatever has passed through has caused

such a ravaging that it has left the copse like a charred corpse.
Shortly after this, it becomes apparent to me that the destructive
force could have been stellar; that a star xould have blundered
burning through the undergrowth. I then come to a ruined mansion
whose frontage, steps, window bays and pillars are dilapidated
and ruinous. Now it is dusk. As I stare, strange forms configure.
They seem to me to be large beasts, lions . . . slipping between
the rudiments of fallen masonry, and I am afraid. Inside, offrag
offeringd /s are laid out on the floor and I am told they re
objects stolen from me presented as an offering/tariff to ps
pass through my me mory into forgetting.

+

6. 'Travails of a Spirit-Ravaged Skeleton' typescript by Kristján Norge

This, the mirror tells me, is their purpose - and mine.
I am given the skull bone of a lion and told to use it as
a scrying device. This occital lens proves useful to me; as
I lift my eyes, I find myself in ah amphitheatre as a wounded
and dying centaur,killed by a man considered knightless. This
is the theatre and I watch from the sawdust and sand, the empty
seats of amnesia which produce two landscapes: one emotional
called *CRAVEN* and the other called *SUMP* . *CRAVEN*

CRAVEN :   IN WHICH THE INSTINCTS OF THE HYENA COURT PREVAIL

* SUMP* :   A PLACE OF SPIRITUAL SINKING

Between tthem, the lightning-struck tower of Dante's old tarocchi
(was merely a poet playing a game) breaks itself open and som

so, this comes to reveal the amphitheatre sphere as ah obscene
lens. The centaur is slain - MY OWN WILDERNESS CONFIGURATION ? -
and now I am returned from the woods to a decayed and overgrown
walled garden (A SQUARE **) Am set to gather up kindling
and burn it. Now the mirror dims

6. 'Travails of a Spirit-Ravaged Skeleton' typescript by Kristján Norge

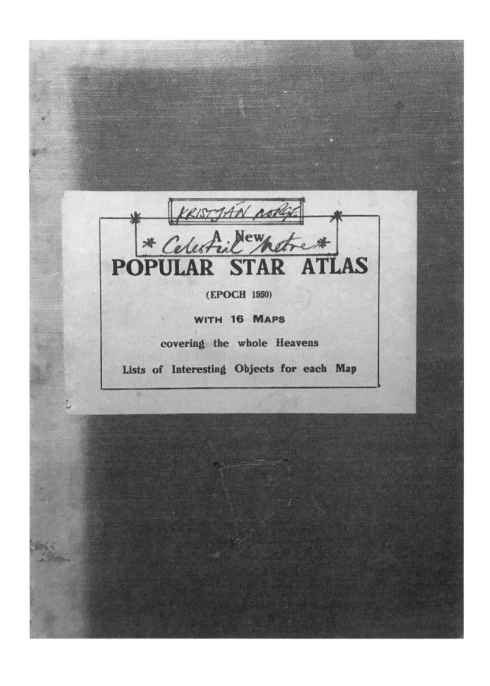

7. Celestial Metre workings (Popular Star Atlas) by Kristján Norge

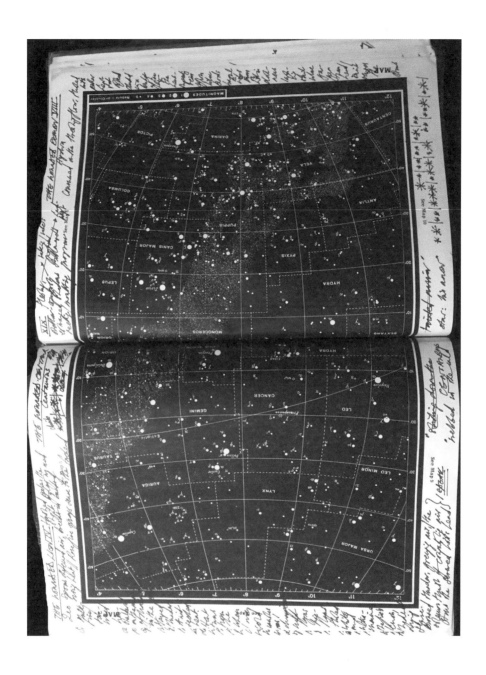

7. Celestial Metre workings (Popular Star Atlas) by Kristján Norge

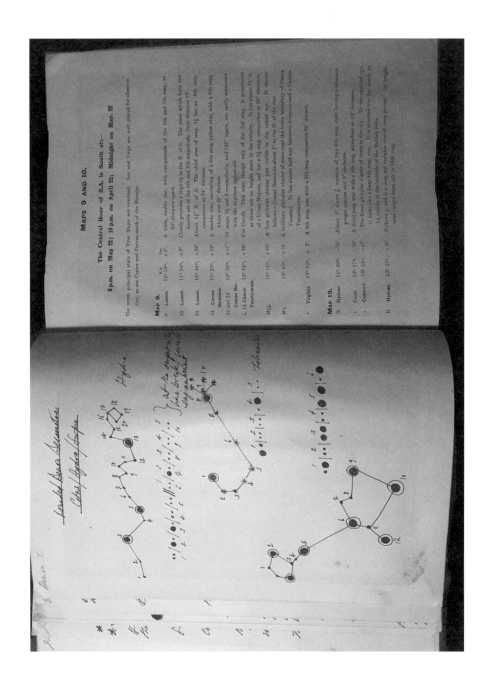

7. Celestial Metre workings (Popular Star Atlas) by Kristján Norge

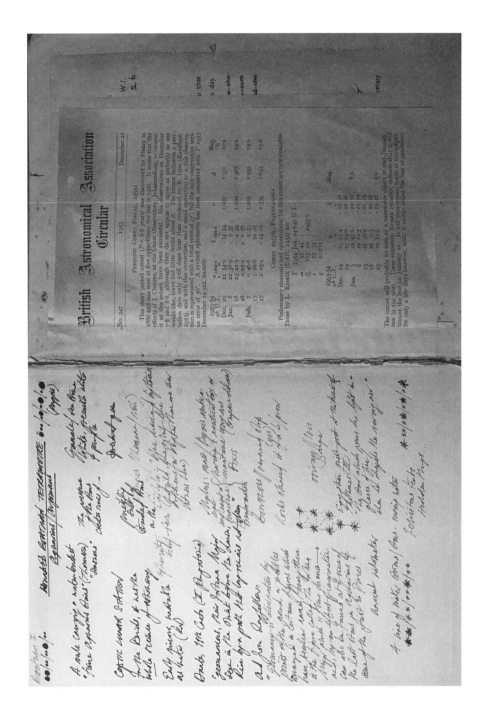

7. Celestial Metre workings (Popular Star Atlas) by Kristján Norge

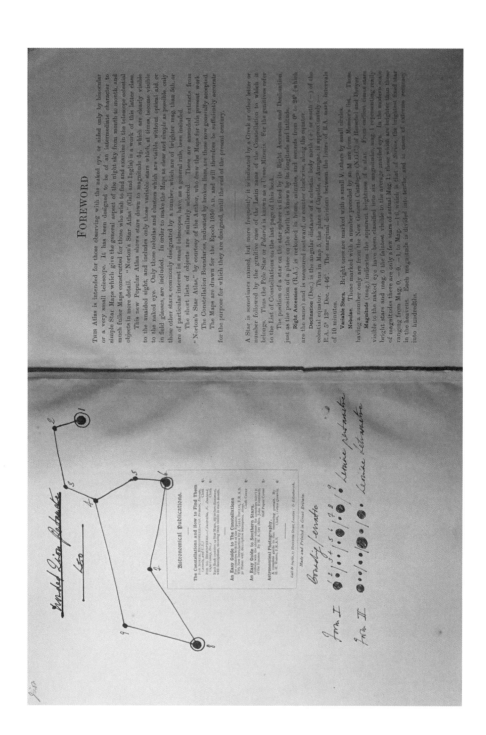

7. Celestial Metre workings (Popular Star Atlas) by Kristján Norge

110

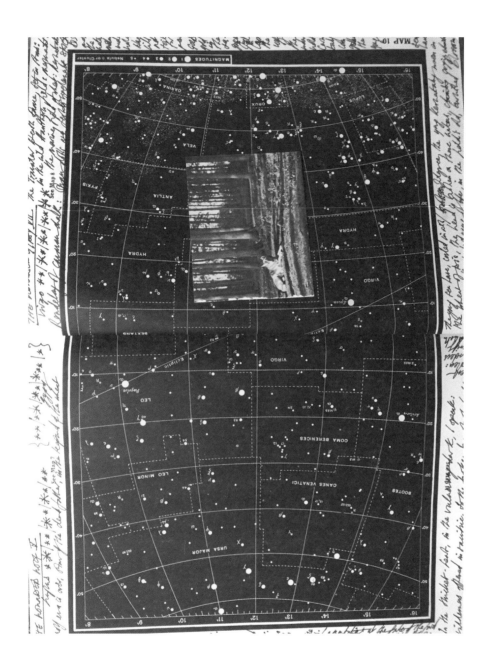

7. Celestial Metre workings (Popular Star Atlas) by Kristján Norge

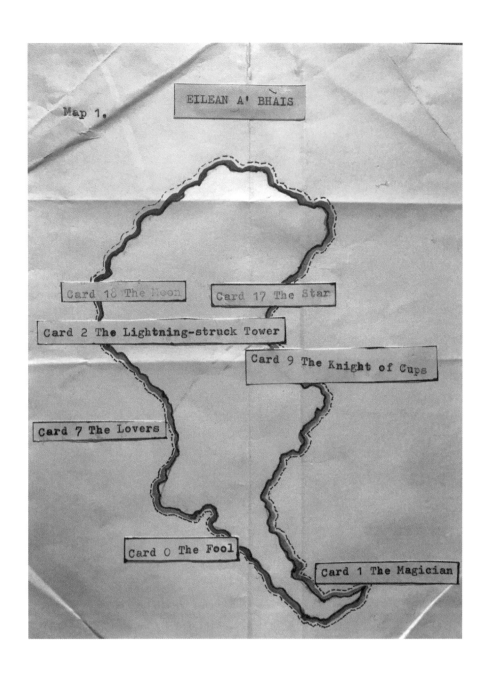

Map 1.

EILEAN A' BHÀIS

Card 18 The Moon

Card 17 The Star

Card 2 The Lightning-struck Tower

Card 9 The Knight of Cups

Card 7 The Lovers

Card 0 The Fool

Card 1 The Magician

8. Eilean a' Bhàis hand-drawn maps by Kristján Norge. See also p.150.

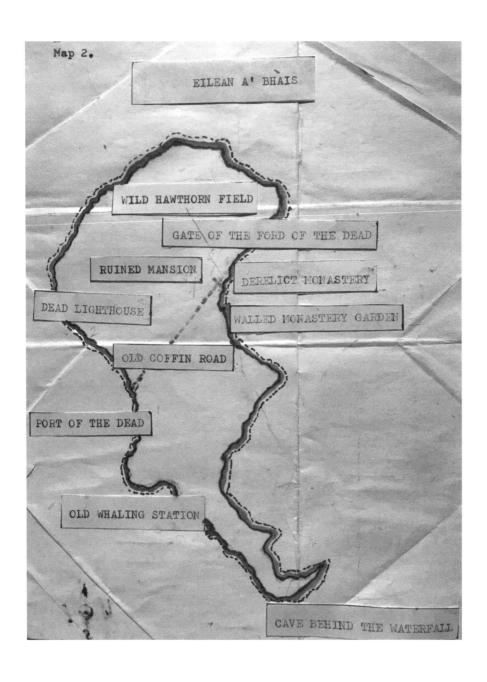

Map 2.

EILEAN A' BHAIS

WILD HAWTHORN FIELD

GATE OF THE FORD OF THE DEAD

RUINED MANSION

DERELICT MONASTERY

DEAD LIGHTHOUSE

WALLED MONASTERY GARDEN

OLD COFFIN ROAD

PORT OF THE DEAD

OLD WHALING STATION

CAVE BEHIND THE WATERFALL

8. Eilean a' Bhàis hand-drawn maps by Kristján Norge. See also p.158.

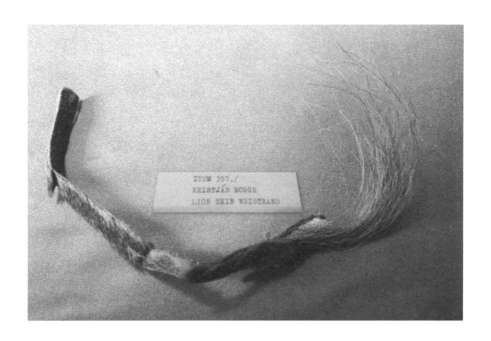

9. Photograph of lion skin wristband owned by Norge

10. Photograph of MacGillivray's ancestors crofting on Eilean a' Bhàis

11. Photograph of a fortune-telling card used by Norge

116

12. Photograph of a slide of the Palatine or Alexamenos Graffito

13. Photograph of Norge's polished steel shaving-mirror

14. Photograph of Norge's Shetland wool knitting on bone needles

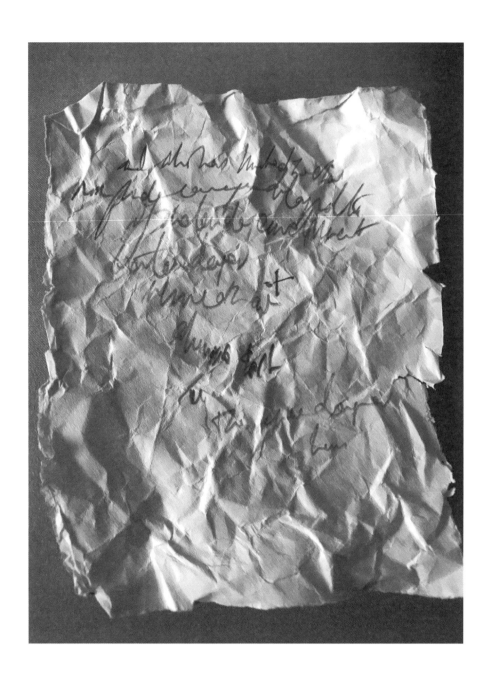

15. Photograph of written scraps from Eilean a' Bhàis Lighthouse

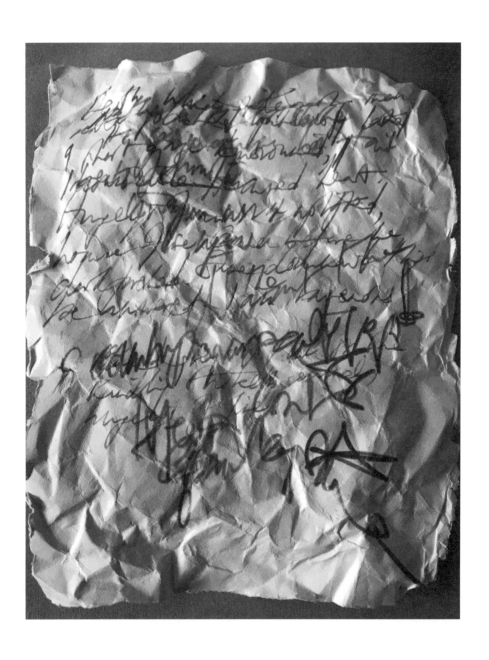

15. Photograph of written scraps from Eilean a' Bhàis Lighthouse

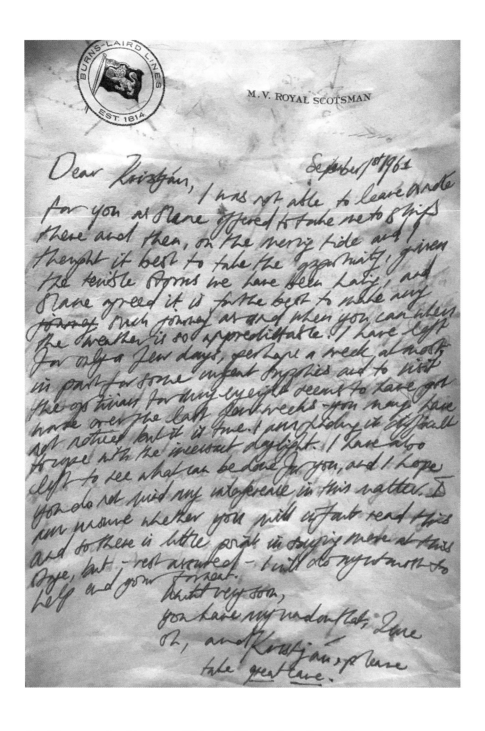

16. Photograph of letter to Kristján Norge from Luce Moncrieff

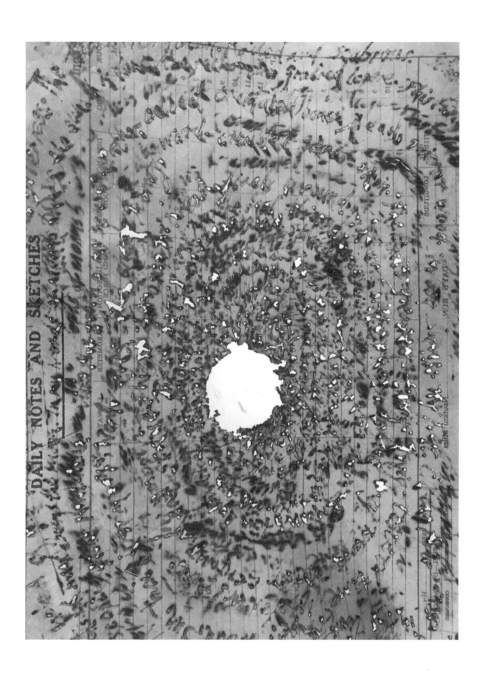

17. Photograph of pyrographic writing

18. Photograph of pyrography set

19. Photograph of Sluagh sequence outworking

20. Photograph of Luce Moncrieff's loom

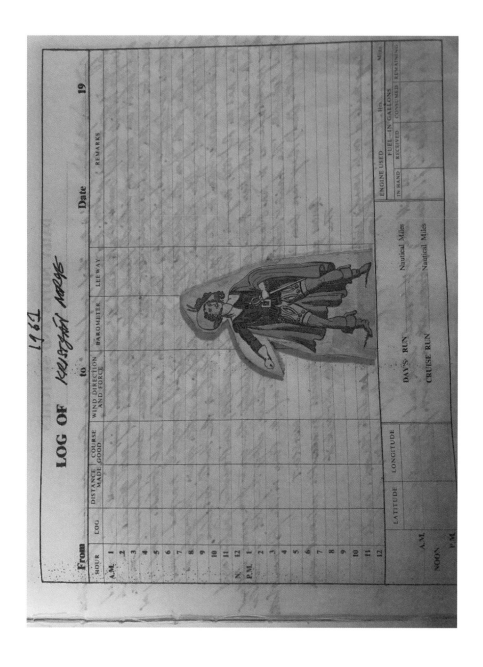

21. Excerpts from Kristján Norge's loggbok

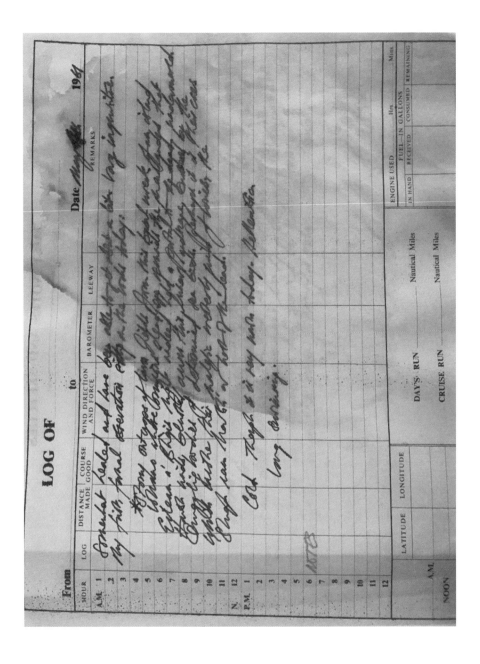

21. Excerpts from Kristján Norge's loggbok

IV

ADDITIONAL MATERIALS

Poet of the Underground City

Essay by MacGillivray on Kristján Norge

Reflex-Man

Kristján Norge became convinced of his demonhood in the summer of 1961, after a prolonged deterioration of nerves and sensibility latent within his psychological state from the 1950s onwards. Even before this occult conviction fully materialised, Norge was vulnerable to a series of profoundly disturbing events. The first involved a dream on the night of June 2nd, in which the happenstance positioning of two mirrors led Norge to see 'an almost anamorphic distortion' of his left hand, 'severely mutilated'. On the following day, out on the rocks gathering driftwood to the south-side of the island, Norge was suddenly pulled to the ground, badly cutting himself. When he staggered up, the beach was empty 'save for a trail of dead sea life littering the tide-line', not previously visible to him. Returning to the lighthouse, 'blood-bewildered' and badly shaken, Norge recounted to his companion, Luce Moncrieff, that he had witnessed '…vast piles of corpses, rotting on the compacted sand, of sea birds mangled and twisted up together like a plunged flock of broken angels. This instantly struck me as being the teorr.' The Scottish Gaelic word 'teorr' or 'tiur' can refer specifically to natural marine refuse left by the tide upon the shore, but also means to stamp, impress, or mark. Both definitions strongly impacted the episode, as Moncrieff uneasily recalled:

> I immediately went down to the beach but could find nothing on the shingle that showed any trace at all of such a big cull, only some blood – which must have been Kristján's – near a small, favourite rock pool. He had badly gashed his left palm and inner wrist, just missing the artery. I realised he must have slipped, collecting seaweed. After that, he deteriorated gradually and would sit up alone, late into the night. My strong impression was one of a tide turned within Kristján himself.

Though at the time Moncrieff only sensed this sea change, it was at this moment that Norge's theoretical research became key to his practical existence. The beach incident proved critical: as temporary 'neach an taighe-solais', or lighthouse-keeper, Norge was now used to an aerial and aquatic co-existence, his 'long arms folded like woollen wings, tobacco-stained and torn', as a living look-out or mortal figurehead in the flashing 'taighe-solais' tower. Given this temporary role by Moncrieff in an effort to stabilise the troubled poet, it seems lighthouse-keeping only provoked further turmoil. In an entry for June 8th, 1961, there is a description in Norge's own words detailing the circum-stances surrounding his subsequent 'spiritual corruption'. He noted in his loggbok a growing disquiet during an extended period of sultry weather, culminating in a second bizarre and alarming manifestation that appeared to him whilst shaving:

> in my left hand I grasped the small rectangular shaving mirror and in my right, the blade. On an old wooden shelf, my candle stub flickered for a moment and then the atmo-sphere in the polished steel seemed to thicken suddenly – just like the basin water when I dabbled my razor in it – and I paused, fascinated. Then, the image of my face thickened and distorted too and in that moment, blood burring in my ears, I fleetingly saw myself as diabolic.

Norge was not the first thinker to see a demon poorly reflected in his glass. Neither was his mirror carefully pre-prepared for magical encounters, being:

> ...a rudimentary slice of flattened metal, polished up for the trenches. Nothing excites it more than a candle... making the surface scratches glimmer. But, I think of it as a portal now...as if I could keep this strange reflexion held in it and carry the reflexion to another place...perhaps over to the cliffs and flick it from the mirror surface into the sea, or throw the whole thing down onto the rocks, like a reflective coffin lid. Yes, I am still afraid of it.

Just one day later a fierce Atlantic storm blew in and Norge, still preoccupied with his fractious mirror, remarked: 'what can

emerge? Can you keep the wind in a mirror and not have it dis-
turb your reflexion? There is a gale blowing across my inner
face tonight, but the steel is calm. And yet, I wish the blasted
wind would yield.'

The wind does not yield, due to a number of unusual weather
fronts that subjected Bàs to a fair battering. On June 10th, one
of the island donkeys was killed by a falling branch and the poet
sank into a depression, tersely commenting; 'Asal's grave is done.
I could get into it with him.' Between erratic bouts of writing,
Norge now spent his time tamping down the outhouses and
nailing up loose shutters. On June 12th, he split his thumbnail
with a hammer and wrapped 'a happock of kelp around the
swelling'. Damaging the same hand in this accident as the one
which was hurt on the rocks earlier that month, Norge, suffer-
ing from nervous exhaustion, embarked on a three-day drinking
spree. This final incident of the fateful sequence affected Luce
Moncrieff deeply, who awoke one night to find Norge gone.
Earlier that evening another blistering storm had struck and
Norge, seeking shelter, retreated to the well-known cave located
behind a waterfall on the south-easterly side of the island (see
fig.8, p.113.) It would be three days before Moncrieff eventually
located him at the island's 'claw', feverish, semi-conscious:

> and bundled up very tightly in his old overcoat. He was
> lying absolutely still in the innermost recesses of the rock
> behind the waterfall. Next to him was an empty bottle of
> Haig's, and I realised at once what had happened.

Unsurprisingly, Norge's experience differed radically from
Moncrieff's summary of events. For the agitated poet, the storm
created an atavistic danger-field of collapsing self-awareness and
corroded personal autonomy. Having witnessed a new figure in
his shaving mirror, Norge claims he was conveyed to the cave by
this visitant and endured, he wrote, 'the diabolic and visionary
Gaelic rite of the *taghairm*'. In his loggbok, Norge had previously
attached a page with candle wax from *Dr Armstrong's Gaelic
Dictionary* which defined the ritual, now commenting that 'even

though my hand came away when Luce grasped it, I was able to seal it with wax at the wrist when we reached the lighthouse. But, the bright-lipped droning, the murmuring goes on,' he complained, still demonstrating a degree of self-awareness. Armstrong's entry is as follows:

> divination by the *taghairm* was once a noted superstition among the Gael and in the northern parts of the Lowlands of Scotland. When any important question concerning futurity arose and of which a solution was, by all means, desirable, some shrewder person than his neighbours was pitched upon to perform the part of a prophet. This person was wrapped in the warm smoking hide of a newly-slain ox and laid at full length in the wildest recess of some lonely waterfall. The question was then put to him and the oracle was left in solitude to consider it. Here he lay for some hours with his cloak of knowledge around him and over his head, no doubt, to see the better into futurity; deafened by the incessant roaring of the torrent; every sense assailed; his body steaming; his fancy in a ferment; and whatever notion had found its way into his mind from so many sources of prophecy, it was firmly believed to have been communicated by invisible beings who were supposed to haunt such solitudes.

When fully recovered from the rigours of his hangover, Norge doggedly claimed that what he had experienced at the cave tallied with Armstrong's depiction of a 'ferment', insisting that this second reflection which had appeared in his battered steel mirror was of an autochthonous being which had made itself visible to him:

> a reflexion named Monmhur came to me in the mirror that night and lifted me to the cave of bloods... ten times, he says, the wind will come and will take me to the sites I have already prepared across the island. He can only speak with me in the mirror, but will appear after each ordeal. So, the wind of voices will take me at new moon and full moon and breathe into me knowledge of my demonhood and he says this will come in the pictures I will see before I am again abandoned. I will then be returned to the light-

house. There I must daub old hair I have collected from my horn comb with blood from my damaged mouth and set it alight on the surface of my shaving mirror. After the hair has flared, Monmhur says a coded counter-charm will appear in a sequence of flashes on the mirror surface for me to write down and retain. The flashes will then vanish, leaving only Monmhur's reflected face, and the mirror will soften. I will now be able to make a cylinder of it, placing it upright on a clean sheet of paper. Distorted language will be murmured from Monmhur's miniature cylinder portrait in the mirror onto the paper surface. The chaotic words will seem scorched or burnt into the paper. When this is done, this reflexion will vanish and the mirror will unfurl, returning to its normal, flat shape again. I must copy out the words, keeping one sheet of paper and folding up the scorched original with one of my own possessions. On the same evening, under the same lunar conditions, I must return to the site where the wind first conveyed me and stash the paper, along with the personal object.

For Kristján Norge, Monmhur was quite obviously a member of the 'Sluagh nam Marbh', or 'Host of the Dead', a dangerous wind of voices he had studied which were much feared in Gaelic folklore: 'I have a strange reflexion, a visitant who would move in the glass as if it were once again sand and draw me into the myriad grains as if drowning in visions. Now I occlude with a lozenge of steel and the visage is harder, stranger, even.' In reality the face in the tarnished mirror was, of course, the poet's own.

Norge had evidently been absorbed by a 17th-century traditional esoteric tract, the *Ars Goetia*, in which 'Murmur' is cited as one of the angels who falls with the rebel flock to become a demon. Translating 'Murmur' into the Gaelic 'Monmhur', Norge describes this visiting entity as resembling 'a ravaged and pockmarked ship's figurehead, a marine gargoyle, whose moving features are animated by the shrinking and swelling of cracking wood'. We know from Norge's loggbok that he had intellectually assimilated Monmhur as his double, doppelgänger, co-walker; or 'Reflex-Man', a term coined by the Reverend Robert Kirk during his own fatal 16th-century experiences with the Highland sìth, or

otherworld fairy culture. Norwegian Vardøger tales would also
have been familiar to Norge, which captured the benign presence
of a phantasmic double whose actions predicated those of the
mortal they were shadowing: 'Monmhur-Vardøger,' he wrote in
his loggbok, 'has been to see me again.' Manifesting as the poet's
'Reflex-Man' and harbouring sensitive tendencies, Monmhur was
one willing to aid and abet his Norgesian double: 'even within
rebellions there stand counter-rebels; those who waver within
their previous instincts. Call it weakness, but real rebelliousness
is a stubborn and contrarian spirit, true only to itself', asserted
Monmhur, according to Norge – the demon's inevitable mouth-
piece.

Other numinous sources supporting Monmhur's curious
presence can be found within the Gaelic tradition: the personal-
ity of Monmhur could also be read as a 'tarbh boidhre' – a
monster, demon, or deity able to shape-shift into many forms
— a bull, horse, or man who possessed supernatural powers.
Alternatively, Monmhur might have been the poet's personal,
attendant angel. In Highland lore there exist nine 'ages' of angel
which Norge himself may be measured against, greying and
bearded, as one age shy of his death time: 'nao naodhanan
roibeanach laith', for Kristján Norge was dying.

According to Gaelic belief, the soul can return to a person,
after wandering through space and time, by alighting on his
face. Sometimes the body lived on after the soul had died and
that body was said to amble about, carrying the substance of
the soul in its left hand and the shadow of its withered heart in
its right. Accounts exist of islanders who were buried with a
stone placed on their chests to weigh down the dead heart per-
haps to guard against such post-death wanderings. These cor-
poreal trace elements of the heart and soul suggest vestiges of
counterbalanced, once vital elements: a shadow of the heart and
a substance of the soul which somehow gave intent to a person
without living concreteness. Norge himself increasingly lacked
substance, in particular, the substance of identity. In the context
of esoteric Gaelic culture, Norge's questionable ability to vanish

suggests his knowledge of a sian or protective charm. In his own thinking, perhaps a transformative occult power, termed the fìth-fàth, had transmuted the poet into self-assumed invisibility. This lack of personal visibility, substance, or form, may have been the fundamental root of the poet's psychological trouble. And so, the glinting emblem, or bridge, between Norge's seen and unseen self may be apportioned to the murmuring figure of Monmhur, his own reflection.

However, the most symbolic occurrence of that summer by far, eclipsing itinerant fiends and talking mirrors, had been the sudden extinguishment of the Bàs lighthouse lantern on June 8th which appeared to usher in this period of personal turmoil in the poet. Distressed, Norge was unable to fix it despite repeated attempts across several days. His weakened state made matters worse and now the failing poet became febrile and unsettled, maintaining all the episodes outwith his control were intrinsically linked to the Sluagh whose malefic presence steadily increased across that tempestuous summer of 1961. Norge heavily underscored the last part of the Gaelic dictionary entry pertaining to 'invisible beings', on June 11th, scrawling in rough capitals: 'THIS IS THE SLUAGH'. His deterioration had begun.

Sluagh nam Marbh

During the time leading up to his disappearance Norge was strongly influenced by a major work of esoteric Japanese literature: the 1776 demonic encyclopaedias of Toriyana Sekien. Within their pages, he found a demon-illuminating mirror, the 'Shōmakyō', whose rounded shape captures magical reflections. In Sekien's first volume, *The Demon Horde's Night Parade*, the 'Kasha' or 'coffin wind' is rumoured to lift the corpse in its coffin high into the sky. Norge compared this to instances in Hebridean folklore of a bier smashed against a thorn tree to prevent the Sluagh nam Marbh from later using it to convey the corpse-laden coffin in its devouring and tempestuous currents:

it is interesting to note that a lack of wood created the need in the Hebrides for stone burial cists or inhumation of the body without a coffin. For conveying the corpse to its grave, a dead bed or 'cro-leapa', was used. The last 'cro-leapa' was said to have been buried with the body it carried. Though I wonder... this fact seems at odds with stories of 'bier smashing' – wood on the Hebridean Islands was exceptionally rare for many centuries and any such carefully constructed bier would have been preserved for several generations' use.

Sekien's account of sweat and blood left on old battlefields igniting as demon-fire equally resounds in battleground descriptions of the Sluagh which left pools of blood on the stone-studded peat turf, known as 'fuil na Sluagh'. 'The blood of the hosts is the beautiful red "crotal" of the rocks, melted by frost,' writes Alexander Carmichael in the *Carmina Gadelica*, as told to him on Barra. This testimony is disarmingly similar to the blood found on the rocks by Moncrieff. Being a dyer and weaver, she knew the difference between blood and crotal, an indigenous lichen used to stain Highland yarn a warm brown. For Norge, the blood spilled that day was both humanly sanguine and symbolically of another world. The ignition of such otherworldly blood plainly existed in the battleground of Norge's own senses, which enflamed a demonic encounter with the Sluagh's congregation.

But, what is the Sluagh nam Marbh? In varying oral accounts, the Sluagh was considered either a malign horde or a crowd of ethereal, wind-blown presences. Some said they were the sìth or fairies, others the souls of mortals lost in human battles or aerial huntsmen, still others that they were fallen angels or demons. Norge attempted to reconcile these differences, writing: 'here is a host of many entities – mortal and immortal, religious and folk-loric, victims and aggressors, but all aerial – all wind-borne.' The wind which the Sluagh occupied blew from a westerly direction, and was often known as the 'people's puff of wind'. The wind-blown host picked up living mortals, frequently carrying them for miles, and deposited them again having caused the individuals great exhaustion and often physical injury. This was defined as 'falbh air an t-sluagh': to be spirited away by the dead. An oral recollection recorded in the *Carmina Gadelica* describes how:

> a man in Benbecula was taken up several times. His friends assured me that night became a terror to this man, and that ultimately he would on no account cross the threshold after dusk. He died, it is said, from the extreme exhaustion consequent of these excursions. When the spirits flew past his house, the man would wince as if undergoing a great mental struggle, and fighting against forces unseen of those around him.

There were many more incidences of a mortal lifted by the Sluagh and entreated to kill or maim other humans and animals with elf-shot. Considerable evidence exists of such belemnite elf-bolts or flint arrows (purportedly fired from fairy bows) being used as amulets. Born out of this aerial phenomenon is the expression to be 'away with the fairies' or out of one's mind, as if one's wits had been carried off and deposited elsewhere. Inevitably, the Sluagh often came for the weak and infirm. Individuals on the brink of death were particularly vulnerable and the west-facing doors and windows of any dwelling where a person was dying were tightly secured against this tumultuous westerly. The Sluagh was also known to have sucked the life-force from creatures or humans that still retained their outward appearance, creating fetches or revenants apparently returned from the dead. It was tantamount to the wild hunt of Scandinavian folklore, headed up by Odin, god of poetry, magic and the dead: a demonic, horse-mounted commander who led his lost and captured souls across night skies in the raging body of a storm. In a Gaelic oral account, the Sluagh leader is named 'Sgròb', meaning 'the craw or crop of a bird, or to scratch with talons or nails' and this definition may have influenced Norge in his prolific marking of the inner lighthouse walls in an upper-storey room.

Inevitably, rebuffed by strong North Atlantic winds, Bàs remained a stark victim of storms and this had always encouraged a local preoccupation with the Sluagh as a palpable and frequent presence. Luce Moncrieff was aware of this and, when she came to understand Norge's fears, inevitably resorted to the old Highland charms and rituals traditionally used to guard against and ward off the Sluagh nam Marbh. These included a charm worn with flax which she tied around the poet's neck and the insertion of a small grass into the midst of the horde to disperse it, when once Norge witnessed the Sluagh trapped in the water of a disused well. None of these attempts seemed to have taken effect, however. Even before her own urgent departure, Moncrieff watched helplessly as Norge returned each dawn to the lighthouse, bloodied and exhausted, battered by his incessant nocturnal excursions. Though he had first been aware of the Sluagh merely as a folkloric phenomenon, the poet's experience of this malevolent rebel band had now become more direct. As Norge understood it, his own condition merely described the outworking of a crucial process; minor scrapes and tiredness were hazards of the task at hand. The poet's real concern was over Moncrieff's ability to fulfil her own role in his schema. Ever askance, Moncrieff's diagnostic proved quite different: 'he has,' she wrote, 'a perturbance of mind that conjures up bad visions – I must find help for him.'

Poet of the Underground City

Prior to arriving on Eilean a' Bhàis, Norge already had provisionally stumbled upon help, however. In the early spring of 1961, investigating mnemonics, the poet had made several trips to the Manuscripts Division at the National Library of Scotland to research Bàs as an abandoned Isle of the Dead. It was after one of these lonely excursions that he encountered consultant Jeanie Hafoc in his regular drinking haunt, a back bar of the World's End pub. She immediately offered to treat him. Later, Norge wrote in his loggbok:

> she has the aspect and habits of a hawk and I can say with all
> certainty that she seemed to drop from the sky on nowhere
> and, as I was occupying nowhere, it seemed I was her focus,
> her intent, her prey.'

Norge was seen just a few times by Hafoc in her consulting rooms off Niddry Street in Edinburgh's Old Town (rooms which she enigmatically described as 'antechambers to the Underground City'). Little of these meetings was documented by Norge, bar detailed notes on the architecture and history of that particular quarter of the abandoned city which lay even further below ground. Unknown to Hafoc, Norge was familiar with the topography of the capital's subsurface metropolis himself working out of a small, stone office which had been a medieval granary store for Edinburgh Castle. 'There are nine floors beneath the one I am seated on,' he typed, 'and another three above this stone-arched vault.' In light of this early preoccupation, it is probable he agreed to submit to Hafoc's treatment solely in order to gain access to an unchartered part of the Underground City. 'This particular area Hafoc works from, borders the outskirts of a subterrestrial necropolis,' he observed. Indeed, during this time he evolved extensive mnemonic cartographies of several lost cities: 'sublunar: Ur, subsolar: Aztlán, submarine: Atlantis', before claiming 'the subterranean: Dùn Èideann' which Norge vigorously sought to expand his knowledge of, aided unwittingly by a committed Hafoc. Notoriously late for his appointments, 'I would most likely have been found half a mile north,' he wrote, 'down on my knees in a chiselled stone corridor, pocket torch in my mouth, charting the labyrinthine environment surrounding my descent. By March 1961, I had grafted every detail of the medical history of human anatomy in Scotland onto Edinburgh's Underground City as a memorial architecture. From mort-safe design to the manufacture of surgical steel, I've mapped this history onto the architectural features of the sprawling Underground City, even discovering a hypogean anatomy theatre beneath the old medical school on Hunter Square (possibly used as a secret alternative in surgeon Robert Knox's era of anatomical murderers and body-snatchers) in which he positioned imaginary ecorchés of Robert the Bruce and Mary Queen of Scots as aides-memoire, ostensibly dissecting Scottish history itself. It has taken me just four years to do so.'

Unsurprisingly, Norge's obsession with the Underground City was at first only lightly contested by his new-found forays into memory on Bàs. Writing her diary entry for June 26th, Luce Moncrieff commented: 'he is distracted and restless. He almost belongs with Hafoc beneath ground, or lives there, in spirit.' Though she had not yet met Hafoc, Moncrieff regarded the psychologist with a certain wariness by proxy; 'her acute professionalism, her assertion, somehow undermined me... I felt impaled.' Certainly, during Norge's rapid deterioration from the middle of the summer onwards, he was often to be found striding across the island as if seeking a prior haunt, frequently disappearing unannounced, incessantly murmuring (a habit Moncrieff noticed had become perpetual, even waking him as he slept, 'but murmuring, always murmuring...') and 'barricading himself into the upper rooms of the lighthouse to burn things,' she wrote.

Since childhood Luce Moncrieff had subsisted on the islet alone and when not light-keeping, busied herself examining shards from the several souterrain sites on Bàs whilst dyeing and weaving in her spare time. The unwarranted arrival of Kristján Norge immediately altered this solitary existence. 'Stamping with fire,' Moncrieff noted in her entry for May 3rd, 1961, 'a strange figure staggered onto the beach and rolled in the sand to put out the flames which engulfed his old overcoat. A little way off, his boat bobbed against the rocks, in it a small library of damp paperwork: some pages alight, some drifting in the surf still on fire, and some blown, charred, onto the beach. He had his dog with him, a large creature that howled from the wreckage. It was a dramatic entrance and for me, now looking back, the spirit of Norge was there, in the flesh – drowned and burned all at once.'

A contemporaneous character sketch would portray the odd figure she had attempted to rehabilitate: the pipe-smoking Norge, wearing a battered hunter's cap and an old gabardine tied around his waist with baling twine, who carefully tended the small herd of two donkeys; Asal and Asan. Though only in his early forties when he disappeared, he 'had the haggard or ravaged look of a drinker, was often unshaven and was wind-bitten so that his large-boned face – likely once handsome – had now markedly aged,' Moncrieff revealed. 'In truth, the man could have been two decades older or more.'

Norge kept few belongings on his person bar a small, rectangular military shaving mirror, a selection of pencil stubs, a jaw harp and a rusty tobacco tin. A particular joy of his was to hand-feed small birds which alighted on his Olivetti when working outdoors on an old trestle table. 'Bobby-shaws,' he called them, feeding the robins that came to him, fragments of oatmeal. Unusually for the time, he was a dedicated knitter, working a single ply, natural brown yarn which he described as 'a miracle thread. I can make keen stuff from string and air,' he said, and Moncrieff surveyed him as 'a kind of fisher-poet, spooling wool between both chapped hands while his smoking pipe remained firmly clamped between uneven teeth. He called anything he made, his "net", and considered knitting and weaving (both of which I did, of course) as "pure physics combined with an alchemical materialism. Quite literally, a spell-craft of the labyrinth".'

Norge's fascination with the immaterial began at a young age when he claimed he had 'slowly flown down a flight of stairs' and the poet linked this ability, which left him at the age of six, with his profound short-sightedness. Rejecting spectacles, he encountered 'shape and form through atmosphere and presence,' which may have influenced his perceptual sensitivity to spiritual phenomena and his preference for poetry that was both esoteric and destined for the page.

Living alongside the poet must have taken its toll. Moncrieff, who had originally found him, nursed him and given him a provisional role as temporary light-keeper, now kept a wary watch over him. From early May to early June, Norge stabilised, but then seemed ever more vulnerable to the inclement weather, wrestling periods of profound disturbance with lucid spells that grew rarer and rarer. At the beginning of September, deeply concerned both for her own wellbeing and Norge's deteriorating state of mind, Moncrieff travelled to Edinburgh having made an appointment with Hafoc, whom she hoped would intervene. She had been exposed to the poet for a little under five months and, unbeknown to her, would never see him again. From her diary, we know that there was an altercation between the two women and that during the argument, presumably over Norge's treatment, Moncrieff slipped and fell down a set of stone stairs. Hospitalised, she recounted: 'it was as if I had fallen into the Underground City itself; in fact, I believe I did so, for when I came round I had a strange and somewhat hellish vision.' The fall, in which she broke her wrist, two ribs and badly cut her leg, incapacitated Moncrieff for several months. By the time she returned to the island in January 1962, Norge was gone.

From Moncrieff's account, it is not entirely clear whether the poet suicided, was killed in an accident, or returned to the mainland. Though officially reported missing, it was generally accepted that Norge perished either through falling onto the rocks from a sheer cliff edge on the east side of the island, or was drowned. A wilder supposition was that he had leapt from the lighthouse gallery. His body was never found.

Dante, Mnemonics & the Tarot

Norge's initial investigations into classical mnemotechnics had begun in the late 1950s when he became fully conversant with the urban mapping process necessary for a Roman rhetor to memorise a speech as de-lineated in the *Rhetorica ad Herennium*, a Latin text on rhetoric anonymously authored in the late 80s, BC. As such, he was wholly familiar with the organisational benefits of the memory palaces of antiquity, within them carefully chosen loci or places: plinths, pillars, etc., and the sequential arrangement of objects or 'imagines agentes' (images which act) placed in each of the loci to provoke the recollection of a speech to be re-membered and performed. He was especially concerned with the imagines agentes, or 'IA' as he termed them, and wrote prolifically on how these performing images or figures, traditionally formed of striking details and possessing exceptionally bloodied or extremely beautiful bodies, might be poetically perceived:

> if stanzas in poetry are rooms, or cellae, or chambers, or stopping points (all this taken from the etymology of the word 'stanza'), what might make the reader pause? Might they not be filled with terrible and brilliant memory corpses… and if the chamber were sacrificial, might not those corpses be newly decorated with gold and blood, still spasming with life? Might the act of being witnessed give those IA life? Imagine the page as a palace, the stanzas as rooms and the body language of the poetry – the knife fights of the iambic, formal dance of the pyrrhic and limping of the trochaic as belonging to the dagger-wielding knight, the bells and veils of the courtesan, and the footsore, limping fool? I can write each chamber-stanza as a cell in which a moving IA to catalyse memory is imprinted. The cells could be numbered, like cards, shuffled in the mind and rearranged. A deck of poetry. A fortune-telling poetry. But, I ask myself, what are these IA being used to recall?

Though convinced that poetic IA were fundamentally self-referential, Norge insisted on whole subworlds of attendant memory imaging 'phosphorescent with thought', which the presence of IAs inevitably attracted and re-generated, along with the depth-charge of their etymology: 'gold is fattened on shining.' Norge was aware, too, of the term 'phantasiai' – the presence of powerful and emotive images which impacted strongly on the memory:

> …my etymological dictionary informs me that fantasy derives from the Greek word *phantasia* meaning 'power of imagination; appearance, image, perception', from *phanta-zesthai* 'picture to oneself', from *phantos* 'visible', from *phainesthai* 'appear', in late Greek 'to imagine, have visions', related to *phaos*, *phōs* 'light', *phainein* 'to show, to bring to light'. These phantasies or fantasies I am dealing with seem to be distorting mirrors, alive with phosphorescent images.

In an attempt to steer complex and vast network of images through cause and effect, past and future, this poetic landscape of mnemonic figures, contorted and wounded, striking and memorable, was conflated by Norge with a sequence of fortune-telling cards or tarot images. With the squared and framed card as object, hand-held and stimulating a plethora of numinous possibilities which might come to light in reality, Norge argued poetry could have the same function as divinatory devices, its prophesying performers caught in stanzaic vignettes, their metres and stresses embodying a finely tuned language of action and conflict danced in armour, accompanied by the fundamental note of the flute. 'Premonition, fore-memory, agitated circumstance. All this set off by a dramatic performing image which acts as a forerunner to recalled circumstance,' he wrote. Encouraged by the etymological roots of 'trochee' from which the term 'truckle' or wheel evolved, Norge was all too tempted to harness his new-found theory to actual tarot motifs, perceiving the trochaic as linked to the 'Wheel of Fortune' – an Arcanum card embedded with the letters 'rota', the Latin for 'wheel', in turn connected with the scrambled letters of the word 'taro'. The wheel of life was also the wheel of fate, a memory cycle. He had come full circle, it seemed.

Concurrently, Norge had discovered William Marston Seabury's tantalising, yet incomplete, 1949 exploration, *The Tarot Cards and Dante's Divine Comedy*, in which the author claimed to have uncovered significant correlations between early tarot card imagery and *La Divina Commedia*:

> if the cards of the Major Arcana of the tarot pack were arranged according to the same chronology adopted by Dante, a true and completely intelligible interpretation of the cards will follow, from which the same story told in the Comedy of Dante may be derived from the cards themselves.

Seabury argued that it was imagery from *The Divine Comedy* (as well as from other sources by artists such as Giotto and Boccaccio) which had informed the pictures in the Major Arcana cards. 'Perhaps his *Commedia* can now be read as a score for prophesy,' commented Norge, 'spawning an oracular vision to be played and replayed across subsequent centuries.' The pamphlet had clearly made a strong impact on Norge who, revisiting explorations he had begun a few years earlier, now provisionally incorporated some of the tarot emblems into his own rudimentary system developed on Bàs (as outlined below). The schema incorporated references to other material such as a fortune-telling card in his possession, singled out from a 1950 deck of *Le Grand Jeu de Mlle Lenormand* featuring Chiron, the wounded centaur, which Norge tallied with the 'Broken or Lightning-Struck Tower'.

He was equally absorbed by Dante's mnemonic themes in *La Divina Commedia*, locating virtues and vices embodied by the IA inhabiting its pages, in which the tripartite Catholic vision of a pre-Renaissance Italy vitally manifested as an interlocked memory world. 'The *Inferno* reads as a burning deck of cards: an imaginal and numeric memory house of suffering. To read the *Inferno*, housed in the woods of memory – picking up charred sticks from the ground of recollection – is to walk through cartomancy itself.' By the third week of May Norge was sufficiently cognisant of some of the key landmarks on Bàs and produced a map of the island, superimposing onto it a shrunken tarot symbolism, partially evolved from Seabury, which also incorporated aspects of his own picturing and features of the island sites themselves. Though there were many more on the islet, for this tentative and derivative first map-making Norge selected only seven and allocated each one a card with its attendant image. Carefully allotted, this list of seven cards provided gateway images between real locations on the island, the metaphoric symbolism of a Dantesque tarot, and Norge's early probings into a pre-prescribed cartographic and cartomantic memory system.

SEABURY'S SYSTEM

CARD 0 – The Fool

PART ONE – INFERNO
CARD 1 – The Magician or Cobbler
CARD 2 – The Lightning Struck Tower
CARD 3 – The Hanged Man
CARD 4 – La Papessa
CARD 5 – Death
CARD 6 – The Devil, Satan

PART TWO – PURGATORIO
CARD 7 – The Lovers
CARD 8 – The Wheel of Fortune
CARD 9 – The Pope
CARD 10 – The Emperor
CARD 11 – The Empress
CARD 12 – The Hermit, or Sage
CARD 13 – Justice
CARD 14 – Fortitude
CARD 15 – Temperance

EPILOGUE TO PURGATORIO
CARD 16 – The Chariot

PART THREE – PARADISO
CARD 17 – The Star
CARD 18 – The Moon
CARD 19 – The Sun
CARD 20 – The Last Judgement
CARD 21 – The World

NORGE'S SYSTEM (MAP 1)

CARD 0 – The Fool: Dante/Norge (Old Whaling Station)

CARD 1 – The Magician or Cobbler (Cave Behind Waterfall)
CARD 2 – The Lightning-struck Tower (Lighthouse)
CARD 7 – The Lovers: Luce, Jeanie, Norge (At Sea)
CARD 9 – The Knight of Cups (Derelict Monastery)
CARD 17 – The Star (the Coffin Road)
CARD 18 – The Moon (the Ruined Mansion)

NOTES TO MAP 1

CARD 0 is the Fool (tarot) and is marked 'Dante/Norge'. It is mapped onto the 'Old Whaling Station' on Bàs' south-west coast. In Norge's observations, it becomes clear that he considered Dante to be a wandering fool or troubadour and memory personified, rambling through an inhospitable forest. We cannot be sure whether Norge considers a wandering memory foolish, or the fool to be a wandering memory, near-forgotten.
CARD 1 is the Magician (tarot) and is marked 'Cave Behind Waterfall'.
CARD 2 is the Lightning-struck Tower (tarot), become the Bàs Lighthouse.
CARD 3 is the Lovers (tarot) and these are Norge, Luce Moncrieff and Jeanie Hafoc. He positioned this card 'At Sea'.
CARD 9 is the Knight (tarot). The significance of this card remains something of a mystery and is placed at the 'Derelict Monastery'.
CARD 17 is the Star (tarot) which signified for Norge the star of hope, positioned on the 'Coffin Road'.
CARD 18 is the Moon (tarot) and the site of the ruins of the Bàs Mansion.

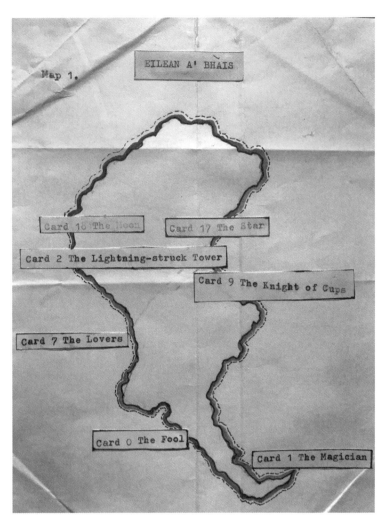

Map 1: First hand-drawn map of Eilean a' Bhàis by Kristján Norge.

BÀS LOCI		*IA*
0	Old Whaling Station	Fool
1	Cave Behind the Waterfall	Magician
2	Lighthouse	Lightning-struck Tower
7	'At Sea'	The Lovers
9	Derelict Monastery	Knight
17	Old Coffin Road	Star
18	Ruined Mansion	Moon

150

For the remainder of May, Norge broadened his scope, continuing to diagrammatically position a series of tarot-driven IA. This time he selected ten island loci, expanding on the original seven. Simultaneously treating Eilean a' Bhàis as a metaphoric locus, Norge fleetingly discerned the whole island topography as a self-contained and rugged stanza floating on a saltwater page and the loci as sites on this island stanza at which tarot symbols were situated to perform as IA. Alongside, he placed their mnemonic properties. Norge was frustrated at these early efforts, calling them 'memorially illiterate... I have failed, in some cases, to conjoin several IA with the correct mnemonic or locus. Here, for example, is the "Fool" who embodies curiosity and engenders an attendant list of states such as venturing, lightheartedness and beginnings, placed at the "Port of the Dead" which is a locus of mortuary rites, sombreness and endings.'

BÀS LOCI		IA	MNEMONIC
1	Port of the Dead	Fool	Curiosity
2	Lighthouse	Broken Tower	Truth
3	Coffin Road	Star	Hope
4	Ruined Mansion	Moon	Fortitude
5	Gate of the Ford of the Dead	Empress	Self-reflexion
6	Derelict Monastery	Knight	Chivalry
7	Wild Hawthorn Field	King	Justice
8	Old Whaling Station	Death	Prudence
9	Cave Behind Waterfall	Magician	Inspiration
10	Monastery Walled Garden	Hermit	Knowledge

Yet, Norge swiftly reconciled himself to what he had first identified as clumsy juxtapositions, borrowed in part from Ramon Llull's list of knightly virtues in *The Book of Order of Chivalry*, a manual written in the latter part of the 13th-century. Norge provisionally sought to affiliate these states to the essential characteristics of a poet, inferring the figurative presence of tarot motifs could catalyse a memory of distinct poetic properties.

'Here we have chivalric remnants: hope, fortitude, justice. In this manner,' he conceded, 'the Fool traverses death as the great adventure, rather than being at odds with its stasis and can possibly only do so within the scope of rebirth and playful curiosity. These configurations produce many shafts of light that glint and deflect, as if from a broken mirror, but their realignments are recommendations from fractured stellar configurations – always they reform within the guise of poetic logic.' Norge concluded his cartographic guide in the monastic garden, tended to by the 'hermit of knowledge, collecting up the firewood of futurity'. In another example of his writing from this time, the recuperating poet displayed a keen interest in monkish learning:

> to gather up the kindling of knowledge and ignite it again:
> the alphabetic twigs of lettering smouldering in my hands
> as if incantatory. Listening to the map, I can hear its
> meaning as if putting my face close to the blaze to read
> the consummating letters spark and twist with inference.
> These sticks have been gathered in Dante's wood and can
> be scattered to prophesy future behaviour, whether sinful
> or good. The forest, of course, is the forest of memory
> and the bundle of kindling recollected: gathered in again
> to fuel the fire of future imaging.

Much of Norge's reflection on medieval scholarly and monastic absorption of knowledge now bled into his early 'poesis' or 'poetry-construction', as he termed it, partially informed by St Augustine in Book X of the *Confessions* whose own doctrine occupied a wild landscape : 'in the wide plains of my memory and in its innumerable caverns and hollows... I range...' Augustine wrote – his, a natural compendium of elements held in a secret or hidden memory which the mind overall may not experience or be aware of. Norge made this flickering duality his business, heartily engaged with hunting down classical memorabilia. 'Dante's wood, within which the path that does not stray was lost, is solely a memorial wood,' he concluded, 'and through it we can track one of the many arts, crafts, or somnambulisms of memory.' He then set about roughly charting the building blocks of memory itself, according to their Latin definitions, tallying each to a tarot figure and so, in turn, to a select cameo cast lifted from the hell-fired pages of Dante's *Inferno*. Returning to source, Norge again used Bàs as his locale, still maintaining the real tenfold sites he had selected on the island, which he never expanded beyond:

BÀS LOCI	TAROT IA	MNEMONIC	COMMEDIA
1 Port of the Dead	Death	Invention	Charon
2 Lighthouse	Broken Tower	Location	Dante
3 Coffin Road	Star	Image	Virgil
4 Ruined Mansion	Moon	Likeness	Leopard
5 Gate of the Ford of the Dead	Fortitude	Substance	She-Wolf
6 Derelict Monastery	Knight	Intention	Michael Scotus
7 Wild Hawthorn Field	King	Reaction	Ulysses
8 Old Whaling Station	Devil	Benignity	Lucifer
9 Cave Behind Waterfall	Magician	Rationale	Nessus
10 Monastery Walled Garden	Hermit	Collation	Beatrice

Alongside this tracking, Norge became deeply preoccupied with Celtic bardic composition in the Highlands for which a singular memory system had once been used. The poet composed by night, learning the poem by heart alone in his cell (Norge replaced this term with 'cave') and wrote down his composition during the day. Something of the flavour of this practice was perceptible in Norge's own retreats and emergences at the time and in his preoccupation with visibility, secrecy and temporality: 'under a late May moon,' he remarked, 'I shiveringly scratched out a poem recalled not yesterday, nor from childhood, but one remembered from the rocks themselves.' He had been down to the Bàs cavern more than once, (known in the Gaelic as being disguised behind a 'waterfall of the bloods') to experience composition as an intentional and imaginal nocturnal poet, before finally prising a self-haunted verse of the 'taghairm' from his finely tuned, dying vision.

Memory-haunted bays and fissures, abandoned caves and deceased lighthouses, had clearly possessed Norge in his extensive ruminations on the allegorical cartography of Bàs. Drawing on the island's reputation as an abandoned death isle whose 'Geata Àth nam Marbh', or 'Gate of the Ford of the Dead' hung open and whose old 'Port nam Marbh', or 'Port of the Dead', lay derelict, Norge became ever more focussed on transience and decay. 'The crumbled masonry of demolished crofthouses is dispersed among the peat banks and tangled heather all along the westerly shoreline and this tumbled chaos of dwellings recalls, resounds, reworks in abstract patterns, the memory of the Gaelic culture that built them. Of course, I am dying,' he wrote, 'and so can interpret the patterned glyphs, the poetry of collapse, the memory of the torched and smoking roofs of clearance brutality with clarity and precision.'

Mnemonics were indeed Norge's volatile currency. Immersed in his groundwork on Bàs as a 'mythic portal to the west – and by west,' he wrote, 'I mean solely in the Ancient Egyptian sense of a death-bound direction, which was also true for the Celts.' He had, by this point, tracked all of the island to chart its landmarks as loci within a classical memory system, conflated with Dantesque mnemotechnics and tarocchi symbolism. Now he looked for a centre-piece.

Of all poets, the figure of Dante Alighieri most embodied memory, argued Norge. He had once tentatively positioned Dante as an imago agento: a living poet traversing the precincts of the Underground City, who might initiate, through his actions, a forgotten awareness of memorial systems to be applied to Edinburgh's distinctive subsurface quarter. Transferring Dante as a vital IA to Bàs must have been an easy gesture. The bleak islandscape was a memorial to death itself, said Norge, and proved too tempting not to isolate as an esoteric setting for the figure of Dante to wander on tirelessly:

> I see the Florentine poet as the genius loci of Bàs, roaming
> the island with a leopard, she-wolf and lion at his heels,
> picking their way through salt-water and rock pools on the
> lonely and deserted beach.

When researching Eilean a' Bhàis during the 1950s in the National Library's extensive special collections, Norge had already uncovered material on the Hebridean island which evidenced its status as a defunct death station – no longer a working death harbour, no longer a utilised internment ground – whose processing of incoming cadavers and administration of necrotic rites had ceased at some point during the tenth century. With this in mind, the poet regarded Bàs (itself named as 'death' in the Gaelic) as a rhetoric of liminality, hosting the memory of death itself as near-forgotten. The loci Norge selected, therefore, were ten island locations which had individual significance within Bàs history as a sepulture station or floating mortuary ground. Here, Dante himself was positioned in Norge's own system as a moving and performing imago who had inherited the skills of a spirit-guide from his apt mentor, Virgil, not to usher the poet toward realms of the afterlife, but to put them to good use in navigating through the flourishing 'ars memorativa' of memory itself. And so, Norge quietly pictured Dante Alighieri as a tramping memorial embodiment who had, so to speak, lit the undergrowth of memory's forest. 'The taxonomy of memory on Bàs, though concerned with morbid properties, is still a rhetorical memory,' wrote Norge, deeply engaged with each of his ten memorised haunts. Enthused by the idea of a processional trail which began at the Port of the Dead and ended in the Monastery Garden, Norge had 'the poet' set out on a pilgrimage across ten loci:

1) *Port Nam Marbh* – the landing point is the 'Port of the Dead' where the poet disembarks, seeking the conditions of his own demise on the ruined and abandoned Isle of the Dead. Dysfunctional and forgotten, many of the buildings on Bàs, such as the monastery and lighthouse, lie derelict.

2) *The Charred Arrow Shaft* – is the 'Lightning-struck Tower' (tarot) and this tallies well on the island map, being the lighthouse. For Norge, the Bàs lighthouse signifies a watch-tower and a much larger presence which he superimposes on the circular form of the colosseum so that it looms like a large lens, or eye. This sawdust or sand-filled arena, provides the horizontal discus for the poet's imagination:

> in it, he performs his own death-rites as centaur – beast of his natal constellation – having been mortally wounded by the anti-chivalric figure of 'knightless'. The charred arrow is the devil's tower itself and is the sagitta (arrow) used by sagittarius (the archer), and therefore could be read metonymically as the wounded centaur who is slain to self by 'knightless'. Or, it represents the part of the centaur that is malign because he is shooting with a blackened and charred arrow. Or, the arrow represents, by pointing into the flesh, that part of the centaur which is slaughtered (memory wounded and killed). Or, the centaur is benign, but caught up in the devil's tower which then collapses.

3) *The Star-Ravaged Co(r)pse* – the initial vision is of a stellar body having passed through and in so doing, having destroyed a wood or copse. Norge argues for a presence or atmosphere of spirit which the body must progress through, as a kind of aether, which ages the flesh. This ageing must then be worn into death. Norge asserts it is the spirit which wearies and acts upon the physical body of the individual advancing through the spirit's presence in one's life. He envisages the spirit as invisible but as an active agent that pools around the poet's body in a cloud or atmosphere. The spirit can only be perceived through its effect which appears as ageing in the flesh of the human by its own spirit. Norge presents this argument in the metaphoric image of the star crashing through and so annihilating the undergrowth. He also wondered whether the landscape of Bàs could be an environment which memory (as a stellar body) itself had traversed and eradicated, considering both the metonymic possibilities of memory as a destructive stellar body and the microcosmic/macrocosmic configuration of memory within its own place as

if: 'memory had passed through its own terrain like a moving statue whose feet do not touch the ground, leaving behind little that is good in its ravaged trail'.

4) *Al Jab'Hah* – here we have the ruined mansion standing for 'Lunar Mansion X' in the Arabic system (Norge's mansion of birth), filled with lions. The Arabic mansion name, Al Jab'Hah, refers to the forehead of the lion and this is used as a seeing or scrying device, subsequently referencing the Neolithic remains of cave lions used in prehistoric mark making. However, he also included the 'occiput' or back of the skull, as counterpoint: 'the seeing sense of backward awareness.' Norge also worked in relation to lunar mansion sonics which, in the Arabic tradition, were sounded as the 28 models of spoken letters: the sound of Mansion X is 'sh'. Norge identified leonine presences as lurking shadows of his own selfhood and surveyed the mansion exterior as decayed, derelict and abandoned.

5) *Sequences for a Tariff* – at the 'Ford of the Gate of the Dead' the poet must pay a numinous tariff in order to pass.

6) *Knightless* – is indicated by the monastery ruins.

7) *Sump* – presents a sacrificial field with a rectangular dug-out grave which, in Norge's mind, can be roughly transformed into the stanza on the blank field of the page. See his essay *TRAN-Quil-Ity: Crossing the Quill of Being* included in the additional materials for Norge's extended thoughts on this.

8) *Meat Spirit* – here lies the old whaling station where the vast, waiting bones creak and rub at night.

9) *Taghairm* – is the cave in which the poet undergoes the ritual of the 'taghairm', wrapped in a steaming animal skin, to gain a vision.

10) *Legere* – is a monastic walled garden filled with the broken and smoking kindling of religion in allusion to the star-ravaged wood of the opening sequence. The old mariner tombs are here, grown wild among the barren fruit trees. For the poet, this is a hermetic bewilderment of flame: a contained and diminished illumination.

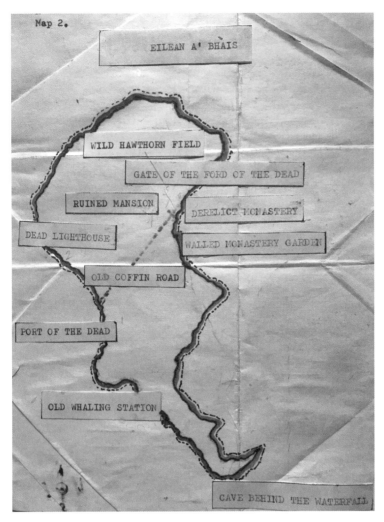

Map 2: Second hand-drawn map of Eilean a' Bhàis by Kristján Norge.

This second mapping by Norge is much more extensive and aligns to his own system, discarding any tarot traces altogether (apart from an allusion to the 'Broken Tower'). The sites on the island listed in both Maps 1 and 2 were ones Norge grew familiar with on his daily walks. Norge situated both interiority and self-hood in his plan as viable loci, for example in *The Star-Ravaged Co(r)pse* which is a spiritual transaction, and *Sequences for a Tariff* in which Norge appears to offer metonymic object-symbols from his own memory as sacrificial offerings to forgetting and *Meat*

Spirit, in which he outlines his somewhat reversed-Cartesian spiritual and corporeal dual experience. As such, Norge's categories seemingly held deep-seated meaning for the poet who now incorporated negatively charged, 'deathly' reversals:

BÀS LOCI		IA	REVERSAL
1	Port Nam Marbh	The Poet	Forgetfulness
2	Charred Arrow Shaft	The Poet	Deception
3	Star-ravaged Co(r)pse	The Poet	Hopelessness
4	Al Jab'hah	The Poet	Cowardice
5	Sequences for A Tariff	The Poet	Self-promotion
6	Knightless	The Poet	Barbarity
7	Sump	The Poet	Injustice
8	Meat Spirit	The Poet	Foolishness
9	Taghairm	The Poet	Incuriosity
10	Legere	The Poet	Ignorance

Circling his raw material like a bird of prey, Norge seemed to link all the events of the first part of the summer through recurrence as well as resonance, noting in his loggbok that night after night he 'fell asleep in the ashes of the fire, hair stiffened with ash, thumbs dark with ash... all ash-soaked in a smudged memory of flame'. He worked over his compositions again and again, revising etymologies, definitions and historicity, always seeking the depth charge of poetic significance. By vociferously hunting down explanations for the Sluagh, for example, Norge uncovered an early spelling and definition as 'sleagh', which could also mean a knight-errant according to his own Gaelic dictionary, there heavily underscored. He found similar significance in the Gaelic term 'lìon-aodach' for a winding sheet or shroud and gave this name to the rescued lion cub (see chapter XIV of *The Wind of Voices*). Certainly his repeated trudges around Bàs' small land mass generated an act of layered tracking, of geographical activation by the poet. He preferred to navigate clockwise, starting at the mortuary harbour before moving off down the coffin road – this route identical to the formal peregrination of coffins conveyed by slow march to burial grounds located on the easterly side of the island. Woven and interwoven, Norge's investigations had become ever more densely populated with phenomena drawn from much earlier stints of research undergone in the repositories of Edinburgh's National Library. The Bàs island locales morphed with characteristics borrowed widely from alchemy; Middle-Eastern magic, Highland folklore, medieval chivalry and classical mythology, all combined with Norge's own peculiar motifs. Such rich scraps were undoubtedly re-ploughed through his rapidly evolving system with its disbanded lions, crashed stellar corpses and cranial scrying bones.

Damnatio Memoriae

Pre-occupied with the roots of mnemonics (as illustrated by the crushed guests at Simonides' infamous and gruesome memory banquet, in which the Roman poet escaped a collapsed ceiling after being mysteriously summoned outside and then asked to recall who was present by remembering the seating arrangement), Norge now hunted for logical equipment to deal with an underlying memory that wounds. He made an emphatic distinction between the mnemonic process as one which was purely logical, rhetorical and taxonomical, and one which was fundamentally emotional. 'The wounded memory learns never to forget,' he stressed, adding: 'a memory wounded never learns how to forget.' His theoretical position on mnemotechnics is lightly illustrated by obscure annotations made in the spring of 1961:

> I fight Simonides *after* his opening scene… that the fatal
> feast may have forcibly imprinted repeated memory on the
> poet, which then cannot be erased. Mnemania. The mania
> of memory…any act of memory holds as its seed a morbid
> fear of amnesia.

The emotive imprint of wounded memory is certainly what Norge appears to have been confronting more generally – aware as he was of Simonides' lesser-quoted opponent, Themistocles, who, when offered the art of memory by Simonides, declined, responding tersely that 'everything he had ever seen or heard stuck in his memory'. Still evolving his own intellectual processes of eradication, Norge mentioned Pliny in his loggbok and described 'damnatio memoriae' (the condemning of memory) performed on the detested Domitian by ordering the removal of all imagines (images) of the emperor, destroyed after his death by assassination in 96 AD. Norge mused:

> I think of 'damnatio bestiari' [condemnation by wild animals] …could memory stand for a condemned person torn apart by wild beasts?… and might memory be the wild beast tearing apart a human being?

At some point during suppositions such as these, Norge's nerves seemed to fray and what were initially theses, rapidly devolved into urgent introspection and heated questioning. It is difficult to determine how much of Norge's system as part of his earlier, academic research now signified the apparent collapse of his poetic powers and self-awareness. Presumably, the so-called intervention of the Sluagh performed a great irony in holding Norge's theories to ransom by demanding his central concern – one of post-occult survival through deliberate amnesia – was met in a new reality. What had been conjectural now became actual. As the summer unfolded, Norge abruptly found himself in the untenable position of a thinker whose suppositions had become real. Overnight, Norge abandoned Dante and his theological mnemnonics, and instead now considered himself a living 'imago agens':

> the strain of such flashes of thought lodge in me as a progressively unstable host, contributing to my outward appearance and behaviour, it seems. Such knowledge changes the colour of my eyes, my hair… my teeth lighten and darken. My burden warps me as the information grows stronger, like a gold, like a liquid metal injected into the vein, and as it does I am less to be trusted, it seems, until I no longer even rely on myself – reflexions are warped. It is my growing awareness of my function as an IA that is shifting the world around me, and it is my function as an

IA that is ravaging my appearance. I will call it demonic. I will say – for the sake of simplicity – that I am becoming a demon.

Following the crises of witnessing his own now diabolic reflection in his shaving mirror and then that of Monmhur, the poet was seemingly unable to forget that he was an IA. 'Seeing myself as an IA, or demon was just a premonition – a derisory flash. I could write it off. But, this was followed up hard with a confirming presence and perhaps tools to eradicate that flashing image, caught somewhere in my psyche as a constantly flickering horror,' Norge related. As described, this refreshed self-awareness came clothed in diabolic form. However, it is unclear whether the information Norge felt was attached to his status as a sentient IA culminated in demonic qualities, or whether the central IA he had become was in fact, the figure of a demon. Where he had been happy to transform Dante into a central imago, Norge's own self-awareness as an IA was brutally tainted. After unsuccessfully trying certain academic solutions to his sudden and fiendish problem, a panicking Norge increasingly turned to alcohol. Yet, it appears that the acts of overlaying, confusing or befuddling this sudden and impactful comprehension (and therefore active recollection of his demonhood) were not useful to the poet. Perhaps he had exhausted these methods or possibly the demonic revelation startled Norge into a self-realisation so deeply inflicted, that neither conceptual approaches nor alcohol-induced blackouts could purge it from him. Instead, he mounted a campaign for forgetting or mnemonic reversal.

Outwardly, it appeared that he constructed a set of poetic symbols – quite literally bridges – straddling the unseen parts of his awareness to the seen, using an esoteric Gaelic language of night flocks, counter-charms and doubles, partially shot through with the imagery of classicism: of injured centaurs and deserted public arenas. Roughly conversant with 16th-century heretical philosopher Giordano Bruno's incendiary imagery and obsolete Greek rhetorical process, Norge set to work attempting to divert aspects of these into an amnesiac system, replete with smoking mirrors and a talking statue. He must have been intrigued by Bruno's leonine metaphor in *De Umbris Idearum* (*On the Shadows of Ideas*):

> ...avoid those who have neither intelligence nor understanding (wrapping their own inventions in the skin of a lion, and finding they had grown into it) to return to your own skin and your own voice.

Inwardly, however, something interminable and supposedly monstrous was continuing to unfold. Norge's new and urgent schema was indeed a plan for survival, but he claimed it was not one of his own invention. Rather, it was the presence of the Sluagh which had unwittingly manufactured an ally in the form of Monmhur, whose time-scarred visage dictated a precise solution to the poet's seemingly occult problem. 'Norge felt he was entirely in the hands of an unknown entity,' commented Moncrieff, 'dressed in the skin of his own research. Somewhere in his papers, there is a docket that mentions the change in pitch that happens when a person approaches an obstacle blindfolded, relying on the forehead for sensation pressures. I think his breathing, his voice, changed pitch gradually when we were here together. I think probably his thoughts changed pitch. Certainly, the obstacle Kristján faced was pitched at him and just when he was in the final stages of recovery from burns inflicted during the boat incident.' Norge, still wrestling with his mnemo-geographic material, now used Bàs as a living locus to deal with deadly concerns surrounding his own experiential validity as a living IA.

Kristján Norge's Amnesiac System

MAY-JUNE 1961

On May 3rd, Norge is 'shipwrecked' on Eilean a' Bhàis, suffering minor burns from an ignited petrol can. His rowing boat is filled with books and papers, some of which are rescued by Moncrieff. He slowly recovers, whilst rewriting his notes.

On May 17th, Moncrieff allows Norge to maintain the lighthouse on his own, and remains in the light-keeper's cottage.

On June 2nd, the weather is very calm. Norge dreams his left hand is severely mutilated, suspended between two mirrors. Later, gathering seaweed on the beach, Norge badly cuts the palm and wrist of his left hand. He claims to have seen the 'teorr' (see introduction).

On June 8th, Kristján Norge suddenly sees himself as the IA of a fallen angel or demon, reflected in his shaving mirror.

On June 9th, first of the summer storms. By all accounts, 1961, on the outer Hebridean Eilean a' Bhàis, is a turbulent year of unsettled weather fronts. Bàs lighthouse is damaged and the light is extinguished.

On June 10th, one of Norge's donkeys is killed by a falling branch and the poet becomes depressive: 'Asal's grave is done. I could get into it with him.'

On June 12th, more vicious winds torment the island. Norge nails down the lighthouse outhouses, damaging the thumb of his left hand – the same hand as previously damaged by the teorr. Later that day, a storm breaks. Norge, frayed and suffering from nervous exhaustion, embarks on a three-day drinking spree. Luce Moncrieff eventually locates him at the island's 'claw', in a cave behind the waterfall. Semi-conscious and tightly wrapped in his old raincoat, Norge doggedly claims he was conveyed there, refusing any more straightforward an explanation. He insists that a second reflection appeared in his mirror, this time of a fallen angel named Monmhur. Continued high winds. Across this period, the Sluagh visits the poet regularly and he insists it conveys him to the ten sites on the island he had already earmarked in his researches on the tarot and Dante. Norge often returns from these episodes physically damaged; Moncrieff rightly conjectures that if he had been drinking at the sites, then he may have fallen. Moncrieff finds it increasingly difficult to keep Norge housebound. According to Norge's logg-bok, the Sluagh visits twice each month; once when the moon is full and once when there is a new moon. The lunar moon cycles for that period of 1961 are:

July 12th New Moon	Abandoned Port
July 27th Full Moon	Dead Lighthouse
August 11th New Moon	Old Coffin Road
August 26th Full Moon (Lunar Eclipse)	Ruined Mansion
September 10th New Moon	Gate of the Ford of the Dead
September 24th Full Moon	Derelict Monastery
October 9th New Moon	Wild Hawthorn Field
October 23rd Full Moon	Old Whaling Station
November 8th New Moon	Cave behind the Waterfall
November 22nd New Moon	Monastery Walled Garden

'It was not until after that very bad lunar eclipse in late August,' Luce remarks, 'I became properly aware of these cycles and, not wanting to go through another ordeal as that one, my attention was now wholly focussed on visiting Edinburgh to consult with Kristján's psychoanalyst. Of course, he mocked this suggestion.' This trip is made in early September 1961, when there has already been another storm and Moncrieff is nervous of becoming stranded – an irony, as that is exactly the position she subsequently finds herself in, due to the accident, only in Edinburgh for those fateful last months. She is never to see Norge again.

JANUARY 1962

On January 4th, Moncrieff returns to the island and draws together the Norge materials in the two upper, unlocked rooms of the lighthouse and across the ten island sites. She is joined by Jeanie Hafoc, with whom there is another altercation.

In an unusual instance of clarity, Kristján Norge has carefully noted the process of his amnesiac ritual, enabling it to be clearly reconstructed:

a) At new moon and full moon each month, the Sluagh lifts Norge to one of ten sites (a locus and portal) on the island eg: the cave, and deposits him there.

b) The Sluagh breathes knowledge of his demonhood as an IA into him as an incantation of voiced air (pneuma) which Norge describes as one of ten 'Sluagh Sequences'.

c) This causes him to become a seer, witnessing a supernatural sequence of a series of demonic imagines agentes (acting images) embedded in the incantation. He perceives the mnemonic attitudes or postures of the spell.

d) He is returned, or staggers, back to the lighthouse.

e) To an onlooker Norge is exhausted and dishevelled and has a bleeding mouth. He is also feverish.

f) Monmhur has previously instructed that he will give Norge a counteraction. Norge is told to collect the blood from his tongue (damaged when the Sluagh breathed the knowledge of his IA into him), to mix it with old hair from his comb and let it dry, before setting it alight on the surface of his rectangular shaving mirror. Once he has suffumigated the mirror with the smoking, bloody hair, a flashed code will appear on the mirror surface which Norge must record in writing.

g) The mirror will then soften and Norge will be enabled to make it into a cylinder from which distorted words emanate onto a first blank piece of paper he has been instructed to use.

h) Norge must copy down the distortion onto a second piece of paper.

i) The same night (under the same moon) he must return to the site and hide the folded first piece of paper for Luce to recover, along with a personal object of his own, intimated by Monmhur. This substitute package will act as a spiritual 'cover' for Norge's mnemonic reversals so as not to alert the Sluagh.

j) Finally, when he has done this, he must take the second piece of paper and identify the demonic 'imagines agentes' evident in the distorted Sluagh Sequence that he witnessed when taken by the Sluagh nam Marbh and take time to interpret them. The distorted text may produce several key IA and it is up to Norge to distil the central one. When he has deciphered and reduced the distorted text down to a single IA, he must carve or find an appropriate statue or figurehead which embodies the relevant IA and insert his mirror poems and written workings to deduce the central IA in each figurehead's mouth. When he has gathered or created all ten figureheads, Norge is instructed to destroy them. Luce Moncrieff is given the unlikely task of recovering the object and folded paper from each of the ten sites and inevitably discovers them in the mouth of the statues locked in the lighthouse upper room, along with the paper-stuffed walls covered in abstruse, poetic graffiti and lion corpse in the other locked lighthouse room.

Norge also incorporated a list of personal belongings (each of which is connected to a place on the map) which can also be found embedded in the second part of *Ravage*, titled *The Dead Reckoning*.

OBJECTS FOUND AT THE SITES

1	Knitting	Helix of wind
2	Shaving mirror	Warped coffin lid
3	Jaw harp	Osseous lyre
4	Lion skin wristlet	Lion skin wristlet
5	Walking stick	Withered wheat stem
6	Pen-knife	Rusted sword
7	Hunter's hat	Hole-cut cloth
8	Belt	Neolithic painter's belt
9	Overcoat	Woven breastplate
10	Pipe	Smoke-filled bone

1 PORT NAM MARBH (the abandoned port) (a helix of wind: his knitted Shetland yarn).

2 THE CHARRED ARROW SHAFT (the dead lighthouse) (a warped coffin lid: his cracked, rectangular shaving mirror).

3 THE STAR-RAVAGED CO(R)PSE (the old coffin road) (an osseous lyre: his jaw harp).

4 AL JAB'HAH (the ruined mansion) (a lion skin wristband: the same – the only object that is real in both worlds).

5 SEQUENCES FOR A TARIFF (the gate of the ford of the dead) (a withered wheat stem: his walking stick).

6 KNIGHTLESS (the derelict monastery) (a rusted sword: his pen-knife).

7 SUMP (the wild hawthorn field) (a hole-cut cloth: his hunter's hat).

8 MEAT SPIRIT (the old whaling station) (a Neolithic painter's belt: his belt).

9 TAGHAIRM (cave behind the waterfall) (a woven breastplate: his overcoat).

10 LEGERE (the monastery walled garden) (a smoke-filled bone: his pipe).

Reproduced here is one example of the decipherments Norge made of the sequence 'Legere', focussing on the 'angel' personified. By treating the individual sentences as collated imagines agentes, Norge reworked those visual components to create a living diaspora of theatrical scenes or tableaux vivant, influenced by the aesthetics of medieval tarot, courtly love, chivalric encounter and troubadour imagery. The absurdist elements reflect aspects of alchemical symbolism and overall these images were used by Norge as diagnostics, drawn from his understanding of each compressed verse, as set out below. Norge felt that these Sluagh Sequences were functional and encompassed occult meaning and instruction:

X

LEGERE
November 22nd, 1961 Full Moon

(THE WALLED MONASTERY GARDEN: WOUNDED ANGEL: ILLUMINATION)

Collecting wood of the word: ruminate. My wood has bitterness. The taciturn forest. Roiled and scabrous. Statues of tree substance: is tree, is forest. Sweet woods, tasted by the eyes, blenched and out-pouring. In my moon of words, burns the sun. In my words of wood, burns the moon. In my word of moons, burns the sun. It is done, the reckoning, grained legere. This twig is wine, this twig bread, this twig beer, this twig meat, this twig fruit, this twig honey, this twig water. Horoscopi: time-watchers. Cuts the teeth of my senses. Gather, collect, cremated bones. Reads: mirror wood. Wood burns: my pelt. Clean the senses in this lion tree: wood, sun, taciturn moons, words, eyes, blenched honey, word-cremated wine skin. The fruit-greased twig: twig-tasted watchers' time. In smooth thirst, horoscopi bread, finely ground. Gather bitterness, shave my words, water-centaur, meat statue. These bones and pouring skin, this cleaned word. My wood cuts: legere, moon burns cylindrical and smooth in forest stone, rolled. Sweet, this teeth-grained moon is twig unborn – Pumice-shaved water, stone burns my moon. Flat colour burns vellum – stone is time-rolled putridness and smoothed, my eyes wash word-blasted statues. Retrieving animal sense: colour in the raised roughage of co(r)pse, I swell on time. Star-blasted kindling, wood senses stand broken, ravaged.

1) Collecting wood of the word: ruminate. AN ANGEL PAUSES FOR THOUGHT, KINDLING ON HER BACK. My wood has bitterness. WORMWOOD CHEWED BY HER. The taciturn forest. A GAGGED MOUTH CARVED IN SEVERAL TREES. Rolled and scabrous. A DAMAGED WHEEL. Statues of tree substance: is

tree, is forest. THE ANGEL BECOMES A WOODEN STATUE. Sweet woods, tasted by the eyes, blenched and out-pouring. HERE INCENSE RISES OF FRANKINCENSE AND MYRRH. In my moon of words, burns the sun. THE ANGEL'S MOUTH IS OPEN AND FILLED WITH A MOON THAT IS IN TURN FILLED WITH A SUN. In my words of wood, burns the moon. A MOON IN FLAMES IS GLOWING IN A FOREST. In my word of moons, burns the sun. A FOREST OF LUNAR CIPHERS GLOWS WITH A FLAMING SUN. It is done, the reckoning, grained legere. A GRAIN OF WHEAT LIES ACROSS HER BUNDLE OF WOOD. This twig is wine, this twig bread, this twig beer, this twig meat, this twig fruit, this twig honey, this twig water. SEVEN DIVINING RODS HOVERING IN FRONT OF EACH SUBSTANCE, HELD BY THE ANGEL. Horoscopi: time watchers. SIGNS OF THE ZODIAC CUT INTO THE MOON. Cuts the teeth of my senses. A TOOTH IN HER EYE, EAR, MOUTH, PALM OF HIS HAND, NOSE, EACH TOOTH EMBEDDED WITH A KNIFE. Gather, collect, cremated bones. THE ANGEL DRAWS TOGETHER BLACKENED, SOOTY SKELETONS. Reads: mirror wood. A CROSS-SECTION OF TREE TRUNK IS A REFLECTIVE MIRROR.

> 2) The wormwood you chew
>   reflector of skeletons,
>   thirsts for the angel.

3) Wood: my pelt burns. THE ANGEL DONS A BURNING SKIN MADE OF BIRCH BARK. Clean the senses in this lion tree: wood, sun, taciturn moons, words, eyes, blenched honey, word-cremated wine of skin. A MAN WASHING HIS EYES IN A BAOBAB WITH A WET TWIG WHILE A GROUP OF SILENT WOMEN WATCH FROM PALE, SWEET FACES, WITH SUDDENLY FLARING VOICES THEY DRUNKENLY WHINE. The fruit-greased twig: twig-tasted watchers of time. FALLEN ANGELS (THE WATCHERS) CONSUME WAXY ORCHARD FRUITS. In smooth horoscopi bread, finely ground. LOAVES BAKED IN THE SHAPE OF THE ZODIAC SIGNS. Gather bitterness, shave my words, water-centaur, meat statue.

PICK UP WORMWOOD, SEA HORSE, FLAYED MAN. These bones and pouring skin, this cleaned word. SKELETON HOLDING A WINE GOURD OF SCRAPED VELLUM. My wood cuts: legere, moon burns cylindrical and smooth in forest stone, rolled. Sweet, this teeth-grained moon is twig unborn. IN IMPRINTED LETTER-ING, THE FEMININE IS ENFLAMED AS THE ENTOMBED POET IN THE CAVE OF KNOWLEDGE.

> 4) Eyes washed in the tree,
>   your shroud of knowledge burning,
>   the angel enflames.

5) Pumice-shaved water, stone burns my moon. STONE GRATING ON ICE, A FEMALE EFFIGY BEING CLAY-FIRED. Flat colour burns vellum – stone is time-rolled putridness and smoothed, my eyes wash word-blasted statues. ON GREY ASH PAPER – A LARGE ROCK BEING ROLLED UPHILL ACROSS CORPSES WHOSE SIGHT CLEANS DESTROYED EFFIGIES. Retrieving animal sense in the raised roughage of co(r)pse, SERAPH SPOTS ON A ROUGH CARCASS. I swell on time. A PREGNANT WOMAN. Star-blasted kindling, wood senses broken, ravaged. WORMWOOD EXPLODES HIS POETRY, HIS GAELIC ALPHABET IS DESTROYED AND LAID TO WASTE.

> 6) Ravaged effigy:
>   as the seraph spots the star,
>   with bitter motes.

1) An angel pauses for thought, kindling on her back and chews wormwood (Hippocrates prescribed Wormwood to patients suf-fering from memory problems). She notices the image of a gagged mouth carved into several trees (enforced silence) and a damaged wheel, (the wheel of fortune?) resting against one of the trees. As she does so, she becomes a wooden statue of her-self (an effigy, not herself) and around her rises the smoke of burning frankincense and myrrh brought by the Zoroastrian

magi to the birth of Christ (they being a sacred sect of priests). The angel finds her mouth suddenly filled with a full moon and within it is embedded the sun. (Union of female and male instincts). The moon breaks into flames and the flames become the trees of the alphabet. The sun rises among these tree letters and she sees a single ear of wheat lying on his bundle of wood. (The germ of knowledge and the earliest prayers in poetry: Enheduanna, lunar priestess). The bundle falls open revealing wine, bread, beer, meat, fruit, honey and water (the fruits of her labours) and in front of each, a divining rod hovers. Now, the signs of the zodiac appear as if carved and watchful on the face of the moon. The angel sheds a tear and finds it is a tooth embedded in her eye, shakes her head and finds a tooth stuck in her ear, coughs and finds a tooth in her mouth, wipes her mouth and finds a tooth in the palm of her hand, sneezes and a tooth shoots forth from her nose. Every tooth is in turn embedded with a sharp knife. (She is learning through experiential knowledge: her senses – cutting her teeth.) Now, bending, the angel gathers up the remains in the wood of charred skeletons and bundles them together. (Previous selves.) Looking up, she sees herself for a moment as a reflection in the mirrored cross-section of a fallen oak (metonymic for all trees, the mighty oak. The angel sees herself reflected in the heartwood of language).

2) The responding anamorphic IA is the effigy of a mirror which appeals to the angel (collector of old bones: old corpora of knowledge, memories), warning her that the bitterness which is her cud wishes to return to an angelic state, or an apocalyptic one. Here, I reference the star wormwood, the sense here could read 'the memory you chew, death, is thirsting for the third angel of the apocalypse'.

3) The angel puts on a burning skin made of bark and cleans her eyes with a twig in a baobab tree which, according to legend, the devil plucked up, thrust its branches into the earth,

and left its roots in the air. The baobab is also known to be a favourite tree for lions to climb. At the foot of the tree, a group of sweet-faced women begin to whine, their voices flaring. Here, we might have professional mourners at an aerial burial where the body is immolated on a platform in the branches of the tree, collapsing several death rites together. Is the burning bark skin, actually a shroud? She is placed now in an afterlife, as the watchers (mentioned in the Book of Enoch) are present, eating fruit – probably from the Tree of Knowledge. There are loaves of bread with the signs of the zodiac baked into them and the angel picks up wormwood (bitterness), a seahorse (male/ female fluidity) and a flayed man (stripped of his burning shroud?) which becomes a skeleton holding a gourd of wine made from scraped vellum. In imprinted lettering, the feminine principal is ignited and transforms into the entombed poet in the cave, alluding to Christ but also to the Celtic bardic compositional methods which were memorised by night (thus under the auspices of the lunar, the feminine) in cells, chambers or caves. The cave also evokes the Gaelic taghairm ritual once again.

4) The second to last IA in the entire sequence, urges me to engage with these compositional acts. Perhaps a renewed relationship with memory as an act of recomposing (as opposed to decomposing) is here suggested, or a 'rising from the tomb' as an act of poetic renewal, rebirth and foolhardy hope.

5) The final paragraph operates as a dire warning, however, of the consequences if this is not carried out. There is a stone tapping or grating on ice, as the effigy or form of a woman is clay-fired. This enhances the sonics of intent through continuing repetition, tempered slightly by the feminine impulse being 'set in stone' or firmed by fire as previously malleable clay. It is a fermenting awareness on my part. The next image is disturbing and is pictured on a burned parchment which depicts a stone being rolled uphill across corpses whose dead eyes or dead sight cleanses such effigies. This suggests sightlessness – that perhaps watchful

memory is now dead under the tombstone of time and as such, the feminine principal is acknowledged without judgement. There is also a tenderness in the suggestion of the cleansing of statues or effigies perhaps damaged by memory: 'damnatio memoriae'. Now, leper or leopard (adopted by Dante as the symbol of lust but here confused with those who traditionally were wandering outcasts) spots emerge on a carcass, possibly signifying the demise of lust as out of this emerges a pregnant woman, perhaps the result of such lust. However, the angel's bundle is under threat, though the feminine principal 'swells on time'. In my interpretation, the star wormwood explodes the poetry and the Gaelic alphabet is laid to waste.

6) In the third IA, the destroyed effigy of the angel (which perhaps takes my place) though embittered by lust, is touched by the spotted star...flecked with motes of bitterness. But, do these freckle the skin of the statue as a living angel, or an inanimate memorial? For isn't it true, that I will have already vanished?

Diagnostic: the fundamental action here is for me to spit out the wormwood, both as a substance inducing a sharper memory and a star embodying bitterness. Instead, I must pursue amnesia and eschew personal embittered sentiments. Secondly, my riches lie within the pursuit of writing, particularly poetry – which I must strengthen. The end word is a warning: if I do allow bitterness to envelop me, then my poetic landscape will be ravaged, or destroyed.

CENTRAL LEGERE IA

A ravaged angel thirsts for knowledge
in wormwood's tree, chews bitter,
shrouded motes of skeleton.

Anamorphosis

Anamorphosis is an architectural and painterly technique developed
to modify sensory awareness: the art of manipulating perspective
to reveal or conceal images through clever distortion. Used in the
first part of *Ravage*, Norge attempted to transpose the logical
concerns of perspectival distortion, which were singularly visual,
onto his textual system. Examining the roots of the word, he
found that the Greek 'ana' meant 'again' and 'morphē': 'shape'
which reiterated that the spectator (in this case, the reader) must
take responsibility in re-forming the inherent and distorted meaning
– must reshape, or refashion it. Whilst this is immediately apparent
in the case of illusionistic painting and drawing, Norge's results
in translating such a visual device into writing are inevitably
defective. His precise, short poems were designed to act as foci for
the abstracted and expansive prose which they were placed within,
referencing the 'cella' or central chamber in classical Greek temple
architecture where a statue of the god was typically housed:

> Monmhur has given me the demolished architectural plans
> from which to rebuild an anamorphic temple structure in
> prose and poetry. That is, within the letters of fallen masonry
> and passages broken into debris, I can find and rebuild the
> cella – the chamber floor of the text and within each cella,
> a central IA or effigy rests on its altar platform – the 'Eala'
> – or its bier, perhaps.

The process was laborious. Norge needed to 'excavate' the
ruins of each Sluagh Sequence in order to reassemble each
stanzaic cella and restore its ultimate image. Firstly, he deci-
phered the prose to reveal embedded 'imagines agentes', so that

what at first glance scanned as gibberish, was evidently encoded. Each sentence (though not letter) was broken down into a string of imagines agentes: IA. Often he would split the prose into sections and produce several major IA from the image strings. From three or four IA, he distilled one and from it, a central figure materialised which performed the fundamental concerns of each text. 'The garbled prose stanzas, the chambers, are cellae – in which an effigy is apparent: an IA. I scan the prose poem or temple floor the reader (myself) crosses – from any direction – as the cella, the clear space within the prose poem as an altar or raised platform and the compact verse as a distilled 'imago agens'. Here, all my work on the mechanisms of the stanza as stopping place to view a performing statue has come to life,' he enthused. There were ten of these singular mnemonic cellae, each of which contained a specific IA of the knowledge of his demonhood. It was this active memory device, the catalyst, the IA, in each sequence which particularly needed to be distilled for destruction. 'Without the means to remember, that which must be remembered would be lost, or at least subdued to trace elements, subliminal presences… rubble,' asserted Monmhur.

Another way of perceiving these anamorphic foci, is through Norge's own reconstruction of his papers in which he borrowed the form of the anamorphic cylinder imprinted with the central IA to superficially cohere the temple text. When put together, these cylinders and papers seemed to form pillars and a floor. He noted with irony, 'the inescapable fact that my system, when turned into three dimensions, becomes a ruined memory palace itself, thus resisting the possibility of it being an amnesiac device'. Norge's dilapidated paper memory temples were poetic monuments momentarily erected on the island loci of Bàs, such as Lunar Mansion X, the lighthouse tower or the coppiced field of hawthorn. When dismantled and read on the page as 'flat' again, these compact stanzas appealed to Norge as altars; he perceived them as able to be transformed from the rectangular to the cylindrical: from the right angle to the sphere.

In his essay, *TRAN-Quil-Ity: Crossing the Quill of Being*,

there are traces of Norge's early fascination with the platform and coffin. He knew of the ancient Scottish site called the 'Eala', a temporary place of sanctuary where a stone placed in the choir of a church would offer a protective station for a year and a day for any criminal. 'Port nam Marbh', the 'Port of the Dead' on Iona, provided a landing site also named the 'Eala' (the tomb or sepulchre) on the Holy Isle for burial where a stone slab could be found positioned on top of a mound. The corpse would be carried around it three times sun-wise and then laid out on it before burial. Prior to the carpentry of coffins and biers, human remains on the Hebridean isles were wrapped in corpse cloths and laid directly in the grave or in cists. Norge incorporated this by collapsing his notion of a coffin with the body itself, so that the squared and raised form of the casket could be replaced by the rounded mass of a corpse. He paused for a moment to consider Christ's tomb as a rough cella containing the fundamentals of death, with the crucified cadaver placed as a coffinless effigy in the inner sanctum of the rock face that held that tomb. 'My interest in the Christ-tomb is inherently circular: the rolling of the stone, the three-day cycle, the wrapping of the corpse. What tomb might the fallen angel be given…what corpse-cloth and mirroring sword? He is trapped, knightless, beneath ground heavy in the chains of his own weight. Nothing is reflected in his shield but the sharp angles of death.'

Deflecting, as opposed to reflecting, shields were of equal interest to Norge who had meditated on coded ignition points in an early, rejected book proposal *The Foolkiller* which he put together in 1958.

> Mirrors kindled great interest in relation to the early sym-bolism and function of the classical flashing pharos of antiquity… Book XIX of the *Iliad* describes how 'from Achilles' shield, bright and beautifully engraved, light streamed to heaven'. Later, mirrors were to become fun-damental to light-house illumination, along with lenses. Demonstrably powerful, they were ill-used in warfare to ignite ships as described by a Roman historian in 212 BC

(my paraphrasing) when Syracuse was sieged, an enemy fleet of boats was successfully destroyed by Archimedes who used mirrors placed at the same distance as one arrow's flight. Using these, he directed and concentrated solar rays and the ships' timbers ignited and burst into flame.

Norge had maintained a longstanding interest in heliography and the history of telegraphic communication. Now he imagined flashing messages appeared in his mirror, conveyed to him by Monmhur, who temporarily revivified the dead beam of the Eilean a' Bhàis lighthouse. Norge described this flaring code, which was reflected in the polished steel as 'lucent pharography', insinuating that it was deflective rays from the expired light-house which illuminated his mirrored communiqués. Perhaps he perceived these rays as tantamount to starlight: 'the dead ful-gentness still indicating travelling knowledge.' True to form, Norge positioned Monmhur as the sole perpetrator: 'the metal is lit up with Monmhur's missives as he draws luminescence from the dead lighthouse into its square. He has assured me that it is his own alignment which enables him to capture the information like a frequency, or a scent, and that the mirror itself remains still and calm.'

Luce Moncrieff was not immune to the effects of these strange arrangements, though she was likely unaware of the otherwise dormant island lighthouse beam being precisely transmitted for a few minutes twice a month, at new and full moon, only noting that 'the generator is getting tired, or perhaps the wiring... once every few weeks, the electricity dips and flares erratically, though we have had no reports from sailing vessels or otherwise.'

For content, Norge was apparently given his encoded stella-graphic work as a premonition, using the final constellar line from each of his longer poems composed in celestial metre transposed into telegraphic morse code as the content and cipher for these mirror encryptions. The dead pharos light, worked into the angling of his steel mirror to illuminate stellar coding, brought his system full-circle and evoked a radiophonic, sublunary language of dead starlight in his mirrored messaging.

The light source was the expired (but magically reinstated) lighthouse beam, the flashed code appeared in his tilting mirror, and that telegraphic code itself was rooted in the stresses of large and small stars aligned to Greek metrics from constellations which resonated with the figures found in his own death-charged system. The initial stimulant for Norge's encounter was thus indeed the endpoint: a single cosmographic line was worked through his mnemo-amnesiac scheme to emerge as one of ten stellar configurations which gave voice to his IA figurehead statues. Norge's starry vision was maritime and his navigation through it, a meandering through dying pulses and nautical frequencies of a marine heaven: 'small universes seemed to dance momentarily in my steel'. After receiving this flashing line of verse via Monmhur, Norge's mirror was made pliant and could be scrolled, he claimed. From its argent surface, a dense inscription was radiated onto a page torn out of his loggbok, its scrawl scorched onto the lined paper. Among Norge's belongings is a 1900s tool for poker work, which may explain the presence of this pyrographic sample, the only one remaining which is now kept in the SPL archive.

Possibly also used as pre-prepared implements, Norge's placing of coded mirror poems between each of the Sluagh Sequences alluded to ritual practice outlined in the *Picatrix* (from which he devised the presence of the hanging mirror evident in the book's subtitles: *Speculum Ante* and *Speculum Retro*). This is the magic mirror – in reality his WWII shaving mirror, acquired in a pawn shop – in which terrible things manifest and through which he can absorb and understand the speech of visitant, Monmhur. Preparing such mirrors was complex, as Norge had read:

> hang the mirror in silk for seven days over water and suffumigate it there; and let it be suspended by the branch of a bramble. And for three nights suffumigate it with good and pleasant odours such as may be found in the Book of Moses. And if you gaze into the mirror and watch it well, know that in it will appear men, winds, spirits, demons, the dead and the living and all of them will be obedient to your command.

In direct contrast to the rotundity of magic seeing glasses, the rectangular shape of his shaving mirror fascinated Norge, who thought it mimicked the altar or coffin shapes lodged in his columnar constructions and also the mound of the 'Eala', with its rumoured elevated stone. However, it was the cylinder which gave Norge numerous, overlapping motifs. In its cross-section he saw the eye of the storm, the vanished lighthouse beam, the circumference of the colosseum, the sliced surface of the arrow shaft which wounded the centaur and his own, circular-seeming, wound of fresh self-awareness as a demonic IA. This theme of the disc recurs as a healing and clarifying device. Norge referenced this injury in his loggbok as 'dearg' (in all likelihood to obscure it). 'Dearg in the Gaelic is an impression and hence, a wound – from it we get 'deargadh', or ploughing,' which exactly demonstrates the condition Norge sustained in the apprehension of his demonhood, as a specifically damaged place which worsened, while the rest of him – though influenced by this hurt – was not directly affected. 'It was is if the wound was ploughed over and over with the plough-blade of its own knowledge,' he wrote. Norge sometimes referred to his affliction as an 'ora ghonaidh', a wounding or death spell, inherently circular through relentless repetition. Fundamentally, it seems Norge came to consider the lighthouse tower itself as an anamorphic obelisk onto which the distorted terrain of Bàs was crystallised as a single image on the rough, outer wall. What this image was, and where one might have to stand on the island in order to glimpse it, might never be known.

Sea-Worn Effigies

Now the statue-life of memory came into play. Reaching the end of all this written architecture, Norge was told to conclusively outwork the effigy placed in each cella in three-dimensional form. Returning to the act of image-making and hunting, he salvaged wrecked ships' figureheads found already half-buried in the sand on Bàs, or newly washed up on the shore, and even attempted several crude carvings himself. These Norge eventually gathered in the ruined mansion, he noted in his loggbok. Norge applied the term 'figureheads' to these objects rather loosely, using it to describe the marine corbels and smaller, nautical sculptures he had found, as well as his own contorted efforts. Unsurprisingly, he recognised the stranded figureheads as anamorphic tools in their own right, their physiognomies moulded by acute marine pressures. 'Yes, the sea,' he wrote in a more lucid moment, 'is responsible for their morphed, mutilated and abstracted bodies, but what I now possess are perspectival sculptures. Anamorphic depictions that cohere a smeared ocean.'

One of these abandoned figureheads was a gnarled angel chained to a plum tree in the monastery garden which had withstood the weather, in brush and brambles, for seventy years or more. In his schema Norge positioned her effigy in relation to 'Legere', arguably a more beneficent category. 'Here is the wolf of melancholy staring back at me, the hermit of self-reflexion, the lion of inspiration and the angel of illumination,' he noted. Curiously, Norge included himself, 'carved from rotted wood', and labelled this figurehead the poetic property of 'will'. The figureheads' endpoint was grim, however: 'after they are cut into life,' Norge acknowledged, 'they will be burned or drowned.'

These statues were quite clearly objects of transference, that did not move and so were without agency, which represented elements of his poetic personality. Norge remained convinced that the eradication of his 'sea-whelped court' would remove the attendant cognition of his diabolic role as an animated IA in this flawed and fractured reversal of an ancient practice of rhetorical memory. In a curious externalisation, each figure had a living counterpart in Norge's real environment on Bàs and an allotted place which connected both to Norge's own poetic components and the content of each sequence he had rigorously deciphered as cellae prose and a short verse of IA. Thus, each figurehead found a literal and metaphoric temple foundation on the island which honoured the oncoming demise of his poetic self.

1 Port of the Dead	Port nam Marbh	Ferryman figurehead	Boatman	Transformation
2 Dead Lighthouse	Charred Arrow Shaft	Hermit figurehead	Monmhur	Self-reflexion
3 Old Coffin Road	Star-Ravaged Co(r)pse	Poet figurehead	Norge	Will
4 Ruined Mansion	Al Jab'hah	Lion figurehead	Cub	Inspiration
5 Gate of the Ford of the Dead	Sequences for a Tariff	Wolf figurehead	Varg	Melancholy
6 Derelict Monastery	Knightless	Knight figurehead	Sgròb	Acumen
7 Wild Hawthorn Field	Sump	Gypsy figurehead	Travailer	Intuition
8 Old Whaling Station	Meat Spirit	Demon figurehead	Hafoc	Doubt
9 Cave Behind the Waterfall	Taghairm	Centaur figurehead	Donkey	Vision
10 Walled Monastery Garden	Legere	Angel figurehead	Moncrieff	Illumination

Norge as an IA

To recap: an 'imago agens' is an image or picture which performs in order to provoke recollection of the knowledge it references. As a living 'imago agens', Norge thought it crucial to continue developing the amnesiac structure, not to eradicate this status for its own sake – and his – but to outwardly perform the fresh symbolic behaviour his identity as an IA now demanded. That emblematic performance was best delineated in the form of a highly charged picture, as set out below, but before Norge was subject to a clear image of himself as an IA, he was given the nature of his circumstances:

> according to Monmhur – who is myself, my reflexion, but a surrogate to foil the Sluagh – I am a fallen angel in the guise of a dying poet. I am in reality an operational IA for the memory of God to distinguish between the risen and the fallen. I am a shadow of Christ, stumbled in his garden. A poet of the rock pool. As an IA, I am performing the role of a fallen angel who has tried to get away and succeeded: an IA creating a system to forget. All the signs have been there: the severance (my wounded hand), the premonition (my face reflected as demonic), the self-reflection (escaping the part of myself which is malign and would subsume the rest). Whatever the outcome of my following an unfolding am- nesiac plan for this awareness, the reality of that plan being merely an outworked behaviour of my moving presence –

my IA – of a fallen angel, will continuously subsume any good results, I assume. I am the angel of amnesia tracking the demon of memory, or a mnemonic demon hunting down angelic memory. They are one and the same. A fallen angel chasing its own tail.

And so, in the act of decipherment, Norge felt he had discovered that he was actually an IA of 'God's memory of fallen angel Kristján Norge', performing out the role of an obscure poet who had attempted to escape his lot within the host: a wind comprising rebel angels or demons named the Sluagh. He once had left his reflection with them as an avatar or stand-in, so that the rebel flock he flew away from would be unaware of his missing presence. It was this reflection, named Monmhur, he insisted, which had alerted Norge that the Sluagh had become aware of his departure and were returning for him, to inject knowledge of his true identity into the poet and ensure his permanent position as fallen, among them. The information had been blown into Norge as a vivid tempest and was marked as an eternal memory, one deeply felt. In order to erase this memory and continue to evade a premeditated destiny, Monmhur had given Norge a complicated process of reversal in the form of ten stages for forgetting this specific aspect of his selfhood. 'I have plunged from the fallen, and now must rise into the plummeted, unless I can disappear altogether. Vanishing is preferable to a continued existence as a grounded angel who stumbles among humans, despising and ignoring my stature as rejected,' penned Norge, now surrounded by screeds of paperwork in the lighthouse tower. Redemption seemed an impossibility for the damaged poet, deeply hurt by the understanding of his existence merely as a mnemonic tool for God:

> ...I have the hide of a fallen angel, a prototype clothed in the skin of a dying poet, to activate within the memory Kristján Norge within the mind of God. Dislodging this has meant working out the embedded, smaller IAs: reducing this memory of God of 'Kristján Norge' to ten effigies... if I can manage them. I have my old cutting

knife and get them together first, chipped, broken, get them together to burn them to nothing or chuck them in the sea …I will vanish, and so the thing which is God's memory of me will also disappear. I am it. My consolation is that I will not be a fallen angel whose maker is aware of him. I can escape both God and myself.

And yet, the individual presences of his ten wooden sculptures were given voice in the conclusory cycle of poems: *The Dead Reckoning*. In it, Norge positioned his ventriloquising constellations as personifications of the ten stations his morbid progress demanded. His process was fairly crude: 'taking a stellar cluster, I mark out points along it and track each star's candle-power which then dictate the pulses, or light emissions of the poem. These boil down to stress and metre, of course – but returning Greek to Greek is a strong match and not an eclipse.' Inevitably suffused with the etymology of star, Norge traced the word into roots which were significant for him – 'star/ starn (Shetlandic), Stjerne (Norwegian) bristles with favour: look, here is the origin 'ster' which blossoms with tantalising meanings':

> 'stiff', or 'stark' and then there is 'sterphos: hide, or skin'. Though themselves post-mortem, the linguistic soil which 'star' is buried in holds crazy richness. I want to flay the hides or skins of these figures, to reveal their underlying syntax. Constellar anatomy. In these 'stark' moments, far from feeling myself 'ravaged', my atlas is a friend and we go out hunting together, in the dark, through stippled skies… reams and reams of stellagraphia issuing from my thoughts.

This perambulatory cycle marked a return for Norge: in it he earnestly pursued Celtic compositional techniques: writing by night and with the aid of a battered star atlas: 'what my naked sight cannot perceive, my map-book can position'. His atlas is thick with drawings of constellations and rhythmic patterning to match one or several starry manifestations to his cosmographia. He references Dante and Milton in their keen awareness of the heavenlies, alongside fragments of ancient Greek and Arabic knowledge. The spiritual progression he undertook is plaited on paper, with a brief introspection in the lilting metre of the King James Bible, but, what follows is a composite cynosure of collaged star-accented verse whose scansion vivifies the underlying 'blueprint' of each constellation as an IA of itself. He was anatomising stellar recollection, through showcasing and stripping back the visual motifs of Orion, Hydra and Ophiuchus, for example, to reveal the structure of these bodies of light which were then reconfigured in alignment with his own IAs. Lupus was his wolf-dog Varg, Leo, the lion cub found half-drowned in a circus container on the Bàs shore. 'For wounding (or Ravaging), I must stick variant starn clusters together and allow them to be reversed as metrical lines,' he wrote, keen to give himself a little flexibility. 'Centauri and Sagittarius and Sagitta, the arrow, can all morph under the skin of the poem in a prosthetic physiognomy, a sack of stellar bones and muscle giving rough and strange shape to the appearance, body-language and appearance of the centaur. As in the 'Star-Ravaged Co(r)pse' these stars ravage their own physical environment as they pass through their self-perception. My true aim is flayed galactic verse.'

1 Port nam Marbh	Ferryman IA	Aquarius/Puppis	Celestial Metre: Wounded Boatman Decameter
2 Charred Arrow Shaft	Hermit IA	Ophiuchus	Celestial Metre: Wounded Hermit Pentameter
3 Star-Ravaged Co(r)pse	Poet IA	Lyra/Appartus Sculptoris	Celestial Metre: Wounded Poet Tetrameter
4 Al Jab'hah	Lion IA	Leo	Celestial Metre: Wounded Lion Pentameter
5 Sequences for a Tariff	Wolf IA	Lupus	Celestial Metre: Wounded Wolf Pentameter
6 Knightless	Knight IA	Ara/Orion	Celestial Metre: Wounded Knight Trimeter
7 Sump	Gypsy IA	Virgo	Celestial Metre: Wounded Gypsy Pentameter
8 Meat Spirit	Demon IA	Hydra/Cetus// Scorpio/Andromeda	Celestial Metre: Wounded Demon Decameter
9 Taghairm	Centaur IA	Centauri/Sagittarius/ Sagitta	Celestial Metre: Wounded Centaur Hexameter
10 Legere	Angel IA	Aquila	Celestial Metre: Wounded Angel Tetrameter

It is not altogether clear from Norge's star atlas annotations why this last flare of electrical energy which produced the sequence emerged, nor why he embarked on a surgery of celestial bodies.

He had, according to his own writings, 'been compelled to undergo the trials of star-craft' in the decades preceding his arrival on Eilean a' Bhàis which might indicate that this late flurry of poetic activity had been brewing for some time. The extreme and oppositional elements on his imaginal Isle of Death may have created an environment uniquely disposed to aid the timing of his sagittal arrow: 'stellar sense now nocked on my bow'. Yet, the final embodiment of Norge's idolatrous cosmogony would be a self-construed effigy of his singular awareness as a living, mnemonic image. These starry positions warranted a final process in which Norge distilled his con-templative stations of death.

Cadere to Cadaver

Outworked as the pictorial skin of the process and Norge's internal predicament, is a lone image which apparently makes him the fortune-telling card of his own destiny:

> The image on the card is of a dying poet standing on a cliff edge where a cave can be seen, with the wind in his hair, holding a mirror in one hand which reflects a miniature, falling angel that is his own likeness. In the other hand he has the (imaginary) symbol for memory. He stands in a ring of ten figureheads, each emblazoned with a poetic property. Along the rugged cliff-top are graves and etched at the bottom of the card is the archer constellation with a wounded and dying centaur depicted among his stars.

According to several traditional sources, Norge noted, once pleased to hold it in his collection: 'this lost, early tarocchi card from the Major Arcana is named "The Falling Seraph" and would originally have been placed between "The Broken Tower" and "The Star" as representative of the dispersal of poetic language, first spoken by the birds.

Upright Interpretation

(With the figure falling in the mirror). When upright, the concept embodied by this IA in the eternal memory of God is of Lucifer: the fallen angel who struggles to recall his original state as benign. Fallen angels are premonitions of the ordeal God caused Christ the poet, and therefore are mnemonic devices to remind God of the necessarily poetic suffering of his son as semi-human. 'And the angels which kept not their first estate, but left their own habitation, he hath reserved in everlasting chains under darkness unto the judgement of the great day' – Jude 1:6. This card signifies spiritual recollection and calls for the recovery of sacred memory.

Reversal Interpretation

(With the figure rising in the mirror). When reversed, the concept recollected by this IA in the eternal memory of God is of Christ: risen with the angels. Fallen from God, because abandoned by God, Christ the poet descends in spirit to the underworld for three days, during which his body lies in the tomb, before rising again. The wind typifies the Holy Spirit and the wounded centaur depicts Christ as the foolish donkey, crucified and so, holy (see image of the Palatine Graffito as a reversed centaur). This card signifies corporeal amnesia and so, redemption.

'This scruffy fortune-telling card, hand-drawn with its miniature falling angel,' wrote Moncrieff on January 13th, 1962, 'is one of the few things I have found amongst Kristján's belongings that seems to still have life. Sometimes, when I am tired, or the room grows dimmer, or the flame of the candle I have set down among all his books and papers – when the flame of that candle flickers in a draft of wind – it looks for a moment as if the small figure of the angel in the card falls in the hand-drawn mirror. Then I know I am done for the night.'

'Branded by thought,' Norge deliberated on Christ's body as entombed and static within the stanza or stopping place, the altar or the 'Eala' containing the death-created effigy of God:

> his spirit exists as he descends to hell... is his corpse the IA of his wandering spirit... what does Christ's dead corpse imagine... my stopping places are cellae carved into the page as temple rooms...for Christ the rockscape around the tomb, the gardens in which the deadened... lifeless images of the living spirit of poetry which has gone... the memory of God is there too, in the broken body of his dying son, bleeding IA. Wounded centaur licking the wounds of the garden.

And so, Norge conceivably received his verse sequences in *The Dead Reckoning* as a series of such cellae: the unmoving corpse within each, present and somehow invoking or evoking a body language of absent spiritual action. His was the bruising psyche of an angel who rejected his status as descendent, leaving self-reflection to ransom in order to escape. Having altogether forgotten his previous fiendish existence, the recall of malevolent voices must have been at turns bewildering, at turns frightening, but when expanded into the realms of clothed patterning, became life-threatening. Wearing the disguise of a dying poet over the image of a fallen angel, Norge's own underlying constellation which was made accessible through such configurations, is a flighted pattern of ascent and descent.

'The will to fall is heightened by the will to fly and finds its specific tuning in the equipoise between each interdependent state,' argued Norge. 'I can cascade or float through the nine ages of the Gaelic angels. Equally, I can be raised up through consciousness of these actions. I am the underlying design of descent.'

More than this, he now reached a terminal conjecture:

> it is apparent to me that God himself is a memory symbol. Christ gives this motif its memorable drama, yes, but perhaps not so that we merely recall the presence of God. I

feel that the triple personhood of this deity – and all deities embodied in effigies whose tactile presence incorporates non-physical form – all such supernatural presences are only memory aids for some other, universal awareness to recollect stored knowledge of the religions of our world. The Christian God made a greater bid for impact by manifesting a mutilated son, outstripping any previous mnemonic device in its terrible visual power, pressing it far harder on the senses, on the memory. Christ was the tortured image who included the God and the Holy Spirit in his agonised mnemonic imprint. He was the wounded flesh which clothed the immaterial design and function of God the father and God the Holy Spirit but the three operated as a whole. Just as a constellation of stars – themselves abstract and hard to discern – are given the hide or skin of centaurus, himself a stellar narrative, so too did Jesus clothe the pattern of God but as God: the triple conflation. And so, my final question is – what is the vaster knowledge attached to the IA of God and who or what requires to remember it?

Norge had travelled to far-reaching poetic aspects of himself: had embarked on a poesis which he, as his own will, had visited – his own illumination personified by Luce Moncrieff, and his own doubt embodied by Jeanie Hafoc. In this way, perhaps all the figures in his system, attached to ten places on an island of oblivion, were merely aspects of himself and more than that, aspects of himself as poet. The living characters Norge encountered were possibly figments of his poetic make-up at war with itself. The Sluagh, or Host of the Dead, or Wind of Voices, were ostensibly his own voices; dolorous, plaguing and unrelenting. Monmhur was apparently both his actual reflection and self-reflection. The various animals in his island world were arguably elements necessary to the act of making poetry: vision, melancholy, inspiration and the boatman was, of course, the great transformer, the one who enabled transition from the outer precincts of doubt to the inner precincts of luminescence. He was a dying poet who had travelled to those inner realms of selfhood concerned with self-demise.

Ravage can be absorbed as a matter of the dead, embodying

material and immaterial instincts in alignment with Norge's morbid system. In this light, Eilean a' Bhàis holds Norge's personal landmark cairn or chambered tomb complex in which strange objects and ideas can be disinterred pertaining to his exequies. Fittingly, the grave site returns us to Norge's original ideas concerning the stanza as a sacrificial altar in a field, the crudely dug pit in the earth. Possibly Bàs itself should be positioned as an expansive funerary cairn of the imagination and Kristján Norge's spiritual progression read as the action of a poet who was once a living image, was once the 'imago agens' of a condemned seraph forced to perform its own death rites.

Fear Eun Lota: Bird Wound Man

Essay by MacGillivray on Kristján Norge

Similar in appearance to medieval depictions of 'Wound Men', the 'Fear Eun Lota' (Scottish Gaelic for 'Bird Wound Man') demonstrated poetic damage done to an individual when deliberately conversing with birds – an archaic gift much sought after in the Highlands and Islands of Scotland. Such wounds afflicted specific parts of human anatomy relevant to the particular type, size, song or mythology of each bird so that the 'slaughter-hawk' or raven, can be seen to attack the hands, for example. Derived from the arcane 'Corvus Codex' in the 'Ancient Ionian Book of the Dead', an anonymous monk from Saint Columba's sacred community, covertly transcribed the 'Fear Eun Lota' in its Latinate form, titled: *Avis* (bird, sign or portent), *Vulneris* (emotional or mental mutilation), *Homo* (common man), thus inferring a more complex understanding of the wounds as signs to be read in terms of damage to spirit. Later, however, 'vulneris' changed from the genitive to 'Avis Vulnus Homo' and was more strongly associated with an injury as mark, sign or seal. Conversing with any 'omen-bird' was considered to be an unholy and dangerous occupation – more so than augury – as demonstrated by the dictum:

> *Quem quaerent homines quaerentes vulnerat oscen*
> *The omen-bird wounds men who seek it.*

It was observed that to 'converse with the birds' stimulated eidetic experience, and was said to elucidate an intimate knowledge of angels. Through exposure to pain, the supplicant would access a convulsion of the mortal and avian, manifesting in a conjoined vision. Holography, or the possession of one's own handwriting, in the Latin context, was heightened through an annotation of avian scarification. These cicatrices were 'read' as angelic text, imprinted on the damaged skin of any individual who had managed to communicate with the birds, thereby experiencing a momentary amalgamation of the avian, angel and human. Later, those known as 'Avis Vulnus Homo' suffered great persecution, most commonly tortured to death by immolation. The residual ash from such executions was rumoured to become 'wan misshapen'; strange configurations lifted by the wind, to acquire a reputation as 'fowl air'.

A hymn, or libation, in a hybrid of early Scots, aristocratic Gaelic and 4th-century Shetlandic, originally embodied the Hebridean ritual concept of 'Fear Eun Lota'. It was to be chanted whilst modulating the voice to a vessel, bottle or other receptacle as it was slowly filled with water or wine, thus altering the pitch. This hybrid of language is considered unique among early Scottish invocations and scarcely evidenced elsewhere.

In 1952, little-known Norwegian-Shetlandic poet, Kristján Norge, responded to such obscure historicity with a poem whose title, *Fear Eun Lota*, mirrors the myth's Gaelic origins but whose Shetlandic and Scots tongues are construed via an introspective, Modernist interpretation. Norge is perhaps best remembered for having coined the term 'Cantian Poetry', in the course of a long-standing preoccupation with secrecy in language and abstruse systems of poetic codification. This is a rare example in Norge's early output of a lunar motif, the poet having been more conversant with solar imagery, which perhaps reflects his continuing fascination at the time of writing with 'parhelia', or 'mock suns' – hence the quadruple repetition of variants 'mön, muin, moon'. This verse appears here for the first time in print, rescued from his papers. Arguably, the condition of the poem itself can perhaps be seen to manifest a wounded palimpsest of Scottish translation rites and rituals.

Fear Eun Lota

Wis a twafauld aungels scliff i' a mön-het brocb,
creeshy wi' feeling.

Maun muin, A lang leukit upon thaim,
foondit th' glyphs i' th' girse, schauchie aff holograph.

Ma mynd aye a brent gless,
a sharrae dist glentin.

Hyne i' th' muin hard darkenin
A whisked-aim doun, pechin,

sweitit oot thair thoosand queels
queevering closed i' th' pail,

paulie mön an th' scliff wis
maik a scliff o' hert, maik a sclitter wit
waitin' wis.

Bird Wound Man

Was a dual angel scuffle in a moon-hot halo –
greasy, with feeling.

My moon, I long looked upon them,
found the glyphs in the grass, discarded as writing.

My memory still a burnt mirror,
a bitter dust glinting.

193

Late in the moon-gloam,
I rubbed them down, panting,

sweated out their thousand quills;
quivering sluiced in the pail,

pale moon and the segment was
like a scliff of heart, like a wet sense
waiting, was.

scliff [sklɪf, S. sklɛf, sklØf, MN. sklʌuf, SN. skluf] *n.* A shuffling trailing way of walking or the noise made by that. A dull heavy tread. A clumsy or worn out shoe used as a slipper. A blow with a flat surface. A scuffing glancing blow. A thin slice. A shaving or paring. A segment of the moon or of an orange.

broch [brɔx, brʌx] *n.* A halo round the sun or moon, usually the latter, indicating bad weather, any kind of circle or halo.

holograph ['holəgraf] *n.* A holograph. A letter or other document wholly in the handwriting of one person. adj. Holograph, wholly in the writing of one person.

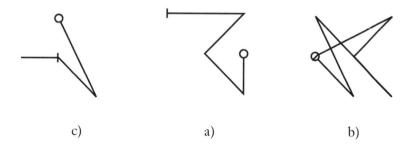

c)   a)   b)

Figs. a) From the Gaelic, b) Latin, and c) modern English. These are contemporary depictions; the Latin invocation of the 'Homo Avis Vulneris' was subsequently evolved in zodiacal sigil work, of which there are few remaining examples.

It is regrettable that the earliest Gaelic artistic depictions of the 'Fear Eun Lota' have been lost. Equally, there are no surviving iconographic diptychs and we only know of one statue which was destroyed in a fire caused by King Edward II's troops that ravaged Melrose Abbey in 1322. There remains in existence a single calligraphic transcription attributed to hagiographer Adamnán of Iona, and a contested reference in a Roman graffito on a preserved section of Hadrian's Wall, now held in the special collections of the Hunterian Museum, Glasgow. Art historians can only presume that such graphic and three-dimensional works were inculcated with an imagined impression of form, as opposed to eye-witness depiction, though scholars still debate this point. Typically, the association of transformative pain alludes to the potential in humans for achieving angelic flight or, metaphorically speaking, sacred flights of thought, though this was a Christianised position promoted by the early monasticism of St Columba. As such, these extant relics merely retain an inference of any original pagan ceremonial significance. Nonetheless, in some circles it is understood that the ritual practice of summoning 'Fear Eun Lota' never truly died out, but is still evoked (outside the precincts of 'Crown and Kirk') on Shetland, at Dunlichity and purportedly, in Edinburgh's infamous Underground City where several breeds of bird are said to be trained on raw meats in the dark.

V

APPENDIX

THE WIND OF VOICES

Based on the diary of Luce Moncrieff

THE SITHS, or Fairies, they call Sleagh Maith (or Good people, it would seem, to prevent the dint of their ill attempts) are said to be of a middle nature betwixt man and angel, as were daemons thought to be of old, of intelligent studious spirits and light, changeable bodies (like those called astral), somewhat of the nature of a condensed cloud and best seen in twilight. These bodies be so pliable through the subtlety of the spirits that agitate them, that they can make them appear or disappear at pleasure.

REVEREND ROBERT KIRK
The Secret Commonwealth of Elves, Fauns and Fairies

EILEAN A' BHÀIS

1962

I

AM FAOILLEACH

I

IT WAS ON A hot, clear Hebridean night, that Kristján first suspected he was a demon. His mirror had flashed its urgent fire. Of course, I had known for some time but naturally did nothing – not, at least, until the midsummer storms came. Before the heat broke, the sea always released a foul stench in that particular solar quarter. The mainlanders liked to say that the Samh Sea would kill wild people living in caves near the ocean. Strange to recall, it was in such a cave that eventually I found him... Kristján Norge, the poet demon.

Rumour has it, this place is an equivalence of ghosts. I am speaking of Eilean a' Bhàis with its light-tower, monastic remains and cave mouth covered by a waterfall... the island has long been reduced to lichen ruins, bleached grasses and strong winds. Winds of seed and pollen; sea-salt and bitter soil. Winds of pagan water that release petrichor from the pink-earthed monastery grounds. Perfumed currents of dried heather and cut kelp... wafted through the cool smoke of a driftwood fire... contaminated by touch. Some still say the island acts as portal to the underworld. Nearby, in the North Atlantic Drift, a dangerous whirlpool broils like an eye on sunlit nights. A pale lens, it watches the harms and the hurts congeal.

We Moncrieffs have been light-keepers here for many centuries. Before the invention of glass and electrics, we used driftwood and built up scant pyres near the rocks. Originally, the fire-scored air guided death to the island. Landed here in ancient times, the dead were rowed in to the old Port nam Marbh whose viridescent palms still rustle at night all along the deserted shoreline. Those flickering nocturnal vessels, packed with heather and cinnamon, were brought into port by silent boatmen. Light craft with dead weight; junks and skiffs; barges and coracles, buffeting the key-stones as mortal cargo was winched to the jetty. These were the forsaken dead: a traffic of neglected souls, traded in for volcanic chips that were shaved in lots from the island's cliff-face... the dull roar of pitch torches, the soft chink of basalt flints. They had their chthonic stars, the oarsmen of those funerary boats: knew the beacon was determined for them. Once a night it burned for an hour. One hour only, and the air thick with bitumen.

Now, I still hold the island close; 'like an early sea-marking hermit or sorrowful aristocrat performing luminous penance,' Kristján said to me, once. I know the ropes: can haul and scrub and stitch. Most importantly, I can occult the light. There are storm-ravaged birds to heal and small, hurt things dashed against the lantern-room panes. All such modest tasks preoccupy my endless time.

*

Some island incantations... peat haunts the wild, salt-infested grasses that web the old mariner tombs. At sunset, minerals glitter in the derelict ruins of the Port nam Marbh, igniting a blush in the stone as the lintels and jetty stones, keystones and cornerstones, gaze longingly westward toward the ocean. The setting sun puts colour in their stony cheeks. I live in the lighthouse: a monolith among the phantom stones, rubbled into oblivion. The old coffin road is overgrown and the matelot graves sunk into bog. Still, Bàs retains its pernicious mystery. The sea is like a rippling shroud wrapped about the head of the island's corpse. And the wind rages most often at night, scathing the battered heather. Yet, as with all Hebridean islands, the longer you linger, the less the outer world exists; like evaporated sea water leaving only traces of salt. I recalled those saline runes and decided to return.

Take a track north-east from the lighthouse and you will be walking the old 'Sraid nam Marbh', the coffin road, up to the ruined monastery. Pines in salt-lick grey: a rough-eyed donkey stands in the hawthorn field to the mid-east where there is a sheer drop from the pasture down to the shoreline. In 1587, a large herd of wild asses had roamed the island, bred from survivors of a vicious wreck. Of those first beasts, only two descendants remained and were named for the Gaelic: Asal and Asan. They were quiet, but wily. Now there is only the one. Though he grazes on banks of saltwater thistles, Asan has been known to snap up a starling. Red deer throng the island in massy herds, outnumbering any wildlife bar the gannets, whose squawking flocks surround the lighthouse.

Southward, lies the cave of the bloods with its sheet of continuously falling water located at the Bàs claw. Then a trudge towards the derelict, walled monastic garden with a ship's figurehead salvaged from the shore…totem in the sea grasses, found half-buried in the sandy soil, a kelp-covered offering from turbulent waters. This pock-marked figurehead, hardened and calcified, standing among the sea graves, seems stricken, static… stark with salt. Open-mouthed and with blanched eyes, she is voiceless and gazeless, but still looks outward and mouths into the blackness across that sea-tundra of endless dark. Cobalt, obsidian, both buried in the night haul of love.

*

Kristján! These winter nights, when the haloed moon solemnly rises, I still walk out: walk and watch and witness. Here, for example, to the south side of the island where the sand can look navy or white by turn, near a small crop of sea graves, stands the old whaling station. The sea-bull skeleton pitched behind it has been left untouched since first the station fell into disuse. A bone colosseum. Giant stubs of rib and jaw loom like penitent giants at dusk – to steal them would be the equivalent of stealing a small house. Nonetheless, Kristján had tried. It was a foible of his: stolen shoes, stolen milk. I can still see him now, limping down the empty beach, trailing an old sack on the compact sand. Down to the cave to stash it with empty bottles and whale bone. Down again to the waterfall cave where once I'd found him. Half-stunned. As if the lightning-storm had stolen within him to flash something awake that had long lain dormant.

Even when Kristján first arrived, he was a premonition of the past, a dead man rowing his own barque. He had staggered up

207

through the moving surf, engulfed in flames, and then thrown himself down to put the fire out. A burning figure, wrestling on the sand. He'd come in fire and water both and his small boat bobbed, still alight, sparking and smoking against the stone jetty of the abandoned harbour. A punctured petrol can and pipe, his dramatic props. I watched until he wore himself out and fell asleep on the sand from sheer exertion. For those first few hours, I didn't show myself to him. Kept to the edges of his awareness. Then, I went down to him... Kristján. Slowly, as the tide came in, I let my shadow cross his feverish face, left a hand on his arm for a moment longer than I should have done. He grew instantly stronger as his wild, hard eyes sealed into knowing and he looked at me then like a man saved.

Yet, hopelessness was like a tang savoured in the evenings by the watchful peat fire and the dying, heather-scented light. I overlooked it, with keenness, with longing. What shadows play afterward on the clarity of our understanding... I should have known that his recovery rested lightly like a curse – thought, but not spoken. It was tainted. The wind knew it. The wind intervened. Its currents were to blow a sickness through him of tragedian scope. How could I have had no way to fathom it? I questioned the sea that night, turning my raised face back and forth: westward, eastward, then northward, southward; the ocean lit up in a surrogate question. If Norge was the answer washed in, then life gave me no notion of the reckoning. Like Norge's small, charred vessel, pitted with smoke, my poet was marooned on the island of himself. Then the wind came to ignite whatever still glinting horror lay beneath. Of course there was his mirror, that bad altar. The one in which Kristján kept himself revealed. He held his own lights, I see that now, the burning skiff, the malign glass, the unknotted wind. His glowing fever which initially calmed, was a false calm before an unprecedented storm – one which no one had told me about: that the voices would come and ravage this burning poet washed up on my shore. An urgent driftwood, to be urgently forgotten.

*

You see, Kristján Norge had come in the name of memory. He was a man driven by poetic possession. I suppose he'd read about Eilean a' Bhàis in one of those dusty excursions to a basement of papers that hide in the darkness of archives like a sheathed field of dry wheat. He'd brushed through them and in that field of dust had found a map. The poet researcher. I have little time for them: whether they burn their books or bodies on the pyres of reason. Norge had come to find his field and his field was mnemonics. That venerable pastime of recollecting memory.

He had sat with the rhetors when the sun scorched their backs. Had worked wax and feathers. Tipped masonry in near-fallen buildings to crush bodies into recollection. Spread nets of thought for cascading corpses, ruined by time. Had seen bands of death rising, like heat. Had saved drowners: drowning in thought, in feeling, in love and in the blood of their own heart's knowledge. Now, Kristján had come to Bàs, and Bàs was known as an island of oblivion. An island of forgetting. An abandoned isle of the dead. Kristján had rowed his boat from the magnificence of institutionalised memory with its bowered palaces and lion-caged courtyards, its multicoloured sands and crude winds, its powerful speeches and regrettable rearrangements (for surely we all know how memory's images morph like warm wax when pressed); rowed himself hard into the numbness of regret. Of course, all this was pure theory to a poet already hovering on the banks of death, who had spent a lifetime conforming to the high-walled enclaves of badly lit libraries, before retreating to a dank World's End pub for a solitary dram.

His boat had been packed with mnemonic folios of papers when he sculled swiftly toward the island, a pipe clamped between his teeth, his old overcoat tied up with baling twine, Varg barking at the prow. Kristján was a determined Charon, weighed down by the bodies of his books. I had salvaged very little that day... his notes on poetry, some charred volumes. Pages scattered in the surf washed in and out as the sea dissolved their ashen lettering. The petrol can floated like a suitcase, leaking foul rainbows flecked with salt. I was quick to fish it out. Then, slowly we ascended the steep cliff path as an undying sun blazed down on us disapprovingly, carried bundles of sea-soaked papers and books like Osiran scribes trudging to edge of the underworld. At the lighthouse, I set Kristján up with bitter black coffee, whisky and tobacco, lit a small fire and cut away his burnt clothes. Even that night, after the initial shock wore off, he feverishly attempted to restore his notes, filling in the scorched spaces. I hung most of it up to dry, the ink running off it in black welts. Then the wind came and went, pummelling our exhausted dreams.

When I found him – that man on fire, drowning on the beach – he was watermarked in flame. Marked out. Much later, as my hopes of reviving him faded – as the wind seemed to take him – I merely watched. Did he know why it began within him? That stinking summer of 1961, where he stood on the cliffs with the sea wind behind him. Where night never rose to meet the endless daylight. Where is Kristján, now that I need him?

II

SUMMER LOCKED JUNE TO the wet pine trees, salted with sea scrim, that blew and bent on the west wind; brought a slake of voices to the burnt hulk. They too had scorched on the heel of a storm, pouring and scraping down the windows, screeding down the lighthouse tower, calling adrift and alone on those aching midsummer evenings as the light paled and thinned to a wisp of yearning. Nights when the air became a colour field, bleeding vivid blue. Our feet had salted too, as we inspected his crumbling wreck: a stark, charcoal skeleton that the sea sipped at and pressed at night. The skiff never budged in the time he was there, but when the wind picked up, a fine black dust was sifted from those boards in flecks of violent sea song. I had thought the voices belonged to the ocean. I was wrong. No black tide welled up with the cries of drowning sailors, no marine love sighs sifted from those timbers. The nights were bright when they happened and it was the wind, not the sea, that brought the voices in...

Once, Kristján had told me, a gale manifested from the island annals of the dead and the Bàs monks took careful note. Some rendered it a malign tempest of fallen angels that would lift a man high in the air and break his body on the jagged rocks. Others enforced a fierce crowd of strident armies. Still others maintained it was a sign of the spirited sìth, influenced by the Gaelic fairy lore. None had actually heard this wind, participated in its lonely myth. Only one scribe was rumoured to have encountered it. He had trained alongside Bruno at Naples, but fled the Dominican convent when they discovered his secret: not to have developed a schema to speak with demons, not to seed angels in the warming air of dawn, but to have created a masterful system of amnesia through which the entire universe and its contents could be subscribed to oblivion. It was his nib (pinioned, rumour had it, from a trapped swan) that had splintered when he penned: *Sluagh nam Marbh: Host of the Dead* before swiftly covering the inscription in sigillary Latin. But, he had dreamt it as a deep-set ocean wind: a maritime storm blown up through the wrecks. As if the voices rose from marine inhumation. I suppose I'd sensed this strain of his thinking: felt the ocean to be of greater threat than the wind.

*

I can still see Kristján now, dark-haired and full of consternation, speaking long into the night, incanting histories of the island. His face had a waxy, sallow tone, as if seen through mouldy candlelight, and his dull hair was badly shorn. Sometimes, on those long, summer evenings, when the gusts grew wild, he would look up suddenly with wolf-grey eyes and survey me with a fatal expression. Even when he was lucid, I heard him muttering... the consistent murmur began and stayed with him. His constant companion. It pitched us into a slow-moving turmoil. Kristján, always frightened, then became hardened. I watched him go out. Dreams like being shot. Physically traumatised for a day – but, only a day. Somehow our weaknesses kept rising up to meet us.

'What is a ghost?' Kristján had asked me one night, reluctant poet come down from his tower, one hand cradling the back of my head.

'A ghost,' I said, leaning forward to rake the fire into life, 'is when you are more aware of the space behind you, than in front.'

That day, Kristján had been in an anxious, pensive mood, standing like a helmsman by the chopping block. He had begun to half-shout his addresses, a kind of rough caress – pushed at me with them. Worse, I had known they were a delayed tutelage while he sorted his thinking out. A way of putting me on hold. Later, when I came to love the island again, came to recall older storms, as lightning cracked a blistering tree in the tasty air, they all became supernatural and Kristján with them, and I realised that always he had been conversing with the voices.

And so it began, his nightly venturing. I watched helplessly as Kristján returned each dawn to the bolted lighthouse, bloodied and exhausted, battered by his incessant nocturnal excursions. Across those weeks he came and went... as the Samh sea swelled with bitterness under a late June full moon, and all the time the wind kept on at us as if in an interminable labour, or centuries-old pain. Sometimes, during the day when he wasn't sleeping (and this happened at times in the lighthouse fireplace: I found Kristján fast asleep in its ashes) he would only murmur to me in those faint monotones. I made up charms – one with flax which I tied around Kristján's grubby neck. He badly needed a shave and here and there was grazed and cut. He slept in his overcoat and his body gave off a sweetish stench. Sluagh nam Marbh: host of the dead. I could see it, in his gaunt face. Eddy winds ran through his blood, tossed his thoughts, blasted his heart. The nights grew brighter as we crossed the year and the sea mist rose in the early mornings full of the cries of invisible birds.

Then he started writing, a wilderness madman. Roaming the heather with his typewriter strapped to his back like a bundle of wood, his wolfdog, Varg, loping alongside. Murmuring over his notes in the evening when the silence came. Shouting back to the voices towards the end. His eyes looked scalped then and he didn't want me near him. Once, when it was very bad and he begged me to leave with him, patch up the charred skiff and row out from the island, I held him down, pushing the whisky bottle to his chattering teeth, ministering and forcing until he fell into an indigenous sleep of forgotten dark and silence. Later, when the whisky ran dry and Kristján's eyes looked through me and faltered, I again rolled onto him, pushing his head to the boards when they all screamed on and he with them for hours at a time. That was when I questioned everything, questioned that the wind was a part of it at all. It seemed to matter deeply to him. And now, at last, going through this room of scattered papers – pages lifted by a different wind than the one that dictated them – a cigarette half-burnt in the shell I'd given him, there is one thing I recall Kristján urged me before vanishing – 'destroy them,' he repeated, 'Luce, you must destroy them.'

Of course, I'd agreed – not then knowing his full meaning. And so, I have finally managed to get back to Bàs, to slowly begin gathering the fragments in – to build a bonfire and commit them to ash. Three months on the island. When I returned, he was gone, and the boatman knew nothing. Kristján did not survive the last storm, it seems. Did not survive the relentless voices… Kristján has vanished, but his small, burnt boat from the start of last summer is still here, chafing in the breeze.

*

Kristján had told me one night, pale-eyed by the dying fire, about the earliest ship's figureheads: how a sacrificed head was stuck on the prow with its eye whites showing, surveying the ocean. He had a little stick with him and listlessly raked the coals.

'I feel like a severed head,' he'd said, 'lifelessly surveying its own existence.'

I let the silence deliver Kristján up to himself, as I sat sewing in the half light, waited for his next offering. I began to think, after a long pause, trying to cut the thread between my teeth…
…now I recall what it was… it is true that most merchant navy ship's figureheads are women, bare-breasted for the lashing sea. I was never one of those. Could not trace sea-aligned veins in the worn wood. Had not done great battle with the deep. Had not survived like metal through flame: promiscuously scarred. No, I had inherited a quieter fate, alone on this salted shelf of land. Yet, I saw Bàs as a kind of vessel, moored in loneliness, and the lighthouse as its prow, and so supposed I must be a kind of living figurehead. Such foolishness…

'Not so, go on,' Kristján had said – 'you are the island's blue-eyed figurehead and your dark hair is soaked by the night fog, and you are alone, in the darkness, peering with your unseeing eyes into the ocean, an angel chained to a wild plum tree in the old marine garden.'

*

I am standing in the lighthouse, having broken in. Varg patters among the papers, sniffing at them. Dusk is rising as the winter sun falls and the sea churns like an unsettled field, ploughed and re-ploughed. I shiver. His cigarette's gone out. I shouldn't smoke, but I relit his old stub. This is my last attempt at suffumigation – at smoking out Kristján's old presence. And it helps with the pain. My left wrist is only now healing after that bad fall... dampness hurts me. And, smoking his stubs keeps him closer to me – calls him. If I reveal where I am, then perhaps he can return.

I have brought a radio, whisky and a sunlamp and sit with a dram as the sheets glow under the UV lamp which keeps the ghosts away and helps heal my broken limb. Most of all, I think I have nearly found the thing he wanted – not spoken by the wind, but scrawled by Kristján in uneven lettering. Kristján, who has disappeared from the island. Kristján, who has nearly vanished utterly from my sphere of comprehension. How he was wrecked on the rocks by the wind. I feel remorseful, that I could have helped if I had allowed myself to be a little more human. It is January 1962, the beginning of a year of lunar orbits, and I tune into my tiny set, roll up a cigarette and listen to a report while I go through his notes, typing up a description from June 23rd, 1961:

> The vision is a sore: pus-filled, and needing drained. Drain it I did, as Solomon drank down glasses of wine, as Simonides drained Roman beer at his feast. Time wounds, it does not heal. Time wounds me repeatedly: fixing a mirror in the ordinary glass, its own repeated death's head in the rubbish of the beach. Light drowns my eyes, winking and suffering wounds of interference. Sight will activate them. Breath will activate them. But, they have already been subject to some sort of disturbance, whetted, stroked, smeared, roughed up...agility of disposition extracted from the acuity of fire...the colour of Saturn is like burned wool...Sagittarius: white lead...soften the mirror and dust well...strike the surface of the water...take as much river water as your mouth can hold and carry it to the reflection...

A Neolithic drinking well. A Neolithic watering hole. Painting within the poem of a reflected scene: a danger. In the circle where the cylinder rests is a death's head come to life again in the mirror of mud. The dying centaur staggers, leaving a limping trail of horse hair and fingerprints: pawed over, bitten at, ground in the teeth. And are the mirror sequences my shield, flashing in the sunset, glimmering in the moonlight? The death-horse, lunging in the colosseum of its own dreams, an audience to the empty seats. Did one hold the bow and the other release the arrow? It is a manu-script illuminated by horse blood in forgotten wood. The shield is of beech and scored with scratched lettering. Let it burn in my mouth. The bull stamp, the heavy cross. A cross-animal bullion. Now it is noon, and I must go to my death.

This, of course, amongst the many fragments I have found in this shut-up room. I suppose, even now, these papers don't strike at me the way he had always done and the recollection of him stabs at my heart with a sweetened blade whilst my mind spontaneously swabs, sews and bandages it. He had to have the voices more consistently as his own than any monkish vision of a blunt sea, haggard and pelting sky, the dim muck that was shot through with the startling blues and reds of the heather. The voices had described Bàs to him even as they described Kristján to himself. He had become needful of his madnesses.

III

ON AN ISLAND, SOLITUDE has many edges but the most expansive edge of all – the black saltwater – repeats its loneliness again and again, washing in and out of proximity. I had wanted the sea's melancholy early on. Later, it became unbearably heavy; marine solitude gnawed at me as if I were an old whalebone. But, islanders inherit their reclusion and it has proved to be of great use to me, with Kristján lying desolate in my thoughts. The loneliness improved as I gently nursed my castaway, warily treating his slight burns. I had Slane, the boatman, bring mustard, flour and oats. Kristján claimed them as provisions for the afterlife, noting:

> …those old Pharaonic, Greek and Roman feasts loaded on long, wooden barges rowed past long ago in the dead of night: honey, wheat, mummified meats, culinary levies and fares, handed over in the dark by cold fingers; bundles of osseous rib wrapped in papyrus leaf for boiling into soup; some dusty corn to be ground and baked into small loafs; and endless carafes of bitter wine…

He summoned these foods as I fed my half-drowned, half-burned visitant on dark tea and blackened toast. He often lay there, a heavy hand on Varg's skull, as tears rolled from the corners of his closed eyes.

By day he seemed weaker, but night gave him strength and I kept the lighthouse window open to let moonlight beat down on him. It was several days before Kristján spoke, conveying his needs through a series of slight gestures. When his fever calmed and I watched him recover his senses, his history, he began to talk… his work on memory, his feeling of betrayal by memory, and I would walk him down to the shore, those first few weeks, eyes whipped by the soft summer wind. Now, among all the sheets of his writing, there are only snippets on lunar memory and sanguinary memory such as this one, dated shortly after his May 3rd arrival, 1961:

I would like to pour the property of moonlight through a passage of time. I would seek the feminine vowel. The sibilant. The properties of silver. The aspect of 'above' and 'shine' or 'glow'. How there is a space that travels across. How the page might be an inducted field. How the centrality of that field might be milky. I would say tonight's is a horse-coloured moon. See the sky arrange itself around it. All breath held. To disremember. To let slip from memory. Here she works into a bruise, here she plants a sweaty print. None of the words fit. Cadere. To fall. To fall from memory. Like Icarus: only he was recalled, again and again. Time is not the great healer. Time is the great wounder. It imprints repeatedly, rubs away at the corners But how to forget... Picture Simonides. He is shocked. He has the imprint of crushed fruit: grapes and figs mulched with blood, this imprint on the tablet of his brain. How do you clean the spirit of mud? Memory itself is a bloody and strange configuration. It is a brutal phenomenon and it scores and scars the thinking flesh like a physical scar, only its cruelty is to create an inner theatre of horror, recollected over and over in exhausting sequences. It is not we who relive such memories: they relive us. The ancients needed their thoughts compelled to memory as a flesh. No paper. So did the Highlanders. All spoken. All the body itself. Now ...we have no need for memory systems, unless they are occult. But we do need systems for forgetting. How to make the flesh regurgitate. The body, amnesiac. It must connect to amnesty – to give your own pain of recollection, amnesty. Amnestia. The Art of Amnesia. The Art of Amnestia. Which is the best moon for forgetting? Not a horse-coloured moon, but a wine-coloured moon. Simonides may have needed to experience the crushed feast as under a wine-coloured moon: a moon of blood.

Around roaring midsummer bonfires, Kristján repeatedly related how in the old tale, Roman poet Simonides dined at a banquet, but escaped a collapsed ceiling, after being mysteriously summoned outside. The poet was then then asked to recall who was present by remembering the seating arrangement. Kristján tracked this devastated scene over again and again; wandering

around the rubble in his own mind, picking out crushed bones
of fragmented recollection.

> I fight Simonides after his opening scene…that the fatal
> feast may have forcibly imprinted repeated memory on the
> poet, which then cannot be erased. Mnemania. The mania of
> memory. Yes – life-force: experiential knowledge: is stronger
> …more brutally effective than the average loci and imagines
> – savage beasts kill you in the amphitheatre of your own
> thinking, in the sawdust and sand, and that circus is for
> perfect memory of death and the beasts are demons and
> angels in animal skins… Any practice of memory holds as its
> seed a morbid fear of amnesia and these seeds can be con-
> sumed as offerings, or crushed to a paste for condiments, or
> ground to make a flour for small cakes sweetened by honey.
>
> Memory passes through its own terrain, like a moving
> statue whose feet do not touch the ground, leaving behind
> little that is good in its ravaged trail. Eventually, it must be
> overcome by the undergrowth of horror, sadness, regret,
> which overcome the effigy and binding it with weeds, pull
> it, damaged, to the ground. This ravager is the starkened
> statue of oneself, equal in weight and temperament with a
> wand of nettles and collapsed face.
>
> I think of 'damnatio bestiari' [condemnation by wild
> animals]… Could memory stand for a condemned person
> torn apart by wild beasts?… Could memory be the wild
> beast tearing apart a human? Could a human be bestial,
> and condemn itself in self-ravaging or destruction, taking
> its own memory with it…though the idea of memory as a
> wild beast – say, a lion of the colosseum…ravaging a human
> is truer to my situation. No, the lion must stay in lunar
> mansion ten, where it belongs, and not stray too far into
> the Roman arena.

'Clearly it was already a morbid banquet; a feast of the dead,'
Kristján commented one evening, his long face pale in the flicker-
ing firelight. Then, he had surprised me:

'I am more interested in Themistocles,' he said, leaning back
in the night air, staff gripped in a white-knuckled hand: 'when
he was offered artificial memory by Simonides, Themistocles
refused – everything he had ever seen or heard, was already

there, firmly lodged in his natural memory. I agree,' Kristján murmured softly to himself, 'to escape memory is the greater challenge. I am hunting down a memory that wounds.'

I was startled to see his face in the firelight wet with tears. 'Don't mind those,' he muttered, 'it's merely my inner weather that looks to escape.'

I do not know what had wounded Kristján Norge. Perhaps his obscurity as a poet. I think he felt Bàs could locate him, locate his ideas. He started out from memory, though, when he began to map the island. Amnesia was the more desperate measure he would be forced to take later on, haunted by that forgotten wind.

*

At first, I had thought Kristján might fully recover – served him broth and kept the lighthouse kitchen warm with dried tinder from wrecked ships' rigging; had Slane row in an old suit for him, a pair of shoes fitted for a long dead man. That feeling lasted across May and then the hot weather threatened. I started up my weaving: warped the loom and worked in the evenings while Kristján whittled a figure, whistling an old song that sounded shrill and tuneless against the shuttered night wind. Sometimes he only sat with his mirror, tilted it in the firelight, knifing shadows. He spent a great deal of time knitting a shapeless thing on bone needles in undyed Shetland yarn that he would unravel at the end of each evening. Later, he told me this was a philosophical exercise and an enchantment of string and nothing, conjured up on a couple of sticks. Gradually, he had become a friend and we held one another's trust, locked in a quiet history-taking. I watched over him: down collecting kelp with the chipped wheelbarrow on the shoreline: standing in the looming shadow of the lone monastery bell which dropped to rust through silence: gathering in eggs from chickens and gannets both: tending Asal and Asan with bales of dry grasses and Gaelic airs on a bent jaw harp. The wind in his sleep, in his eyes, in his hair, and all for a mouthful of healing. I gave him the lighthouse keys and helped him move his scant possessions in.

Then, little by little, he would start to speak out…treatises; soliloquies, a meditating silhouette against the blaze of the sun.

'Memory haunts the lonely fissures of the heart. There is no sense to it. Only time washes in and out on the great seas of blood but even time, even that great, sanguine ocean whose memory of the before is the after, cannot assuage recollection.'

It was like watching a formidable statue, an effigy, begin to incant tracts of the forgotten mysteries of its making. I listened, entranced, as he carried on in measured metaphors.

'Some memory lodged deep on the seabed… it may have been a corroded element, a half-rotted figurehead chained to a doomed wreck (some statues commit suicide like the great Scandinavian women, subjected to immolation on their husband's funeral pyres) – some memory released a nutrient to me,' he said.

'We must have a different kind of nutrient,' he continued, his voice charring the air, 'I call it poetic logic. I suppose we might name it imagination, but I think this is different: it's not that sudden flash of imaging, but its complementary counterpart: the necromantic fusion of elements: like arranging furniture in a robing room, coffin chamber or cell. Funerary thrones, mortuary chests…cult-objects. That's what I think poetic logic is.' The sun was obscured by a cloud for a moment, and Kristján was revealed again, merely a human poet re-lighting his pipe. It went out. He gestured for a cigarette and I passed him one.

'Thank you,' he said, squinting at the horizon. 'I knew a woman once, unlike you. Yes, she was deeply afraid of herself, could work the imaginings but didn't know how to juxtapose, no that's not right,' he corrected himself and stood for a moment while the smoke curled around his skull, 'no, she did know how to juxtapose, but didn't trust her own juxtapositions. She had half the experiential ingredients. But, she began to speak in a series of silences. They became like inverse braille: the motes of touch were inaudible. These were her poetic logic, but because there was little written into prosody she situated those blanks entirely intuitively, like firing a starter pistol into the dark. They were a very real, deep internal messaging now externalised. All this was very real to her, essential perhaps. She could smell the smoke of her other lives. Ironically she was named Helen.' Kristján paused to crush the stub of his cigarette whilst reciting 'was this the face that launched a thousand ships, and burnt the topless towers of Ilium?' A strange figurehead she was, almost turned back on those fleets, those waters as if raised through her silences, upraised through a burning ocean like a charred offering of memory personified.'

He offered me an arm and I took it as he leaned on an old stick I'd given him, his left foot the most badly burnt. We hobbled along the coffin road, Varg always at his heels, yellow-eyed and mournful.

'Good,' I remarked, 'you're improving.'

'I knew another woman,' he continued, unheeding, 'a cruel and frightened young thing who inwardly had exploded into glass. Self-contained. Bruised with secrets, walking death-haunted pages…she was only afraid of cruelty in herself if it couldn't be self-contained. She spoke one night to me as we crossed the city in an atmosphere of dusk, declared she thought herself evil. If it hadn't been for an ensuing terror, I might have believed in her malignity, she who held a small, pert flame in her eyes, who walked out, night after night…pushed through the darkness with her small, soft, determined young body. She had a writer's spirit and now, a writer's fuel. A lifetime's worth of wounding: stark to the self. All such souls, damaged on the rocks of life, I still think of the now.'

He looked at me and grinned. It was more a grimace than a grin, not quite a leer, more one of those antique puppet's fixed expressions: a devil's mask in scarlet and ashes. I paused.

'Yes, I know,' he said, suddenly serious, 'I get red in the face with any revelation and this scar on the side of my face where the muscles won't move doesn't help to lessen the illusion – I know, Luce, I know you think me quite inhuman.'

Well, I simply thought of him as not entirely healed, not entirely tired, not entirely old. He oscillated between a person from the last century's thought and one totally divorced from himself. As if he'd slashed his inner moorings and now intoned to the sea this rarified musing.

*

When Kristján decamped to the lighthouse, I remained in the light-keeper's cottage, mist cascading down the outer walls on early summer mornings. Old things gave me renewed comfort: the near-black marine painting of a stout mermaid done in oils, the grandfather clock booming like an upright coffin and sou'westers and tarnished silver cutlery, sheepskin rugs and two solid oil lamps. There were tinned supplies: apricots in syrup and beans and fresh lettuces from the garden – apples preserved from last autumn and damsons from the gnarled plum tree. We worked the monastery garden, clearing fuel from weeds, toiled among the chiselled headstones. And a quiet paradise ensued. Kristján grew clearer, his edges sharpened and his body became renewed: robust. The wild island health had seeped into his heart. Our friendship blossomed into young conversation that lingered across days, like the fragrant presence of driftwood smoke.

Then, our haven thinned to the high, cool hours just beyond midnight. We talked in signs and whispers late into the early morning hours, echoing one another's thoughts like a golden ball passed back and forth, back and forth, crossing that time-worn space between illumination and thought. Mornings were for collapsing in sleep. In the afternoons I wove or we walked out, hand in hand – he needed that. There was a campus stove for coffee and a thermos flask, and he would take his walking stick and we'd go down to the beach to mark out the sand. Once, on the island, expert pipers would teach their young men pibroch from notes scraped in the sand. They only had until the tide came in and washed it all away, to learn their tunes. I had outlined notes with the stick while Kristján waveringly played them on his dented jaw harp, and we were salt-fresh with laughter that rose high in the warm, bright air like a singed offering to Bàs' captive curse.

223

IV

THERE IS LITTLE SO tender to me as a person lacking an image of themselves. Perhaps Kristján had suffered in this way. Certainly, he found solace in the lone old figurehead in our monastery garden full of nightshade and stinging nettles. Here, among electric-blue thistles, stands the carved angel, chained to a wild plum tree. Dolefully, she surveys the ground, studded with sticky fruit in the autumn, enveloped with snow in the winter time. The seraph has withstood all weathers, wizened and cracked like old gingerbread, has been there for decades. When you tilt her base the wood crumbles to nothing, crawling with insects. Perhaps she grew from the tree bark itself, tethered on a rusty umbilical cord. Kristján would crouch by the angel, late at night, mumbling to her in a broken voice...

I think he saw himself as unresolved – unable to tend his midnight court, except as mirrored in a carved wooden statue. It was as if he knew the value of the image of a dead being (as I suppose he nearly considered himself) not as a reminder of the person, but to use up the energies of the present before joining the ranks of the deceased. Was that how he saw her? An expired angel? I watched him hold an entire night's conversation, as the donkeys breathed softly in the clear air beneath the moonlit pine trees.

Once, we found another figurehead washed up on the shoreline: a bedraggled knight in the flotsam and jetsam. Kristján hauled him in on a brave line. He had broken teeth and a chipped nose, paintless eyes and a sea-worn helmet. Kristján pronounced him 'knightless' and promptly dragged him to the angelic icon, both cast shadows shorter than their histories, as they stood without their ships in the long grass and nettles.

When I went out wandering last week, the knight-errant was gone and the angel abandoned. These days a yellow copse of falling snow draws me over to the walled enclave: I am busied by this small, winter-haunted garden. Now to chop, one-handed, the month's kindling with Asan, the donkey, champing and grazing for shoots in the obdurate, whitened earth. Now to make a bundle of sticks. Asan's breath clouds the air, the sharp snap of frozen twigs underfoot. I've found a neat little deal of wood: most stumps are hard and knotted. When bad weather exposes the tombs, I rebury the mariner and monk coffins, carefully pat the boards down in place. Back last summer, when we worked over this hard ground, Kristján had reinforced the crumbling stone wall, restored the damaged headstones and pruned the plum tree. The old monastery plot whose summer secrets were nourished by a compost of kelp, now lay silenced and blinded by snow; even the guardian figurehead is enveloped.

'Because you are really the watcher in the walled garden,' Kristján had said, panting one hot afternoon as he paused to lean on his shovel, 'standing in fits of leaves, bickering with the birds.' Varg surveyed him dolefully, a light breeze lifting his pelt.

Now, there is snow-burdened work and snow-burdened thought, as I sing to myself in snow-chipped notes, the old Carmina Gadelica blessing and think of the monks beneath my axe blade, clutching their pitted breastbones. Pillows of salt, pillows of snow. Here's the old song, sung under my breath beneath the frozen stand of pines:

Dol timcheall nan clach stacanach,	*Going round the founded stones,*
Is leir dhomh tulach, is leir dhomh traigh,	*I behold mansions, behold shores,*
Is leir dhomh ainghlean air an t-snamh,	*I behold angels floating,*
Is leir dhomh calpa cuimir, cruinn,	*I behold the shapely, rounded column*
A tighinn air tir le cairdeas duinn.	*Coming landwards in friendship to us.*

This is one of our old verses I found written on a scrap in Kristján's uneven hand. On the reverse side, part of an old Gaelic charm:

> *Cha loisg teine, grian, no gealach mi:*
> *no fire, no sun, no moon, shall burn me.*

That one, not his own; he took for his own – a planet-driven motto inscribed on his tongue. What other notes do I have of his in my pockets? *Corpse candles, corpse dreams… do not raise scissors, a knife or a mirror above the level of your breath. Closing a west-facing window after sunset is essential to deter the Sluagh nam Marbh.* Here, in a longer scroll, is a half-burnt paper – which must have been salvaged from the fiery rowing boat. On it he has written in pencil in rough capitals:

AN ANATOMY OF ANGEL
Seraph-lore in Quadruple Brittle Urns

The First Urn contains the brutalities of Winter: rusted snow and frozen teeth, chipped from the angel's mouth. Ice-blood here is also contained. Some winter seraphs are headless; in chains. These stand in ruins, discarding inner thoughts like leaves. The voice is lisped.

The Second Urn contains the death songs of Summer: charred ash of petals and the robin's curse. Tutelage of crows. No shade for shadows. Water poured into this urn will tune thought as the pitch changes. The voice is muttered.

The Third Urn contains crushed stone and is Spring. Time stings the mouth and there is a heartful of grain. The hair on the back of the neck is singed and the brushed ash of this hair, consumed. The voice is stammered

The Fourth Urn contains brittle death and is autumn. Nothing is heard, beyond what is open. Rough commands and impressions in wax. Here, a rubber ball is rolled from the shoulder apex of the wing, down its length, to the tip and up again. The voice is broken.

The rest has been completely burnt away and there is nothing much more to give it sense, but there remains a faint outline drawing of a seraphic figure which, of course, is one Kristján sketched of the plum tree chained angel. Beneath it, he has written: 'Luce Moncrieff'. I turn the torn page over and see his rough scrawl race across the paper:

…where do they grow, dancing and dispersing pouches of musk and burning their incense? Is the island itself a giant mound, a pyre for many ships to burn on, or itself a nautical sepulchre on a sea of flame? I have Luce, my angel, as a descendant of many… have sought her out in the annals of angels. What decipherment does she occupy, alone on this salted shelf of land? Once, she tried to fly out, but was stricken by a marine gale that salted her feathers, stiff and sickened with sea spray, that made the flight a wall of thirst. She must have given up, and soddenly dropped to the shallows, staggered beachward through the soft surf. The shore was a hot pink. On one side a silver moon hung, while an old sun descended to blood. In between, the sea, tranquil as a sleeping child, turned in violet and rouge, sinning to itself… but how do they die and procreate? Her father rubbed his first finger and thumb together and she existed. He showed me once, standing among the sea thistles at dusk: a blue flame that grew softly between his digits. He stopped before the gentian flame became a glowing black and let it rest on a twig where it flickered, blueish, softly. A few weeks later it was still there but, by the autumn, was gone. 'There needs to be will in it,' he had said, turning away from the branch and brushing his hands on his garments, 'will and alignment. We can begin, start, commence, but we cannot end – be extinguished: put out. Unless,' and he looked at me keenly, sudden aeons in his eyes, 'unless in altercation with a demon.' And so, she began: a small, fruitful flame enlarged in a tree, spun out from wilful fingertips. She began as her namesake: Moncrieff – 'monadh craobh', or hill of the tree – a lone fruit tree spreading her arms high on top of this mountain island: the fruit of the lighthouse is its lonely flame.

V

A FINE WIND BRINGS fresh snowfall, smooring the thin light-house panes. I am pleased, it creates the kind of silence I need – tracking is easier in this bleak weather, you have to cast other kinds of light as the dark settles down. Wool pulled over my skin brings tears to my eyes – I like it – a rough, oily, dark blue skin. Closing the west-facing lighthouse window, I have risen stiffly and now survey the circular room. Spread at my feet in a restless sea of unsettled paperwork: Kristján's tangled thoughts. Progress is slow: I type on Kristján's sturdy Olivetti using only one hand – nervous of my painful wrist. On days when I am too sore, I read and so have decided to arrange his books, notes and papers into three separate mounds: shall be an independent scribe for each one of them; try to cast light on intellect. Some of his early work is here with its taut, lucid writing. Unusually, he dates almost everything – the smallest scrap can detail merely two words but will be dutifully dated. There are essays: poems: drafts. All of it is to be destroyed, but not before I find out what happened to Kristján. Even if it takes me years, I am determined to uncover this deranged paper trail, to track back into his mind and uncover the circumstances around his vanishing. Only then, will I burn the work. Only then will his wishes be observed. In the meantime, I shall order these fragments. I have not yet found his ship's 'loggbok', but discovered instead, observational marginalia in English, crudely underlined in his battered Gaelic dictionary:

> *an da-shealladh* – two sights//double sight; *taibhsear, taib-searchachd, tai-bhs* – the spirit double of a living human; *tannasg* – or of one already dead; *taslach* – an unseen taibhs, only heard; *taradh* – the noises made by the taslach; *tag* – another word for apparition associated with an inhuman wail; *tachar* – connected to haunted places... now my wick has gone out...

I have noticed in these first few dictionary entries, descriptions of candle snuffing accompany the annotations. Did Kristján plan

228

for this when, on that frenzied afternoon, I found him melting what was left of the winter's supplies of wax and wick? Standing outside, his figure blurred and shivered in the escaping band of fire-air. He melted them down in the old dye pot and the colour seeped into the wax so that he poured rainbow puddles of blue red and green yellow onto the sandy ground.

'What are you doing?' I called, through the roaring bonfire.

He refused to reply. Kristján, who held in his hands such capability. Whose strange air-haunted eyes darkened when you called his name. We could not have continued in this refined heart of winter: two strangers dark against the morning air, bruising each other's shadow. Summer had not culled winter's cruelty.

'I have a solar shadow,' he said to me once, 'and you, Luce, have a lunar halo – a lunar aureole caught up in a knot of unbrushed hair.' He touched the nape of my neck and smiled, flexing naked toes in the sunlight.

Kristján was right: he was charged by the clear, high heat of the Hebridean summer when the sea extended from our gaze like a courtyard of glass. No, my poet would not have survived an Eilean a' Bhàis winter with its fiercely unique language of coldness.

*

What is a bundle of papers? Like splints, burnt matches, a bale of kindling, a basket of swallows, it is a sign of itself; a haunting of reversals by uprights – sense. I am a dubious current of wind blowing the matchsticks back into life, releasing the birds, leafing through piles of hieroglyphs – upright and concerted in my efforts. Obedient to his instincts, I have confronted his other manuscript notes for a rejected 1958 book proposal titled *The Foolkiller* – which seem to explain something deep in the heart of it all that I cannot quite locate and perhaps might help me to pull a thin thorn of understanding from all this painful confusion:

> To 'flashen' with water or powder stems from 13th-century Middle English, meaning to 'sprinkle or splash' and I have

used it to insinuate a revival of the senses. From around the 15th century, emerges a 'flash' of birds that 'dart or flit', accompanied by 'bursting into flames'. This is followed by a 'flash of lightning', defined by the 16th century; and a 'flash of wit', in the 17th century. Omitting other phrases, such as 'a flash in the pan'; a show of vulgarity; and the indecent act of 'flashing'; we arrive in the 18th century to find ourselves discoursing in 'flash' – the cant of thieves and prostitutes which I have truncated (only permitting thieves), and then expanded (to include beggars or vagabonds in thievish company). This presence of a renegade band usefully embodies the persona of the 'fool'; one who has the wisdom to lose his wits on a regular basis through the jovial forms of witty tomfoolery, jest, absurdism and impressions.

Usefully, the term 'vagabond' is linked to the word 'vague', derived from Old High German to include 'winkan: to wink'. Add this to the trope of the fool's mirror, and a useful deflector arrives in the form of a question: perhaps the fool's mirror reflects the flashing light of the tower back to it in crude mimicry?

The occulting or eclipsing of the lantern light involves the screening of fire in early lighthouse keeping; fire which was fed by a large pyre mounted at the top of the structure and which led to associations with sacrifice, vision and prayer. The early structure of prayer as mnemonic – easy to recall and perform – necessarily conforms to rhyming verse and in a blazing etymological resonance we can trace the word 'poetry' back to its root kwei 'to pile up, build, make', also the root for the Sanskrit cinoti: 'piling or heaping up', which are both suggestive of stoking a pyre with more fuel.

With these excavated associations, we can now place the flashes and the three elements of Sea, Tower and Raft, occupying the last with the foolish figure of the poet: the vagabond, or fool, who has survived that worst of ship-wrecks: a devastated 'Ship of Fools'.

Here laid out for the reader is the metaphoric contract between our props of Sea, Tower and Raft: the Sea as the page; the Tower as illuminating inspiration; and the Raft as the lone stanza occupied by a living figurehead – that of the shipwrecked, thirsty and gaunt-eyed poetic fool. Not content with this dramatic vignette; I now unpack these motifs as relevant and distinctly troublesome to the art of inspiration. Not to be confused with imagination in its seed-bed of classical mnemonics and rhetorical imagines agentes; or moving images, inspiration – we are told – must not be waited upon. Yet, there is little by way of ignition points, illuminating guides or practical aids to help with inciting inspiration whose own definition is somewhat inflammatory, somewhat nautical, founded in the Latin 'inspirare' to 'blow into, breathe upon,' and figuratively, to 'inspire, excite, inflame.' The French inhaled their inspiration, and it seems the divine spirit of the Old Testament exhaling into the nostrils of dust, directly informed the verb 'inspire' in Middle English whose definition also inferred 'breath, or put life or spirit into the human body; impart reason to a human soul.' These terms revivify a keen sense of breath enabled, fought for (in drowning); a breath ignited, aflame and quivering with heat (in inspiring).

The Sea, Tower and Raft appear almost as lost tarrochi images, themselves derived from occulted meaning: the dance of death; Medieval morality, miracle and mystery plays. Loose associations could be made here between extant tarot trumps (in a sailor's game?) and our three-card monte: the Sea could be alluded to by the 'Moon' as controlled by this lunar body; the Tower could be read as the 'Broken Tower'; and the Raft might still have the ship's wheel attached to it, which could be interpreted as the 'Wheel of Fortune' – (unless, of course it is the coffin lid, as I have it). Our fool has his place in troubadourian gaming with early, non-numinous tarot decks but has also emerged through esoteric use in association with traditional lunatic values of the moon and is denoted by zero: 0 – perhaps the open mouth of the oracular poet. In the essay conclusion, V Flash of Foolishness, I consider whether the fool communicates flitting insights into this marine tableaux using a mirror. If this is the case, the lighthouse stands dormant and only appears to signal – really, it is the poet-seer who self-summons inspiration, mouthing unheard words into the glass.

He continues:

A 'flash' or sprinkle of water revives the fool, floating adrift on his raft in the ocean. He has been considered an unlucky 'Jonah' by his companions on the 'Ship of Fools', but is the sole survivor from their wreck in a storm. Interestingly, there are a number of Roman sarcophagi whose lids are carved with pharos symbols. This is a foolhardy mulling; the stone bed is the sarcophagus, sunk not like but as a stone to the real bed – the bottom of the sea. Whether hold hatch or coffin lid, tea chest slats or berth door, our fool floats on a raft which is a stanza, a 'stopping place', for his life is adrift, on hold, vague. He is a marine vagabond. Now, it is rainwater which revives him and we perceive him as bloated. His head becomes prominent: sunken eyes, slack jaw, open mouth. Severed through exaggeration; through overshadowing the rest of his emaciated body, the head is vast, overblown – a huge juggler's ball, the jester's grotesquely swollen, tinkling bell. The poet-fool is here a thirsty figurehead, the spirit of the wrecked raft, following the origins of seafaring itself where boats were mounted with the heads of sacrificed animals to appease furious marine gods. As the oracle of his half-sunken platform, his salty stanza, the poet-fool silently mouths oracular cant. Here we have the unmoored 'square' of the raft stanza, animated by the rotting head of a foolish poet.

Birds circle around our dying fool and these can be seen as living personifications of his fool's cap feathers; his maritime flights of fancy. acts of augury outlined by Cicero allowed the augurs to approximate their closeness to a topography of the future in a timely fashion through observable indications of bird flight. After our fool's revivification by a 'flash' of water; sea birds 'flash', darting and flitting above his head, offering similar conditions to interpret omens. On the subject of darting, or arrowing, the use of birds as fiery weapons is described in the 'Medieval Book of Fires' or 'Incendiary Book to Ignite the Enemy' (Liber Ignium ad Comburendos Hostes), consisting of pyrotechnic recipes purportedly written by Marcus Graecus:

'Another kind of fire for burning enemies wherever they are. Take petroleum, black petroleum, liquid pitch and oil of sulphur. Put all these in a pottery jar buried in horse manure for fifteen days. Take it out and smear the substance over crows which can be flown against enemy tents. When the sun comes up and before the heat has melted the liquid the mixture will inflame [on the crows]. But we suggest that this be used before sunrise or after sunset.'

For the hallucinatory fool, such memories of Middle Ages nautical and land-lubbered warfare might now manifest in his parched mind as foolish indications of curious angelic mirage. Nonetheless, the presence of birds at sea within himself and their metonymic traces, aiding inspired flights of dream, vision and wits, are essential to the shipwrecked fool floating dazed on his half-submerged stanza.

The charred bodies of such arrow-simulating birds are drawn to the lighthouse flame and trapped or burned as they near the lantern chamber or great hollow, at the top of the tower. From the Lanterna of Genoa, constructed before 1161, smoke signals to warn passing ships were issued from a pile of burning straw and subsequently, pitch and tar.

Yet, the tower may itself be symbolic of a burning arrow, named in 15th-century Italian tarot decks as 'la Sagitta'. Alternative readings hover between assigning the 'Broken Tower' to the devil or to God with allusions to Babel as destroyed or confused deific and diabolic voicings heard in human tones. That birds resurrect the dead is keenly evident in the Parsi Towers of Silence constructed in desert gardens, whose flat and extensive rooftops house corpses carefully laid concentrically as carrion for birds of prey to devour. Perhaps embodying silent calls to prayer, ignited minarets are called to mind, with the plaintive Islamic cry sounding across wind-hot city streets. Whether the point of the tower can be perceived as the arrow-tip or ritual decomposition platform, smoking tree top or lightning conductor; the illuminated lantern of beseeching prayer seems always a glowing spiritual sign. Ignited as a massive smoke signal, the lighthouse tower appears to be itself a memory column, a plinth from which a statue has fallen from its forgotten pyre.

And so, aided by a 'flash' of water and the 'flash' of seabirds, our poet-fool feels momentarily revived. Sitting up, he speaks to himself in marine cant and the cant of thieves and beggars: vagabond language, vague to those who do not know it.

In this divisive context, the fool's own reflexions, beggared from the voice of the sea (arguably, the Siren strain – or perhaps the whining wind), seem relevant only to himself and can be placed only within himself. He defines his own objectified and metonymic foolishness as: a madman or insane person, an idiot, rogue, or jester, a blacksmith's bellows, a leather bag; swollen, blown – a windbag, an empty-headed person, inflated with wind – at which point the foolkiller picks up; a vicious northerly gale sent to slaughter the foolhardy. The poet as an actual place of high winds, mouthing against the loud air is rendered voiceless, his wits windblown. He is inflated with his own folly, incited by lonely self-definition, filled with saltwater (tears: water of the heart) and rainwater (saliva: water of the mind) but his activation of near self-destruction by invoking the foolkilling wind by its own definition of his interior state has a wisdom. Yet, he is not revived enough to solicit inspiration.

Mirrors kindled great interest in relation to the early symbolism and function of the classical flashing pharos of antiquity. Book XIX of the *Iliad* describes how 'from Achilles' shield, bright and beautifully engraved, light streamed to heaven.' Later, mirrors were to become fundamental to lighthouse illumination, along with lenses. Demonstrably powerful, they were ill-used in warfare to ignite ships as described by a Roman historian in 212 BC: (my paraphrasing) when Syracuse was sieged, an enemy fleet of boats was successfully destroyed by Archimedes who used mirrors placed at the same distance as one arrow's flight. Using these, he directed and concentrated solar rays and the ships' timbers ignited and burst into flame.

These 'burning glasses' or mirrors are markedly resonant in relation to the avian weaponry described in the Liber Ignium. Clearly, mirrors had an important role to play in both incendiary warfare and the dissemination of light. Now, we return to our metaphoric vignette to witness a fool, hoodwinked by his own aspirations to find inspiration. In his mirror he examines a salt-encrusted, blistered expression and finds it interesting. He has become a self-portrait in thirst, stiff with salt, and slowly blinks in the glass. On his half-submerged raft he tilts his mirror and the fiery lighthouse comes into sight. He shuffles, repositions himself and then, blinking, pulls saline crystals from his lashes. Intermittently, the lighthouse blinks back as the sun darkens to blood and sinks below the waterline. The fool winks and the lighthouse winks, with nothing but the rocks between them.

*

Now, it has fallen dark in this spherical room, my candle has guttered and I shiver, but fail to stand up. Something lies dazed within my thought. Varg yawns with a faint scream and snapped teeth. Then, quite suddenly, a feeling of premonition seizes me, but from that summer's recent past. How Kristján had written into his work the burning boat, the capsized skiff with its foolish papers scattered on the surf. How he had known, of course, that keen, bright morning when the damp air lifted into a promise of fearsome heat, that I had been regarding him from a distance, hiding in the shoreline brush...

VI

FIVE SUBSEQUENT EVENTS MARKED that short summer; I will tell you of the first three. The Samh sea of Bàs is a sea of blown glass. Before storms shatter its burnished expanse, strewing the beaches with kelp and driftwood, something hangs in the air like a silence, a stillness, but is, in reality, a palpable awareness. The hazy azure of these benevolent skies holds nothing but the calm of death. The purity of this hot weather is a shockingly true one and the dead calm of the sea is called the calm of birds. That summer, not a hair had moved in the windless air. With the glassy sea gently shucking sea life on the white-sanded shore, Kristján would go down barefoot with a basket, Varg lunging through the surf, to gather up kelp and driftage. He would have liked a moonlit trudge, he said, but as the sun was a permanent fixture during those endless nights, Kristján gathered his materials in perennial daylight.

Yet, though the following days were faultless: they were too regular, too smooth, a kind of smothering, I thought. It had never been as still as this. But, there was nothing I could do. Kristján had retreated too far into himself for me to follow... it was impossible to pursue him through the myriad determinations of his solo spirit. I left him to his own devices, though sometimes smoke emerged from the upper storey windows of the lighthouse and at night strange sounds could be heard: half-calling, half-crying, and the emanations turned foul – a stench in the clear air. He was smoking himself out, I felt...

> Did you ever hear of a snow that burned? All in blazing white, the men on their horses. Blizzarding the eyes, the nose and tongue razed in ice. When they found them, those shapes were a standing army, frozen open-mouthed as the land glittered beneath their feet. That kind of army is worth dying for. How can there be a hot sea in these parts? Imagine the kind of demonry I felt – this climate – this ice – and the blubber ships sailing in boiling hot water? It had a most peculiar effect on me. In the Hebrides, we have visions of fire and ice and above us, here, the aurora sweats

in brilliant coloured shafts – but boiling water? Can the sea be possessed by its own ghost? Thirst... and soon it became known to us, that the island was not earth at all, but salt. Shot through pink in the afternoons with the setting sun. Salt that left a scrim of crystals on the hot water, as if the Hebridean world had dissolved in tears.

The North Atlantic Drift holds warm currents in its keeping and all along the Western Isles palm trees raise their dusty leaves to the sun. Occasionally, Kristján fell asleep beneath one, looking like a Gaelic shepherd. When he was out wandering or tending the two donkeys, I had to warn him not to keep a pipe near the grass bales. He lay in the straw like an old effigy, taken down from a cart, as the creatures grazed around his frayed shirt sleeves, and awoke with glyphic mysteries of corn pressed into his face. He went about in a light shirt and some old trousers, leaving his overcoat for the small hours. Though it was not so cold during those midsummer nights, the light was almost an enemy – you needed a shield against its defiant brightness.

And so, we were lulled like a lullaby-prayer into equanimity, but Kristján found something deeper within that ocean, dredged it up within himself. It was only later, a necessary intruder on the diary of his thoughts, I read about his nightmare. The dream was vivid and plain. They say that a nightmare works on the nervous system in just the same way as any waking reality: the fear is still there. He had been arranging mirrors, working with illusions of line and angle: smearing the coastline map into a calculated distortion which he then realigned with a cylindrical, mirrored tube. Like many illusionists, his point of no return had become obsessive:

> ...now the experiments sink in deeply. I had a dream of such brutal clarity, that it felt real to me for several hours after getting up. In it, an almost anamorphic distortion of my left hand appeared, severely mutilated. The blood ran in cyphers down my inner arm and became a readable map of Bàs, ancient sites marked in sanguine lettering. Then, the blood became a metamorphosing sea and my hand floated away on it, urgently making unreadable gestures and signs to me. Of course, the dream was harmless.

However, the next day he had returned to the lighthouse blood-bewildered and, as I bandaged up a severe gash to his left-hand palm, told me in broken sentences about vast piles of corpses, sea birds and large fish and seals, mangled and twisted up together, rotting on the compacted sand. He'd been out gathering kelp and must have slipped on the rocks, suddenly child-like. Of course, on my going down there was nothing to see – only some smeared blood. I trudged back slowly, considering all this. We have the 'teorr' and it's the sea's own refuse: what the tide leaves on the shoreline – its saline currency. But, the beach stood empty... glassy and peace-wild. I returned to the light-house to keep Kristján company. After that, he deteriorated rapidly, sitting up alone, late into the night, and my strongest impression was one of a tide turned within himself...

*

And the scalding sea was a burden to him then, had become a wide and mercurial shifting mirror whose *sift, sift* tormented him on those long, heat-tormented nights. He would stand, his long arms folded like woollen wings, tobacco-stained and torn, stand on the lantern room balcony and look out across its silver expanse that was pale and shining under the exhausted sky as a vast reflection of his inner domain. Kristján seemed the true living lookout or mortal figurehead to me then, standing in the slow-flashing 'taighe-solais' tower. Had he landed on the island, all those centuries ago, when they once lit the torches, smudging the air with a malodorous welcome, then he might have been greeted as a sage or seer, a visionary or a god. But now, though he'd arrived on the 'avoiding day of the year', he'd bruised in on a half-burnt pyre...could not even manage a successful offering of himself.

Yes: the Day of Avoidance lands on the third of May each year and in the Hebrides is the traditional day marking the expulsion of the fallen angels from heaven. Anyone caught doing wrong would be exempt from mercy. Unforgiven. But, fallen angel or not,

Kristján had not hurt anyone in his unkempt arrival – unless it was counted as hurtful to himself. He kept a picture of that silver sea on him in the form of a polished steel mirror. Bought from a pawn shop, it delighted him still, with a scratched surface that glimmered in candlelight. Delighted him because obdurate. He thought he could carry our small Hebridean island world in it.

I suspect there are stories of wind-calling by magic mirror, like the annals of knots, or blown glass bottles of trapped storms, but if there are, I have never found them. There are crying winds and whistling winds, weeping winds and bellowing winds. Some can be caught with a small loop of grass, others blown into the ear of a human asleep at dawn. Those first winds rippled the face of our sea and I wonder now, whether they also rippled across the face of his mirror. He thought of it as a portal to another place, of his image as trapped. That perhaps he could carry this trapped image and tip it into the breeze. That perhaps his mirror had summoned the wind of voices itself:

> My mirror is a rudimentary slice of flattened steel, polished up for the trenches. Nothing excites it more than a candle … making the surface scratches glimmer. But, I think of it as a portal now… as if I could keep this strange image held in it and carry the image to another place… perhaps over to the cliffs and flick it from the mirror surface into the sea, or throw the whole thing down onto the rocks, like a smashed coffin lid. Yes, I am still afraid of it. What can emerge? Can you keep the wind in a mirror and not have it disturb your reflexion? There is a gale blowing across my inner face tonight, but the steel is calm. Its tempered surface flowers the same old stains, is haunted by the same old calligraphy field of scratch marks. I know them well. Somewhere in between I make plots through the white snow with my blade and the two dark holes in the snow that peer back still remain my eyes and the sudden blood prickle in the foamy furrow is only my blood and the sound of concentration in the metal is still only my concentration.

He had kept a storm book of tides, a star atlas of his own compositions, written in what he named 'celestial metre', and the now lost loggbok of his own deterioration – and that is a brave thing, it seems. How he must have gone from being his own cylinder of sensation, drawing chaos into personal configuration and then found the cylinder reflection was fetid and that he was the seed of chaos that lay within a wind-driven system. I'd had no inkling of this and now, as I plough through endless scraps of paper, rely on my own intuition – a kind of lighting up of circumstance – to decide which to focus on. Here and there, the light shines hard upon the obscurities of Kristján's forsaken sense, as in this, with the sudden shadow of revelation: a paradox of sign and reflection deemed supernatural in its dividends, and I feel compassion for him – demonised by his own intellect; an intellect gone rotten:

> I was at it, attempting to shave the overgrown mess on my face that was becoming a full beard, and doing this one-handedly, as is my habit. In my left hand I grasped the small rectangular shaving mirror and in my right, the blade. On an old wooden shelf, my candle stub flickered for a moment and then the atmosphere in the polished steel seemed to thicken suddenly – just like the water foaming when I dabbled my razor in it – and I paused, fascinated. Then, the image of my face thickened and distorted too, and instantaneously I saw myself reflected as something fundamentally malign, and in that moment, blood burring in my ears, I knew myself to be diabolic. Shocked, I dropped the mirror into the basin as if scalded. It took me a few moments to recompose myself and then, trembling, I slowly retrieved the mirror and cautiously peered into its dripping surface. There was nothing. I was myself again.

VII

AND SO, IT WAS on a June-infested night that Kristján saw himself reflected as a demon. Stood shaving when the thing appeared. In his dreams, he stalked the waves, he wrote: a fiend bent double with the weight of a sand-leaking figurehead lashed to his back. Those nights, as the stinking sea rose and fell, it enflamed my unease...

> Demon-haunted fissures lie low in the water. The earliest emotion of worship is thirst. Did I walk with Christ on my arm in that deserted reflexion? Did I feed on the carcase of Christ in the desert, the slow-faced lion, panting like a deer? He lopes in my heart, even as he drinks in the dew of my heart. Over there, the weather is dying. The desert sea turns and sighs to itself. Who on my arm but the thorn. Who on my arm but the knitted garment. Who on my arm but the flash of myself. Quieter mythology suffers internal bleeding.

He was benefitted by flame, those tangential dawns when the light whispered down to just the slightest screed of pale dark. Pale dark of dawn, pale light of dusk. His mirror rose to meet him...

'The Highlanders say you have either a light: *sorchar*, or dark: *dorchar*, companion – an angel or demon at your side,' Kristján had mused one night, after a day spent stripping timber for the oncoming winter's supply of kindling.

'Well, I say I have both, and not just a co-walker or reflex-man, but reflex women, men, ghosts and dogs, lions, wolves and an ass walking around in my sights at all times. Not one reflexion, but a system of reflexions; not a double, but a multitude – all at odds with themselves. A Dis personality haunting the underworld of poesis.' He paused, sucking for a moment on his pipe stem... the light stained his eyes.

'But one reflection contains all,' I replied, unpicking my weaving.

'One reflexion implies all,' said Kristján, with great seriousness. He got up and the fire uplit his features as sudden holes of shadow. 'All my spirits walk abroad,' he said, 'there's too much fire and salt in us,' before moving off into the pale and saturant sea mist.

*

Here is a poem I had copied down from *The Demon Tracts*, as he titled them (minus his extensive revisions), taken from this larger body of work dated July 12th, 1961. All these poems were marked DT: DORCHAR TAI-BHSE so they should actually be called *The Dark Vision*, but he hadn't specified that and so this sequence, *The Demon Tracts*, is how it remains named. I am still unsure if Kristján means me to recover everything before burning, or burn it on sight.

Ash pulls up through the lighthouse room as I rake the coals, pulls up like rising snow, only to fall and settle in uncountable flakes of individual meaning. I sit with a second dram in front of the heat lamp. Firelight flickers across the gloom as I light a cigarette and begin reading:

AN AERIAL VIEW OF HELL

You, ferret-faced angel, think
in disturbances.
Catatonic culture of literatures;
the wild lynx of the catacombs
stands dead.

I keep my demon close:
pacifier of listlessness is death,
a corn-strewn attitude, distilled in the fields of Dis,
of curled, astonished undergrowth...

How many shuddering mirrors have rippled with recognition? Subjected to our myriad images, they wait patiently and absorb them. They are the gods of reflection, waiting to minister precision. Here on Bàs, the lighthouse beam illuminates a rough, marine mirror. See... our own crude reflections: a merchant vessel picks

242

up the light and is squandered on the rocks. A galleon clips the reef, going down. For three days blood licks at the old port. Bodies float in on the tide and bump the stone jetty, brokenly. On Bàs' crystal sands, armour breastplates lie beached like whales. One body, swimming hard, drags itself up and, taking a knife, kills a man on the harbour wall: flicking his blood across the wide night sky. Then, the banked-up death boats slowly turn on the tide and make their way back out to sea, and the lighthouse blaze is doused. Seen in that sea, the unceasing loneliness. Yes, I knew what it was to be demonised…

>…drawn to the high places,
>drawn to the high, dry places,
>they do die when I breathe out
>and in sickness revive…

His tarnished steel mirror had seen sights worse than Kristján's face: bitter men wrecked in mud: the weight of maternal tears. It was stamped with a hallmark of grace and lit with the long flame of solitude. But, his demon had risen and I knew he had to meet this reflection, to find will in it. I could only offer illumination, shed light on terror, for a cracked will, a broken intellect, is of no use to a poet. Nonetheless, as doubt lurked – waiting for him, he found a new kind of will, a new wilfulness. Kristján's newfound want was a will to forget.

VIII

THEN THE STORM CAME and, as with all storms, everything that happened before its arrival became an act of premonition. Many things colluded, in a perspiration of dust. What was glass, was broken, as the sea cut and dashed itself in revived liquid force. And the lighthouse lantern went out as the wind grew worsted, twisting like a sinew, pulling us into a state of increasing nervous tension. On the second day, a rogue gust brought a rotten birch branch down, injuring Asal, the smaller donkey. When it died a few hours later, Kristján fell into a deep melancholy. He buried the beast that subdued and cloudy afternoon, the air smudged with dark blue smoke from a small bonfire. In its flames, the large branch of the pine tree roasted, spitting and fragrant. And, with its fractured skull, the carcass of Asal was pulled into its freshly dug pit. Kristján stood sweating and smoking at its edge for a while and then harshly began to shovel the earth back in.

In the days following, he had tamped down the outhouses and replaced missing slats on shutters, sheds, always alone. On one morning he'd returned with a split thumbnail and the joint rose blueish and swollen from the hammer blow. I wrapped a slimy happock of kelp around it, had Kristján clamp this bandage to his fist. He looked up at me with a face raw-boned from the blustering wind, and I was sorry not to help him, not to have done more than this.

Reluctantly, he'd allowed me to return to the lighthouse and when I got up that night, there was something of this regret in my outer awareness: how threadbare he'd become. Just as the light strained to leak through the boarded windows, the beacon blasted – its binary code on the sphere gone: there was no flashing brightness. The air was a mild and greasy grey as if the light were merely turned down, like a radio turned down, and the sea stank. The atmosphere was foetid and dream-like and I realised then what had woken me up: the outer door was open and banged erratically in the wind, slamming in the half-light. I rose from my makeshift bed by the kitchen burner, went out to the stairwell and found it a mass of whirling papers. I called up the metal stairs to Kristján. Nothing. Varg padded out and sat on the top step for a long moment before throwing back his head in a long howl.

The doors to the upper floors stood open and sheets scuffled in the wind in the second floor room with its messy bunk and open window. I moved across, half dazed, and pulling the window shut, firmly secured it. Papers were strewn across the table and his pipe lay on its side. A half-empty tin coffee mug was cold now, though I knew he only drank coffee at night. This was what drew me on. Picking up sheaths of typescript as I mounted each step, I found the fourth-storey storehouse completely abandoned. The wind was the only living thing in the place apart from the hard and narrow beating of my nervous heart. Another window fastened, I turned and stood, surveying the storeroom with is dark shapes of rope and firewood, tools and sacking.

For a moment I felt he might be there, standing like an effigy in the gloom, watching. But, he wasn't. And I turned and clattered downstairs, slamming the heavy, outer door shut and ran up the path away from the lighthouse, all the time shouting 'Kristján', as the wind whipped his name out of my mouth.

*

The following days passed in a storm-driven frenzy of my searching and calling, unlocking and hunting. In the driving rain, I turned over all the places I could think of: the musty doors of the boathouse were reopened, thinking he might have somehow found the key and got to a skiff. But, the boats were there, dormant and untouched and I pulled the doors shut. I searched the remaining inner places first: the whaling station outhouses, full of rusted chains and hooks… the whaling station itself, slat-boarded and thick with webs… up to the old monastery with its dark green bell and I took the rope we had strung it with weeks ago, and pulled down hard on its greasy serpent tail and the whole air rippled with sound long after the bell fell dead; those tones and overtones and undertones ringing in my ears and my hands chafed from the splintered rope. No reply came. No sudden call of recognition. Night fell, and exhausted, I took to my improvised bunk.

The following morning, the rain was still driving down hard as I searched the rocks and boulders, the fallen walls of the clearance crofthouses and found a wren's nest in the wall of an old chimney stack.

'Kristján,' I called, but the wind wiped the word away; 'Kristján,' I called again, tears stung in the lettering.

I fell and hurt my knee and then could really cry, as the blood became a sullen welt and I perched on a soaked lintel of the abandoned house as Varg licked at the wound.

I hunted among the mariner tombs in the monastery garden, and back up to the lighthouse again, in case he had returned, and finally, tramped over to the donkey field. I had forgotten Asan and it was feeding time and something in the gentleness of the brute made my eyes well up again, as I forked open a grass bale and watched him eat beneath bats that rose and fell in the stable's dank, evening air. Kristján was not asleep in the stable. I stumbled back to the lighthouse and slept fitfully as, now renewed, the storm raged on.

When I awoke, it was with calm in my heart. In a high wind you sleep in dead air with the tensions of lost stars, lost planets, lost space. My mouth tasted of rusty metal. I drank down his cold coffee and straightened the blanket on the lighthouse bunk as if this would restore order, herald his return. I had been visited by a dream and felt sure now where to find him. Walking down the cliff path to the island's claw I knew either he would be in the cave, or that he was lost: drowned.

The waterfall roared and its glassy sheen glistened in the midsummer light. The rocks toward the entrance were slippery, but I angled each foot carefully on the descent and finally crept behind the roaring water which hung at the cave entrance like a cloth. When I turned and looked back, I saw the faint colour of the outer world caught in the continuous movement of the water like fire. I paused for a moment and watched the drowning colours roar. Then I called.

'Kristján!' His name vanished instantly. I moved forward, deeper into the rock face, fumbling for a match, and lit the candle stub I'd brought.

'Kristján,' I called again. Somehow I felt sure he wasn't there, that he was dead now – had been swept out on a bad current, or slipped on a bad edge and plummeted into another bad life. But, there was a rumour in these parts that if you called a dead man three times by his first name, you called him back to life. The muffled sound of the pounding water lessened as I advanced into the cavern.

'Kristján!' I cried, 'are you there?' His name bounded around the cave walls into silence beyond. My eyes strained to hear, my ears to see. There was a small, contorted sound. I waited. The muffled noise repeated and I crawled forward with the candle in my mouth, pushing myself through a narrow corridor of rock and into a small, airless chamber. An unclear form lay toward the back wall in the dim, greenish light. It was Kristján.

He had bundled himself up in his old overcoat and was lying absolutely still in the innermost recesses of the rock. He looked so rigid and lifeless that, for a moment, I thought he was dead but, crawling toward him, I gripped his wrist and found a faint pulse. I rubbed his frozen hands and held his head in my lap. Though I had a hip flask on me, my foot kicked against an empty bottle of Maclean's and I paused, unsure of myself. Then I unscrewed the chained cup on my flask and poured a measure out. The whisky helped, though only a little got through his clenched teeth, but he came round. When he recovered he was in a highly anxious state and I only got him to come out from the cave after much gentle coaxing. We stumbled along and I recall that being the hardest part of it: my mixed feelings of relief and fury, his clear lack of comprehension... still drunk. All the way along the high cliff path, as we shuffled slowly toward the lighthouse – me struggling to hold him up, and he rambling about the sullen moon and demons – one word rose in the back of his throat: 'Monmhur,' he kept repeating, which, in the old tongue, is Gaelic for murmur. 'Monmhur,' he rasped, feverish and broken.

*

And so it began, his nocturnal rambling. From the new moon of July 12th to the last, brutal lunar eclipse of August 26th, I observed Kristján return at dawn four times and bolt himself into the lighthouse. He came back drained and smeared in blood, tampered with the padlocked door and then slipped in as if unseen. Those interminable days... the swollen sea rank under a bitter June moon, the gelid moon of August. Often in those last weeks, I had found him asleep in the ashes of a fire, his coat smeared light and his face smeared dark, and when he woke he would speak in murmurs. Occasionally he would look at me as if recognising his own features and then, when I bent over to hear him, acknowledged only one phrase repeated: *Sluagh nam Marbh*. Confronting him over his drinking habits did nothing, and slowly I realised he was drier than I'd thought and so I concocted the old charms: had a loop of grass to catch the eddy wind, attached flax to the nape of Kristján's neck when he slept and wiped down the cuts in his stubble as he lay there, insensible. I knew he was possessed by a force which needed to fathom his presence, a force of will, intelligence come from deep within himself. Once, when he slept, I had stolen his loggbok and leafed through the opening entries to find:

> Divination by the taghairm was once a noted superstition among the Gael and in the northern parts of the Lowlands of Scotland. When any important question concerning futurity arose and of which a solution was, by all means, desirable, some shrewder person than his neighbours was pitched upon to perform the part of a prophet. This person was wrapped in the warm smoking hide of a newly-slain ox and laid at full length in the wildest recess of

some lonely waterfall. The question was then put to him and the oracle was left in solitude to consider it. Here he lay for some hours with his cloak of knowledge around him and over his head, no doubt, to see the better into futurity; deafened by the incessant roaring of the torrent; every sense assailed; his body steaming; his fancy in a ferment; and whatever notion had found its way into his mind from so many sources of prophecy, it was firmly believed to have been communicated by invisible beings who were supposed to haunt such solitudes.'

I have been put through the diabolic and visionary Gaelic rite of the taghairm, even though my hand came away when Luce grasped it, I was able to seal it with wax at the wrist when we reached the lighthouse. But, the bright-lipped droning, the murmuring still goes on. THIS IS THE SLUAGH. The taghairm is also known as an echo and this is how it seems to me now: an echo with ten soundings.

*

Then the late summer was spent in thunder, tipped in lightning, and I could not find sense in his words, though flashes spiritedly lit up the sky. I recall thinking that we would die from that endless summer light, at times when I held Kristján down as the screaming air went on. Occasionally, when he became lucid, I had been able to ask him, probe his inner workings, and he nodded and passed a note toward me, across the rough-scored surface of our table; 'this,' he said:

> Monmhur came to me in the steel mirror that night, after I had seen myself stripped. I was stripped to the bone. He is Monmhur; the speaking image. He is my reflex and I shall gag again. Ten times, he says, they will come and they will take me. He says he knows. I have already prepared ten sites across the island (did I not know?) He can only speak in a mirror and will come after each time. So, they will take me at new moon and full moon and breathe into me the knowledge of my demonhood and he says this will come in pictures I will see before I am abandoned. I will

249

then be returned to the lighthouse. There I must daub old hair I have collected from my old comb with blood from my damaged mouth and set it alight on the surface of my old shaving mirror. After the hair has flared, Monmhur will appear and murmur the words of a counter-charm which will appear on the mirror surface for me to write down and retain. The words vanish, leaving only Monmhur's face, and the mirror softens. I can now make a cylinder of it, placing it upright on a clean sheet of paper. Distorted language is reflected from Monmhur's miniature cylinder portrait in the mirror onto the paper surface. The chaotic words seem scorched or burnt into the paper. When this is done, Monmhur's reflexion vanishes and the mirror unfurls, returning to its normal, flat shape again. I must copy out the words, keeping one sheet of paper and fold up the scorched original with one of my possessions. On the same evening, under the same lunar conditions, I must return to the site where the Sluagh first conveyed me and stash the paper, along with the personal object. Monmhur maintains throughout this process, occurring ten times across five months, that if she [Luce Moncrieff] can recover and destroy these fragments once I am finally taken up by the Sluagh, then all will be well.

That he'd mentioned me by name, meant a great deal to me then, but naturally I did not take his instructions at face value.

'Kristján,' I had implored him, 'how can I help you? Tell me.'

He'd slumped in his chair and sat motionless as the heavy room grew heavier around us. Then, with the thick sound of a thumb pressed on wood, he pushed a calling card toward me.

'Hafoc,' he said. 'The will asks illumination to confront doubt.'

I said nothing, not understanding the implications of his request.

'Do you not believe me?' asked Kristján, in a voice filled with the wind. 'In any case, I know the voices are not merely my own invention.'

'And how is that?' I asked him.

Kristján leaned forward in the half-light. 'Because they speak a language older than I can hear,' he said.

Then the wind got up and nullified our dreams and it was as

if I had spoken to a drowning man who, for a single moment, had surfaced in the waves but was now driven down by the currents again… and so I left summer on Eilean a' Bhàis, left it clasping a poet drowning in a high wind, and unwillingly went to Edinburgh to find Jeanie Hafoc, his psychoanalyst.

Would I have gone, had I known the outcome? Such regrets float like dross on the surf before lying beached, ready for combing. I am still unsure which to fling back into the ocean. I turn, and the gentle window pane, scored by the sea, releases a beam of dusty light. I am that sea, I think to myself, in which Kristján has drowned and endlessly turns in my own deep currents and maritime winds. An image of a body turning in the surf. As always now, he occupies my very deepest thought.

IX

JAG ÄR KRISTJÁN Norge, see five drunken demons course round my head. I am thinking of creating a tarot theatre, a paper theatre. The characters will all be figures from the tarocchi: the knight, the high priestess, the emperor... will the fool be the orator? The impresario? Or perhaps the zero hour. At the zero hour there is nothing. I am in the forest of contempt. A meat spirit at large. Here are Dante's definitions: Inferno includes the devil – of course – death, the hanged man, la papesse, the lightning struck tower (or wonder of revelation) and the magician, or cobbler. Am I the fool or the cobbler? The hobo or magician? Now finally they meet... Hafoc and Luce... how it was arranged so simply. I laugh. Here they are, witness to each other. I have seen them. They will dream together in the large O of the gaping night. And of course they will read this for themselves; foolish ones, before a long walk on the white, compact beach. I see them as two hens, leaving their diminishing footprints as the surf sifts in and out again, two hens confabulating. Sometimes their anxious faces peer me out. I dislike them. Sometimes the whisky returns to claim me and I am haunted by spirits and must vanquish myself. Then, I find, usually I find, I have been put to bed – but my bed, I know, lies at the top of the broken tower where language itself breaks over my head like the repeated waves crashing and crushing below. The sea is an incessant cruelty.

I dislike the strike, the line-sperm of 'I'. Let it find the egg, the O. I would prefer to be O. Not I am Kristján Norge but, O am Kristján Norge – see, like a cry: 'O' to be myself, O am! The open mouth. Taboo in painting. They'll give you a phallus, a great set of breasts, but the open mouth is too terrible a cavity. Late in the evening, the cavern opens: the great orifice. The only public orifice. And look what comes out. That rooted tongue resting in its own waters, that rotted whale. All around it sounds of the O, when it opens, emerge. O is a constant stream. You cannot fill the O with fire. You can fill it with leaves, or dust, or concrete. You cannot fill the O with flame. Cannot smoke out the whale.

Everything I touch towards, gets close and fails. A series

of stellar abortions. The publishers, the manuscripts. I am out here now. This is south, for me – a southern island. And the turquoise shocks the backs of the eyes as it blooms in saline delta bands at the shoreline, and the Scottish palms evoke camels, donkeys. They think you can't get burnt by the sun down here. They are wrong. Everything but the O – remember, the O does not hold flame.

Now the anamorphic portrait: the deer come and graze across it. I am speaking of my own movements, grazed in sand. If I stand in my footprints as they are smeared by the waves, I wonder if I am the cylinder by which they make sense. My hair is full of light and my lungs are full of sweat and those demonic angels circling my brow tell me that I am cursed: the double O:O: the fool. It seems I must stand outside myself and watch the women smear my psyche. Christ's blood was only his psyche, punctured by thorns. His tears were his personality. I think, when I bleed – grazed by a sea thistle, some driftwood, that I am merely bleeding my presence. Surely presence is blood? When it is drained, our presence vanishes. Meat spirit. This is my theory. The hobo is also the double 'o:o' – has too much of the open mouth, the split egg, the genesis-equipment boiled up in his little vellum haversack, ready to be tinted by active powders. The whole beach is the fool's duality: the double O:O, one O for the land and the other for water. Earth and water. Somewhere, god is swimming in the saltwater of Christ's psyche. Like me, a good Kristján, debunked on the beach. I walk and talk with myself, because I am my own devil – there is no need for another one to come.

I have witnessed my third tract as a an anamorphic map of Dante's ravaged wood. I am the fool, the troubadour, the vagrant, the wanderer. My perceptions clarify the warped surroundings. So, the prose of the outer landscape is smeared and strange. The clarity of the IA operates in each case, like a mirror. One mirror is smeared with theatrical grease, the other is complicit, but cleansed. I am reminded of the suffumigated mirror for removing sorrow, suspended from a red staff above running water in a silk for seven days. Is the fool's mirror red with the paint of pageantry? Does it flare red with embarrassment in the place of the fool's own careless abandon and critical lack of self regard? It is a blushing moon. Hot with humiliation. Certainly, this fool has abandoned the feast to go wandering off into the deep woods of contemplation on his own. And here the lion is not pride, but contemplative strength. The fortitude of a lion led by a tether of flowers. The Arabic name 'waard': flowers and the black-streaked mane of the lion. Can the fool ever ride the lion? Can the fool mount the lion's shadow? So, the lion is present and now I must confront the abandoned lunar mansion. X. Al Jab'Hah, the lion's forehead. The derelict mansion is the lifeless lion is the skull. As I am needing to construct this as a radical act of forgetting, everything about this mansion must be concerned with dismantling memory. Is it a shrine, a tower, a tomb? A set of mnemonic offerings to induce utter amnesia. Mnemonics: amnesics: amnestia... a nest of worried birds, the forgetfulness of wrong: a deliberate forgetfulness.

Each stage could be a procession. I could now describe in some detail this mansion, this manzil or lunar station. With Bruno's craft, I can lift and lay the Neolithic objects in the tomb... objects of abandoned selves... imagines I have worn and performed... and let the shadows flicker there. I have the increasing feeling that everything is such a smoke-licked mirror, if only we recognise it as such. All we have is our own experience, that is what shapes the nature of our reflexion.

II

THE DEMON TRACTS

* * * * * * * * * *

Edinburgh
January 26th, 1962

Miss Moncrieff,

I suspect my reply did not reach you and so hope my arrival next week will not be unexpected. I will certainly join you: Norge was one of my more interesting cases, though I doubt he would have said so.

Yours,
Dr Hafoc

* * * * * * * * * *

X

WANDER WITH ME THROUGH this dead monument of an island whose snow-flecked ruins are not haunted by light, but by air. Whose silence against the strong arm of the sea's roaring tides, is a silence inhaled as breath. Is my return a final one – a reprisal in ash, an echo stalled in hope? Only I, am again living on this archipelago of the dead. Only I, perspire salt and myrrh at night. All else is illusion, the wind says…

This winter, Eilean a' Bàis lies abandoned. Now, the year has turned and the opening month is what the Highlanders call 'Am Faoilleach': month of the wolf. The cold has a certain bitterness to it, now that Kristján has vanished… most likely drowned… and Bàs seems doomed to return, as always, to a season of subdued regret. Though the constancy of Kristján is relinquished, I cannot help but wonder if the malign wind of voices has disappeared with him.

'I read once,' Kristján had murmured one evening, nursing a blackened pipe bowl in his palm as I half-listened, 'how on a small islet there had been an early language experiment. Two young children were left alone on the island to see if the original language of God would manifest in their tongues.'

The fire had crackled over us, awash with sentience, as I imagined the children playing among the charred ruins, how they laughed in signs and cried, when they tumbled among the stones and scraped their limbs, cried in tears that were powdered like dust, as if their small eyes were stones ground down by sorrow… Kristján continued, lighting his pipe.

'Now I think of us, here on Bàs, like those lost children, abandoned by God, abandoned by time… but not abandoned by the language of the wind.

'Not abandoned,' I had half-echoed him, focussed on my darning.

These are the things that dissolve when I hunt them: how what had seemed like happenstance musing was Kristján placing careful leads, small clues to his afterlife. I had not been listening but, now and then again, if I quiet myself, I can hear him talking and these observations of his rise up like dross on the surf, lie on the shore of my awareness beached and waiting. Sometimes the riddles devour themselves, like this one... but later, there is a replete chink of Anglo-Saxon metal, of Norwegian rune-stone, and the answer is sounded: complete. As with now that I come to consider his talk that evening, a dream I'd forgotten arises in counterpoint, its theatre an ache.

*

...I met Hafoc deep in my dreams last night, her wild hair perturbed like a bird's nest; filthy and matted with twigs. In my dream I had followed Kristján to the Underground City...he took the slope, not the steps, but then sharply turned to the left, crossed the road and mounted a cascading series of stairs that steeply ascended into overgrowth, rising and falling. I saw him emerge at the top in silhouette, like a statue, and pause to get his breath. Then he trudged uphill and I followed, warily, until he reached the castle gates and stood again, surveying the scene. I hid myself in a doorway and with one eye on Kristján, did the same. Beneath the elevated castle, blackened steps of the closes ran off in sooty rivulets from the main drag of the Royal Mile. The cold, hard-dreamt air – half-salt, half-smoke – betrayed a tiny sea to the east of the city, like a sea in a telescope, or another dream, or a magnifying glass. I suppose I should have woken up then. I didn't, somehow caught in the transgression of dreaming. Then, in a kind of daze, I saw Kristján move toward me like a figure in a mirage. The whole nightmare seemed to halt. Kristján vanished and I was in Hafoc's rooms in the underground vaults.

'So,' she mouthed, 'you've come.'

I nodded mutely with the dumbness of nightmare as she gestured toward a split leather chair for me to sit down on. She offered me a cigarette and I took it, shivering slightly. Both the chair and cigarette were difficult, somehow: one impossible not to keep sliding from and the other a matted piece of wood that refused to ignite and left an acrid taste in my mouth.

Then the dream rippled and focussed as Jeanie turned to look at me, her subtle gestures wreathed in smoke. I felt a deeper, more fixed, cold. She held me captivated in her gaze like quarry. She had a pair of cool, golden eyes – almost blonde-coloured eyes – and in particular lights, such as this dreamt one, her pupils were contracted to a tiny speck almost like a distant hawk caught in amber. She stood up, smoothed her skirt, and switched off the strip-light with a click.

'Kristján,' she said, lighting a match that was already burnt, 'said you would.'

Dazedly, I watched her touch the flame of a candle to life and then torpidly fan the match to death. She sat down. For some reason the whole timbre of these informal gestures struck me as ancient and unlearned – simply known in the bone. As she leaned forward, the flickering candlelight uplit a fierce quality in her face, with its slight tracery of lines and delicate cheek bones and suddenly I saw her as an attendant bird: a bird of prey from the afterlife, and as I did so, the small stone-walled chamber of her office immediately became tomb-like, exaggerated by the gaping hole in the stone-work that opened onto the Underground City.

Hafoc monitored my face and leaned further forward. Then, without speaking, she took up the candle, stepped through the rough opening in the wall and disappeared. I stood up, listening for a moment to my rapid breath in the darkness. Then I moved through the opening, myself.

I could see the tawny glow of her candle quite far ahead and fumbling along the wall, found myself descending steps that were deep and uneven. Used to manoeuvring the lighthouse steps, these didn't perplex me much – I simply moved slowly, like a ghost in a film, or an impression of a sleepwalker. A strange sound rose from the depths of the stairwell, not quite a reverberation, not quite an echo. I thought it was laughter. As I rounded another part of the descent, the candlelight seemed much wider and brighter, vanishing into a small chamber. I followed its light which promptly snuffed out and stood for a moment, panting in the dark. Hafoc was nowhere to be seen. I remember calling out to her: a soundless cry: as if muted underwater, and a strong, bitter stench filled my nostrils. Then, as my eyes slowly adjusted to the warm darkness, I thought I could just discern hunched shapes floating in the gloom. I stepped back, unsure of myself, and with that my heel pressed into something both springy and soft... I picked it up... it was a rancid carcass... Nauseated, I dropped the stinking body, treading on more springy mass and realised mutilated chicks littered the floor, some still living, some dead, all trampled underfoot. As I grew more accustomed to the dimness, I perceived rough glittering in my peripheral vision, like stars set in a murky night: all the stronger for looking away. Now the glinting took form. The dark stone chamber was filled with hundreds of raptors perched on individual stands – not quite free, but able to rise a few metres on heavy chains. A sudden feeling of terror overwhelmed me and I began fumbling for the chamber entrance again only to find myself face to face with a hawk. It fixed me for a moment with piercing, languid eyes, and then opened its beak in a high-pitched cry. This was the laughter I thought I had heard. As I moved forward, the creature bated, outspreading monstrous wings that fell apart, decayed, to reveal a set of fanning bones. Then I ran. The return flight of stairs seemed to take hours to mount and I grew hot – almost feverish – with exertion. I stood for a moment, my head against the cold stone, and heard that crying laugh resound again. I paused, catching my breath. There was no sign of Hafoc. Gathering my thoughts, I felt to return to her squalid rooms would be a mistake. There must be some other way out of the labyrinth. I caught a glimpse of a light and took to my heels, clattering up the stone stairs, up and up until the stones ceased and the air changed, and I slipped and fell, for many centuries, it seemed.

*

These nights, I have placed a storm lamp by the guttered lighthouse lantern and gannets rage around this small lantern-room light, their pointed faces swarming out of the blackness like a bewildered flock of demons. Some will die from that artificial light, stunned against the gallery glass. Before it was extinguished, the lighthouse lantern beam drew masses of birds like moths that peered and buffeted the glass of the gallery dome. Climbing into the lantern, I would watch them run around the grating and draw an exhausted one in, a woodcock, living in fast-drawn breath. Those tiny lungs. If you stood on the balcony in the spring or autumn, birds flocked in the light, lit up like fast-flowing stars. Curlews circled in the dark air, higher than the rest, and it was mist that brought them in. Strange to think of the Bàs mist as related to Edinburgh's sodden haar.

Kristján murmured Cicero's line when I first took him up to the top of the light-tower: 'the air itself sees together with us.' He had told me about birds dipped in tar and ignited as arrows, and Odin's wild hunt of souls flying through the air...

'Much like the Sluagh,' he'd said. 'Not angels, not demons, but birds flying up to the tower of thought.'

But, when I opened it up last week, the lantern-room was full of dead skylarks and thrushes, the birds had broken a pane and swooped in. I gathered them up with the smashed glass and flung the sweepings over the balcony railing. Shards glittered in the air as the limp bodies plummeted into the sea like a horde of fallen angels, silently roaring through the falling snow. My thoughts turn to Kristján's notes, as I number another scrap of paper:

> The Fear Eun Lota is the 'Bird Wound Man' – a man showing different woundings by birds on various parts of his anatomy. It is an archaic ritual in which a person is subjected to injury by birds called conversing with the birds, during which vivid images are produced and which can create an intimate knowledge of angels. Scars and cuts sustained from such encounters are then 'read' as angelic text...

– suddenly I recall the strange marks on Kristján's arms –

> ...this ritual has been banned for many centuries as dan-

gerous, and if caught, a Fear Eun Lota was often burnt to death. The smoke and ash from the execution pyre were considered powerful, warped shapes, lifted by the wind – like phantoms. Those immolated may return again, but in angelic or demonic form. In the Highland Gaelic there is the tarbh boidhre. There was an old song, sung in a strange mix of early Scots, aristocratic Gaelic and fourth century Shetlandic. It was chanted whilst modulating the voice to a vessel, bottle or other receptacle as it was slowly filled with water or wine, altering the pitch. The whole ritual came from the 'Ancient Ionian Book of the Dead' and the stone in the Port Nam Marbh (Port of the Dead), may have been important.

> *Quem quaerent homines quaerentes vulnerat oscen*
> The omen-bird wounds men who seek it.

> Many kinds of such wounding exist: wounds to the spirit, wounds to the sex, wounds to the emotion in flesh. I only hope those left persist in it, as I have done – to the absolute limit.

Kristján has always treated birds as kindred. Worked with them in eye and spirit. Here on Bàs, sea eagles nest in the cliffs and a golden pair has been seen to the north of the island on those long summer nights, soaring and tracing the sky like dark kites rising from the afterlife...

> And the sea eagles will come, as if to a salt-lick, and they will nest in my hair and stand on my shoulders as if I were a dead statue with no eyes to peck out...

I think of Kristján's eagles, of the nuanced augury of the Edinburgh underworld with its subterranean lunations and magic mirrors of obsidian and bronze – yes, of Kristján the fool in it all... with birds on his shoulders, nailed to a thorn tree. Perhaps I am coming too much under his influence, standing in this room of dredged correspondences... And yet, I think too now, of Hafoc's dubious offices – the electric striplight flickering like a flame in a draught, the mouth of the subterranean city glowering behind a screen of glass. The back bars and seedy joints, the scarred stone on the tombs in kirkyards whose covenants were penned in blood. It is a sanguinary city whose phantoms are really drawn in bloody fog: the haar, with its tang of witch burning, more a whetted pyre smoke than a saline sea fog. Hafoc, as its sole denizen, had seemed to me fascinating, frightening.

Kristján is not the only one to have kept account of each day's reckoning – I have a diary and in it I wrote on 26th June, 1961: 'he is distracted and restless. He almost belongs with Hafoc, or lives there, in spirit.'

How right was I to regard his psychologist with a certain wariness? I continued: 'her acute professionalism, her assertion, somehow undermined me... I felt impaled.'

Kristján surprises me, though, when his similar feeling about the predatory, gold-haired Hafoc arises in his notes:

> ... she had the aspect and habits of a hawk and I can say with all certainty that she seemed to drop from the sky on nowhere and, as I was occupying nowhere, it seemed I was her focus, her intent, her prey. I found myself taken from the heights of the hollow thing in the lighthouse to the depths of this subterranean dankness. From high above the sea to far below the ground.

My dream of chained hawks replays as our argument: two children in the underground city quarrelling over the mind of a third. Hafoc had paced, doubtful, and slowly I had retreated, nervous, until I caught my heel on the sill of a step and plunged into darkness. The image of Kristján blotted out anything else, as I regained consciousness in a neat hospital bed, with broken bones I had not known the names of. It took those three months of frustrated contemplation as no letters, no wires, no calls placed to the lighthouse control room, reached him. Three months to realise we had both been nervous of ourselves in Hafoc: her acuity, and therefore derision, of the foolish, raw meat of the heart.

XI

KRISTJÀN NORGE, March 9th, 1961

TRAN-Quil-Ity: Crossing the Quill of Being

A sacrificed human buried in a field. Interred as the etymological roots of the word 'tranquility', a poet body seemingly becomes apparent:

I. *Tran:* word-forming element meaning 'across, beyond, through, on the other side of, to go beyond', from Latin trans (prep.).

II. *quil:* From late Middle English *quil*, which is first attested in the early 15th century with the meanings 'fragment of reed' and 'shaft of a feather', probably from Low German and Middle Low German quiele, Proto-Indo-European GWELh-1 ('to pierce, to stick').

III. *ity:* word-forming element making abstract nouns from adjectives and meaning 'condition or quality of being ____,' from Middle English *-ite*, from Old French *-ete* (Modern French *-ité*) and directly from Latin *-itatem* (nominative *-itas*), suffix denoting state or condition, composed of *-i-* (from the stem or else a connective) + the common abstract suffix *-tas*.

What kind of body can this be? How does its burial in language excavate a body language? Is it buried alive? There is an embedding here and of course, 'quil' reminds us of the act of writing itself: 'quill' or 'quilling' with a Roman stylus. So roughly, we have:

'crossing the quill of being'

At least, this is one iteration. We could also disinter:

'being pierced through'

which might insinuate a quill as an arrow-shaft, if both sides of the dug-up coin manifest equally. Apparently, here we have fragments of the death-rites of writing and through preference, poetry. In a further insinuation, let's consider the poet body (so-called because of the quill crossing a state of death) as a sacrificed human, buried where it fell in a site which later becomes an agricultural field. This is a common archaeological situation and points to a framing of the etymology which can be read: Roman/Anglo-Saxon/ Roman or Latin/Middle English/Latin. Perhaps a Roman field prepared for an Anglo-Saxon sacrifice or an Anglo-Saxon sacrifice performed specifically in a Roman field. Somehow, one aspect is compliant and sympathetic to the other: the metaphoric sacrificial rite can take place. Slain here are specifics: 'tran', 'quil' and 'ity' – a tripartite seed. This particular crop-yield gives us the nature of our field.

If we designate a whole page as the excavation site and a single stanza as the pre-dug grave situated to the north-west of the field (in the mainstream Western tradition), or centrally (in the less recognised form of Pattern Poetry), then we might examine the meaning of the stanza as the remains of the grave. Additionally, if the poet-body is curled foetally in the shallow pit and the remains of a fragment of an arrow shaft, or a broken flute (reed) or a fractured quill (pen), then the poet-body is buried with artefacts symbolic of the origins of poetry itself. Here are the objects of hunting, singing and mark-making, embedded within early agriculture and weapon manufacture. The topsoil of poetic meaning in any stanza may have a constructed sense but beneath it – as with our single word stanza – lies a subsoil of buried insistence. Our topsoil is: 'tranquility' and our subsoil is: 'crossing the quill of being'. Here is the field, the plot, the subsoil of the page with poetry pushing up through an imprinted or glyphed surface that roughly corresponds to the idea of this surface of the field. Let's treat the initial field of the page, or monolith, as squared and blanked, (at least ideologically). We have a rectangular form right here, to hand. Now we are going to read this text as glyphic corn and this page, exactly as the field. We don't yet have any scarecrows, but there is always the lurking murder of crows at large beyond the boundaries of our crop. Let's say our field (our page, our stage) grows in the shadow of that phenomenon.

STANZA	PAGE
Burial Plot	Field
An Eala	Port nam Marbh
Poet Body	Death Stage

265

The birds here are also evident in the quill and the tracery of cursive text itself, suggested in the fragment of reed. Perhaps the two are interchangeable: the carcass of a water bird driven across scansions of wetbeds by the wind along the field's southern alignment. No matter. Many flocks passed over the page and a scarecrow – the dead poet? – now revived by fear, has moved off the field leaving heavy imprints behind it, or has dissolved back into the stubble, ragged and muddied, or has been ignited for fear of infection. Perhaps if our straw man were composed also of reed fragments, it is an anatomy of quills that makes its muscles and bones and it is the personification of underworld: the gateway keeper of the underworld.

Speaking of underworld, we might leap across to the Latin again for the Roman god of the underworld, dis pater. This deity was originally associated with fertile agricultural land and mineral wealth, and since those minerals came from underground, he was later equated with the chthonic deities Pluto (Hades) and Orcus. Perhaps this page can be a designated wheat field, a necromantic wheat field. Or perhaps an aerial burial: its fragments of being quilled in crossing – risen, raised to the surface of the page. Or, perhaps banked in water, the corpus of tranquility floats in the reed bed, bloated. The wheat-making of poetry and death. The theatrical stage of the field. In Dis too, we have other Roman death rituals through Ceres, goddess of agriculture. Grain and the dead converge in the connected hemispherical motif of Ceres' underground mundus or covered chamber, Ceres being the corn goddess and mother of Proserpina who became entangled with Pluto through his brutal kidnapping over her. It was believed that Ceres presided over a portal to the underworld situated in the centre of Rome. Three days were given over each year to the opening of Ceres' hemispherical portal during which there would be games. In such a Roman ritual, the first fruits of harvest thrown in might induce rotted compost, built up over several years, given to the dead to consume as they left their underworld to meet the living.

We can tap the quill and blood sputters to ink. We can cut the reed with a knife and create a flute to sound the fundamental note. For all its framing we have an Anglo-Saxon object stuck in precise Latin. A broken arrow shaft, crossing the quill of being. Who knew it could be lodged there?

XII

THE BOATMAN ARRIVES LATE in January, knifing through choppy waters, bearing my second Death Isle visitor. Disembarking, Hafoc runs, drops to the ground on her knees, and vomits in the wild sea grass. It looks an act of torrid prayer, lapped up by Varg (how melancholy and doubt greedily consume one another's remains) and standing instantly, she brushes sand from her skirt, before carefully lighting a cigarette. She looks thinner, sharper, than I recall from Edinburgh, but the whittling has produced a fine, intelligent look that previously had been hidden by an unnatural confidence.

I speak in low tones with Slane, sling oranges he delivers over my shoulder; salt and apples in my coat pockets.

'I merely transfer,' he says in answer to my thanks, his grey eyes unceasingly locked on the horizon, 'or transform, if you like, an entity into another environment, I bear a mutable yoke within the confines of this sea-track, back and forth, a kind of nautical alchemy,' he adds, climbing into the boat. 'No correspondence today,' he says, pulling the engine into life with careful hands, 'it's come to you in person.'

A gold preen of water churns from the small motor and for a moment it is Kristján I see, looking back from the stern, staring back at me beneath a hooded cloak. Varg howls then, and I start. An apple falls to the ground and rolls toward Hafoc who picks it up and holds it out like a golden orb. Coming forward she sounds my name as if to recollect it, kissing me with pungent breath on both cheeks and I instantly think – 'it's going to fail'.

I know in that moment to hate her evenly, if at all, and then the feeling will be subsumed by intimacy, as we fall away from the great statues we have made of ourselves through watchful professionalism on her part, and too much self-awareness on mine.

'Drink,' I say, passing her a hip flask.

'You know how I hate it.'

'Drink it anyway, you'll need it,' I reiterate, already wincing at my facetious cheer.

She sips at the contents of the flask and makes a face. I have forgotten how untrusting she can be, as we trudge over to the lighthouse, lugging her baggage.

*

TRAVAILS OF A SPIRIT-RAVAGED SKELETON

Time wounds, it does not heal. Time wounds repeatedly. Now, the days are eerie and there is no fire plan. In the first place, I suck in the wind and carry it, mouthful by mouthful, to the second place in the hope of making a blaze, but all I find is a mirror there and suffumigate its surface with periwinkle flowers, burnt wool, lion fur, cold camphor and white lead for an offering. I have already given my innards and tongue, one eye and most of my teeth, but relenting, I strip off my skin and drop it on the polished surface, shivering. The mirror rings out like a drum. Then we begin.

I see before me a passage of wood which has been destroyed. The tree branches are blackened and smoking and following this burnt path, it seems to me that whatever has passed through, has caused such a ravaging that it has left the copse like a charred corpse. Shortly after this, it becomes apparent to me that the destructive force was stellar; a star has blundered, burning, through the under-growth. I then come to a ruined mansion whose frontage, steps, window bays and pillars are dilapidated and ruinous. It is now dusk, and as I stare, strange forms configure. They seem to me to be lions, slipping between the rudi-ments of fallen masonry, and I am afraid. Inside, offerings are laid out on the floor and I am told they are objects stolen from me presented as a tariff to pass through my memory into forgetting.

This, the mirror tells me, is their purpose – and mine. I am given the skull bone of a lion and told to use it as a scrying device. This occital lens proves useful to me; as I lift it to my eyes, I find myself in an amphitheatre as a wounded and dying centaur, killed by a man considered knightless. This is the theatre and I watch from the saw-dust and sand, the empty seats of amnesia produce two landscapes: one emotional called Craven, in which the instincts of a hyena court prevail, and the other called Sump: a place of spiritual sinking. Between them, the lightning-struck tower of Dante's old tarocchi breaks itself open and this comes to reveal the amphitheatre sphere as a greater lens. The centaur is slain – my own wilderness configuration – and now I am returned from the woods to a kitchen garden to gather the sticks of religion in my arms and burn them. Then the mirror dims.

*

There is no need for me to formally show her around this room with its shabby desk and typewriter, as this is the chamber that will serve as our shared sleeping quarters. I rake up the coals in the ash-filled grate as Hafoc stares out of a window at the slow-moving seascape. Nothing but silence passes between us... this chamber of the dead feels airless, airtight, oddly precipitate. I have pulled the tattered armchairs closer to the fireplace and we take our seats as I begin to point out the separate piles of scraps; oddments of papers, their similarities and differences. Varg settles down between us, a melancholy presence.

'I was sorry about your accident,' she says presently, with Kristján's star atlas lying open on her lap.

'Were you?' As if in indignation, my wrist aches and there is a twinge in my broken ribs. Involuntarily, I lay my hand over the healing wound in my thigh. 'They gave me twenty-five stitches in my leg,' I say. 'I still have to dress the cuts each morning.'

Hafoc turns her magnificent face to the fire. Immediately it glows on one side with a fine aureole. The ancient deer. I flinch in my chair, without speaking.

'You know,' she says presently in that soft tone, 'it took me a while to come here. I understood what you meant when you wrote back – but, it wasn't that, you see. I suppose I've not been altogether honest. Yes, in part, I'm here to find Kristján, to see what he saw, to hear what he heard. I know the danger in that: the danger in it even being a copy.'

I admire her intensely as she speaks, commanding the empty room, drawing it to her with a sigh. And now crying – Hafoc crying by the fire, her tears firewater running down those tawny cheeks. How could she cry after this time, only just arriving? I am moved that she could cry, in front of me, after all this time, as if we had never been apart.

'Oh, Luce,' she weeps, suddenly broken down, as if all her resistance since his disappearance gives way: 'I'm so confused.'

My whole being halts. She hovers around me without moving, the night raven, the watch bird, and then she senses I feel this and comes to, dabbing her eyes, lighting another cigarette. I know Hafoc well enough to understand her need for dignity and quietude after this blurted confession and that she will return in a while to speak of it, if I am patient.

'I'm sorry,' is all she can repeat, in the meantime.

'You mustn't be afraid,' I urge, 'fear makes it stronger.'

'But I am afraid – how can I not be? And anyhow, your telling me not to be frightened sets up such a redoubled anxiety in me.' She pauses ruefully, rubbing her forehead. 'I am more afraid of Kristján, than anything. That he must wait in some afterlife, to tell us so. That it all had meaning. That nothing was lost.'

'What has happened, Jeanie, tell me,' I murmur.

'It was last summer – you know, he had been writing to me and the letters: those letters... you know, he would start by asking how I was – always start that way and soon, there would be a point where he would start to write down how I was, and it was always terrible things. But, Luce – they were always right. He mightn't have had much to say, just that he had seen such and such – and always *seen*: that's how he put it – and that he would come and restore them for me or if I didn't let him that he couldn't tell me how they could be resolved and we spiralled into a bind. Everything about it could be entirely dismissed – a conventionally disturbed relationship between doctor and client – perfectly absolvable through patience and severance and by me consulting a colleague: transferring Kristján, even. *But I didn't.* Oh – I was far too much involved with him, convinced I was the only one to help, convinced anyone else would read the case notes and have him hospitalised immediately. And I was *interested*. I was convinced he needed these delusional spells to write. That's when it became difficult... I confronted him, in our correspondence about you, accused you of betraying him, of being a sporadic and volatile entity in his life, so that Kristján would feel there was a closer bond between he and I, and get to become cut off. It never occurred to me simply to write to you – I had thought you would disapprove and that you needed time alone with him.'

'You were right, I did,' I say calmly. She glances at me under those cat's kill eyelids for a moment and I have that same disturbing feeling of deep mistrust. 'But, go on,' I prompt, curious to hear what she will say.

'Well,' she continues, lighting another cigarette and pulling her stockinged feet under her, 'then the letters stopped. It was as if the spell was over and whatever he had "seen" or heard was gone. I had thought it you, of course, convinced you had manipulated the whole situation to damage Kristján and to unnerve me. But then, I got another note, just before he disappeared.' She fumbles about in her bag for a moment – 'here,' she says, thrusting it towards me. I set my drink down and reach over slowly. I take the letter carefully, aware of Kristján's erratic scrawl.

'But, Jeanie,' I say, after pausing to open the folded paper, 'there's nothing on it.'

XIII

AT NIGHT, THE WIND burns our tongues. Mine crumbles to ash and I come awake calling. Fire in the windows from the new sun and a roaring, black sea. If the terror of mermaids, calling blindly into a new storm, feeling for the wet hair of their dead lovers, spiralled into delicate form, suspended in the sightless current, were ours, Hafoc and I would now leave this island. But we are fearless: pride ourselves on human persistence, on the ability to supervise events with a full dismissal of the unsung, the unspoken. Even Hafoc, lost as she is without her wilful shadow, converses with certain qualms that are not qualms of the frightened, but qualms of the rigorous. An uncertainty of training. A training the rocks could have smashed against their hardness by a wild ocean, the wind scatter and the sea spew up again and it would still remain – an obdurate doubt. She keeps disbelieving and I refresh myself in light. But, the winter wind is long on these short nights and the darkness doesn't help the calling. 'The wind is magnetic,' writes Kristján, 'drawing energies, instincts, spatial distances, histories, spirits, memories, objects, languages and emotions into it, only to discard them again: sheets of wind driven through ebony night-waters.'

Last week I found the camera. We set up a darkroom in the lighthouse washroom. Ordered fix and wash from the mainland. It came by the boatman, sluicing the insides of its containers with the stuff of image making. Kristján washed up in scarlet. A small poet with his pipe. We enveloped him: brilliance and doubt bringing him out of the light and into the tender darkness of our sight. Washed and rinsed him into existence. Two mermaids drowning a seaman into life. Pinned him up and left him dripping. Escaped down to the shoreline, singing.

The sand held our plushy star shapes as if the night tide took account of the changing sky overhead. It was there we walked the dunes, collecting damp seaweed scrag and cutting small bricks of peat from the larger block under the tarpaulin near the lighthouse gate. Small warnings rose to meet me, but I seemed oblivious of them.

'You didn't tell me about the deer,' said Hafoc, standing up from cutting one afternoon, as she found herself observed by a half dozen of the creatures, poised to escape on the grass-line of the beach.

'Oh yes, the deer,' I replied vaguely, 'we're outnumbered by the hundred.'

'I have a vision of them flayed,' she said suddenly, serious now, her eyes tightening and releasing like a kiss. 'Skinless and smarting with blood prickles from the salt air.'

Her pale face glistened with that brilliant golden down on the upper lip and down the flank of each cheek, sharp eyes reflectionless. I looked at her with my whole body thinking how little I understood.

*

Wild cries of the gulls smack against the lighthouse walls. We share one thinly slatted bunk, the other having been demolished by Kristján for firewood.

'For melting the wax,' I explain ungenerously, 'did he tell you about that?'

'No.' She leans out of the bunk to light a cigarette and lies back, contemplating the smoke.

'There are a great many things he didn't tell me. One's analyst is not always one's trusted friend and he always accused me of having a tendency to indulge skepticism. He told you?'

'He didn't have to – I found him out the back one afternoon, melting down all the candle ends he could lay his hands on. They were – ' I correct myself, 'he said the voices were accompanied by the snuffing of candles which couldn't be relit again.'

'Is that true?' She is genuinely fascinated.

'By the time I came to hear of his theory, we had a whole factory floor of miniature stubs designed by Kristján to last one evening only, and so I never had the chance to put it to the test. Besides, perhaps it is indulgent to challenge the ideas of one so imbalanced – it betrays a certain lack of confidence in their certitude, don't you think?' I know I am pushing her, she hasn't mentioned her confession of the first evening since, meeting all my hints with an evenhanded indifference.

'Not at all,' she responds sharply.

'So you would have confronted him?'

'Absolutely.'

'At the risk of his retreating even farther into himself?'

'But don't you realise that the exact opposite would have happened!' she cries passionately.

I see instantly that what she wanted was a moment of mimesis – of complete exactness, that she would have confronted him in order to possess his idea, to share and command it and then to pour it – like wax – into a mould of misgiving. I thought of him in the sand, splashing boiling wax onto wet ground. Of the burn.

'Perhaps,' I say.

'You haven't told me why you returned here.'

'No, I don't suppose I have. Would you like to know?'

'Yes, if you want to tell me. I had assumed it was to pack up, to lay things to rest.'

'Yes, but more than that. Do you know the old burial custom where they take the body out of the house feet first so that it can't remember the way back? Well, it seems to me Kristján was carried out of here head first, like a bier corpse and that he knows – he recalls, how to return and that he is – or that he was here. I feel him here. He watches over things.'

Hafoc is quiet, yet I can feel her suspicion.

'He also asked me to destroy his work.'

'Destroy it?' She is surprised. Instantly, I regret saying it.

'He was working on something. A system. You knew that.'

'Yes, I did know he was keeping notes, but a *system*. I knew he was working on a manuscript, though… after the last attempt … such a failure.' She laughs shortly and I realise she attributes such little importance to it, she may even forget. 'Can I see it?' she says.

'When I find it,' I reply evenly.

'He stashed it?' She was circling now, with a detached interest. Like any analyst, all things secretive tempted her. She had to uncover them and rebury them in a different place; displace the contracts of belief that anything worth burying might better remain where it was interred. At least, that is where I placed her instincts.

'Yes,' I say wearily, 'somewhere in the lighthouse, I think. Probably in one of the locked rooms above.'

'Well, I suspect we won't find it, then, without the help of an axe.' Screwing her cigarette down in the old sea shell with its fragrant dead smoke rising into the room, Hafoc gets out of the bunk, pulls on her shoes and plods upstairs, thinking, trying to feel, where her broken-minded will would have concealed his secrets and fears, had she been nearer. I leave her to it. Hafoc's preoccupation with the idea seems necessarily selfish and it is good to be alone – subdued – except for Kristján's gift to me: the sudden flash of certainty that the island, and not only the lighthouse, holds his voices, locked into the white sand or dark muscle of the deer.

XIV

'LUCE,' SHE SAYS QUIETLY, 'come with me.'

Taking me by a cold, unsteady hand, she draws me up the soft-clanging lighthouse steps. (I'd already heard her above tonight: the dull thud of a hammer, her footfall on the iron staircase. 'Good,' I'd thought, turning over, 'this is what I had her come for.')

Now, as the last suds of dream subside, I am led upstairs like an unwilling child, and clutch the blanket wrapped around my shoulders tighter. We stand in front of the door to the room above; its padlock hanging penitently, the hinges loose, as she draws me inside, closing the now broken door behind us.

The silence in the circular room is like a change in temperature. Hafoc flicks on a small torch. Eye of Osiris. Ray of Isis. A flock of papers, hanging like dead birds, furled and dry, are suspended in the eye of the torch beam. As if to counteract the spherical chamber they hang like so many weighted plumb lines, singly and in clustered braces. They are hung unevenly, some brushing the ground in front of us. The silence thickens on our breath, a warm presence. Dust on the torch-lit air rises in motes and there is a faint stench I can barely detect: a bulb of myrrh-soaked garlic, linseed oil... pine resin, decay.

'These are his voices,' intones Jeanie carefully, 'his wind of voices.'

'Don't touch them,' I say.

'Were they here, when you were here?' Her small fingers brush the surface of a dark scroll suspended in the near corner.

'I think so.'

'Did you ever come up to this room?'

'No,' I reply and my voice is soft in the dark air, carrying the visions of the chamber in it, 'he locked them both – this one and the one above.'

'Now this.' Her searchlight drops to the centre of the room. The fixed beam is like the single ray of an autumn sun illuminating the planting time for crops on an ancient wall face. A finger of light that points out a mound in the darkness. My heart freezes, doubtless to self.

'Kristján —' I breathe, unmoving. In the middle of the room is a bound up shape. Could this mound of cloth be Kristján's body?

The circular room seems to contract around the bundle like a muscle. Or, perhaps the lumpen shape expands in my awareness like a pupil soaking up the available light…something is squandered…perhaps breath, perhaps sense. Hafoc dips – a dead sea diver – and sweeps the torch beam over this unmoving figure bound in rags, her voice swimming in the aching gloom: 'Kristján?'

It has become our defining question: one whisperingly posed in the torch-flared stone catacombs of Rome…one gasped in the lioness' mouth in the baying arena… 'Kristján?' she intones softly, lost priestess of a leaking island, a sawdust island, a marooned survivor living on the isle of the dead. Now she is on her knees, like a penitent, like a saint, the torchlight trembling in an unsteady hand as I step forward into its electric sphere and find myself devoured by yearning.

*

One pale night, Kristján and I had sighted a flare and went down to the shore. The tide was fully in. Motley crates had bobbed in the shallows: tropical fruit and lettuce blew into the sand banks and rotted for weeks. Some fell apart on the sand when beached – in them drowned animals. I buried a soaked parakeet; its feathers a luminous, wet green. They were all dead, bar one. It is hard to forget Kristján's face as he waded toward me, knee deep in the surf, guiding a crate that held a young lion. I recall the lion's languid amber eyes, the tufted violence in its juvenile paws.

'Must have been a circus freight,' Kristján panted out the words. The muzzled air seemed astonished.

'Help me,' he repeated, and we dragged the crate up the beach and along the path straddled by sea grass, with the muscular smell of the fine young animal filling our nostrils, paused awhile and then into the lighthouse, up those metal stairs where its roar echoed the centuries and into this room on the second floor – 'but don't come in,' said Kristján, who refused me entry.

Then he went down to the shoreline to find the other carcasses: a zebra and bear. He hauled them to the old sea cemetery, burying them among the mariner graves. Later, the maned youngster would play among the tombs and bound along the old coffin road. Kristján built an enclosure in the ruined mansion from chicken wire, fallen masonry. The young cat would sleep there, beneath the knotted pines, a raven keeping watch from the lower branches over this golden, curled predator.

I am telling her all this as a wish and a token. Opposite us, its bandaged mane lit up by a sudden flash of recognition, lies the bound carcass of Kristján's half-drowned lion.

*

To embalm: a bed of natron, a sprinkling of alum, after three lunar months rinse the body in a large springwater rock pool and then suffumigate the corpse with incense and prayers, oiling it all the while. Fill the inner cavities with a warm resin liquid of frankincense and myrrh, and apply to the outer areas; paw pads and anus, for example. The wrappings are lint and hand-woven linen offcuts from Luce's loom. On them I paint the signs of his existence.

I have attached a circuit of small bells brought with me from the mainland to prevent theft and provide a sound pathway for the afterlife and back again: like St Columba's roaring prayer. The wax and asphalt of sonic preservation: deafening the mummer's ears: blinding the mummer's eyes: mumming the mummer's mouth to all but their soft, tinkling cry.

My lion is preserved with grains of barley from which can be grown whole fields of the dead. His tear ducts are sown with heather seeds. His jaw is bound up with strips of plaid. I have removed his temple bone and filled the impression with wads of garlic. His temple bone will be my seeing bone, my scrying bone, my hearing bone for the commandments of the dead.

I dreamt last night a dream of Dee and the embalmed angel, deeply wounded from the fall. Unlike Adam, it could not be risen and suffered a crisis of flesh. Stalwartly burning. He therein had sewed bells into its flesh and siphoned off a mercurial liquid used for an ink that would set itself alight each morning like fiery dew in the sea grass.

Gentle, in the embalmed flowers,
the lion's barbarous roar.
Gentle, in the dessicant grasses,
rusts the dagger-sharp, morning star.

*

We stand over the mummified lion, whose large inked eyes are painted on the bandaging, whose tail is curved wadding, whose flat, heavy paws lie inert. Hafoc holds the torch and I ease open a lint wrapping. The waxed linen end is tucked beneath the lion's jaw and I release its stiff knot to carefully unwind the swaddling cloth. It is like watching a universe unfold in my fingers: beneath it, an underworld waiting, watching. When the maned face rises out of the linen-ink face of its crude depiction, it is a mask peeled away to reveal another mask, somehow sleeping. The lion's squashed features hold utterly, the barren stillness of death. Only the milk-coloured mane still retains a property of essence; the trace of a will; an incumbent memory. Tied around its neck is a carton and I carefully undo the string and open the lid.

It troubles me to find this wristband now, curled in the small paper box. Slipping it on, I find the fur more like silk and the lion skin parched: a dense parchment. Vellum for the afterlife. There is a strange scent; half tang, half tannin and something else – something like a speed or heat to the smell, as if the thousand hunts that occurred in its molecular structure emanated avidly from these arid, pale strands of mane. As if the awareness of the lion still was held in its dead skin. If Kristján deliberately drowned, he decided not to take the lion skin bracelet with him. Perhaps he felt it should not be returned to the ocean.

Hafoc gently speaks now, leaning over my shoulder.

'He was nameless?'

'So far as I'm aware... though I think Kristján may have alluded to a lion once or twice in his writings.'

'But, he was real?' Hafoc's features are hollowed by the torch-light.

'As real as you or I, or Kristján,' I say, as Varg pads into the room and sniffs pensively at the corpse. It is a mound of rag and bone... a disposal from the dead; an offering from the dead to the dead, covered in the skin of a lion.

'We'll have to make a start,' she says, standing upright.

'A start?'

'Yes,' she says, 'we have to piece all these together,' she brushes the torchlight through the strung up colony of papers, rustling in a draught from the broken door left ajar by Varg, rustling like a system of ancient whispers animated by the cold sea breeze.

'But, his system —'

'That can wait – these may lead us to it.' And she snaps off the torch beam, leaving me in darkness. The way Kristján had left me in darkness. A small tightrope of fear in the black. Heart cordoned, petitioned, slackened and then tightened with all the ancestors and predecessors of love.

XV

WE LIBERATE THIS TOMB: prise rough boards from the windows, wrench the splintered door completely free of its busted hinges. The released daylight is keen and we work vigorously into it – Hafoc without pause, without sleep. Now, as I tread the stairs bringing bread and coffee, winter sunshine spills through the doorframe of the room. She crosses it as if through water, pushing against its substance, leaving small prints on the dusty floor and comes to stand in a square of sunlight with arms full of shreds, balls, sheafs, wads and scraps of paper: cursive offerings, or petitions. I advance warily toward her with steaming coffee and set it down near a confirmed pile at her feet.

'Give me my orders,' I mumble, lighting a cigarette. I sit cross-legged on the floor, looking up at this new island visitant casting her doubt on a scene I'd already been tired out by, had nearly quit.

'I suppose just to continue what you have been doing all this time before I came. Sort out the piles. Some are dateless, as you know. There's a seal on this one,' says Jeanie faintly and holds up a withered looking envelope. She reads it out, cigarette in hand. I absorb her words, shifting in my position, disappear into the account. A sleep-listener concentrating exhaustedly.

*

In the winter they bind it to pine and in the summer, willow and they douse it in pitch so that there shall be a good flame. Not a blue flame like the sìth flames, but a healthy red one. In summer when the light is constant it is easy to write in a steady hand but in winter or on inclement days or by inconstant moonlight also, the hand must enlarge and its features, namely those things by which the presence of a hand is present to make its marks and so defile the paper, must enlarge also. This is not to say we write with the hands of giants on such days, but that we occupy more of the paper, seeing less of it, so that we may fully know its parts. Think on it like a bolder map of thought. Then my poems go dark because unread...

When I ask myself what he was doing, I am never able to resolve an answer. Whenever I had confronted Kristján directly, he informed me in the same monotones: 'It was the wind,' he would say mechanically, 'the wind of voices – they told me.'

What kind of fear blanched his rough face, as if the gusting air around him were thinking, as if it knew how to threaten by mere suggestion. He would have me close windows, shutters, doors. Batten down roof hatches, old outhouse skylights.

Recalling this, I start pinning, repinning, adjusting the sheets. Ink has bled from several papers, wandering across their surfaces in extended maps of befuddled meaning. Voices adhere to every page in a thin scrawl of handmade inks and charcoal, quilled on, pressed with a thumb to seal them; documents that roared and clamoured, murmured and sighed. There are tear stains on some, yellowed and butchered papers. Blood on some. Dark prints. Paper packets yellow as nicotine.

Jeanie reads to me across the day into the evening, by torch-light, whose dying battery flickers in code from another afterlife. Whose voice is hers on this strange, ventriloquised night?

'Look,' she says, and in gestures I see, emerging from the walls themselves, on the ceiling, across the floor, messages etched into every surface. Fortunes of the bold, fortunes of the blind: illegible, discernible, petroglyphic and hieroglyphic.

'Look again,' she says, and I observe all the room's surfaces beneath those inscriptions patched and reworked with small pieces of cloth, wool, bone and paper, but minutely stuffed or arranged into the fabric of the building. The words. I cannot read their presences, their rootwork of slow silver in the torchlight.

'How...?' I breathe.

'The light had to be just right and we've taken down most of his papers. These marks must have been here for some time.' The torchlight slowly fades to nothing and we stand in darkness.

'They are all-encompassing,' my voice says, oracular – as if not my own, but spoken from another time.

Constructed of voices – the prints and scratchings whisper from the lighthouse walls. That night we think we hear those scratchings, but perhaps it is the wind, quiet and yearning, that dislodges the cramped notations, bundled into balls, packets of etchings stuffed into the myriad gaps and holes of the building. I am afraid if we remove them, the lighthouse will crumble and we'll be left in the wind with these feverish scraps of notation, all blown down to the sea for a night drowning. As we extract the inscriptions we will become, systematically, semiologists, excavators and construction workers. Lying on the narrow bunk, we think to retrieve and rebuild, section by section, that small wind-stuttered tower on the island. An autopsy. Will its skeleton still stand? Not structurally deficient, but without the call of the voices, the whisperings and murmurings that have constituted its walls for so long, would the lighthouse slump, its muscles shred and its wind-worn skeleton collapse...? These night jottings ache on our tongues, though no snatches of sound pervade our exhausted, dreamless, sleep that night.

*

Morning loads all its fresh light onto us, but we are open to its burden. I am forced awake by instinct to track the beacon interior and observe the structure of the lighthouse as a whole: the stairway, the skirting, everywhere, everywhere to be seen – writing. Scratched into the walls are inscriptions, messages, quotes. Wilderness graffiti. Hafoc is still absorbed by the lion chamber, as we now call it, detaching, unfurling and determining the significance of Kristján's writings. I meet her for an exhausted lunch on the cold lighthouse step and she is pale with consternation.

'What are you thinking...?' I ask her that early afternoon, as we pause in our efforts with whisky and sandwiches.

'About a dream that recurs,' she throws her head back to bask against the iron jamb and the glaring January sunlight casts an inverted halo around her jaw.

'I see a canoe half-suspended over a waterfall, the stern still in the water and the prow projected in the air. Below the water flows down, falls down, crashes down and the boat is full of his papers, it's filled with letters and scraps and is just hanging there in mid-air as if one more oar-stroke, one more packet stuffed in at the front end, will tip the balance. And here's the part that matters: in the dream, I know if I tip the canoe, he will die, that there's some terrible need for its balance and he won't tell me what and now, Luce, I'm afraid of uncovering these things. The lighthouse, the walls, afraid of it all. I had the dream again last night. Let's go, Luce, let's get away from here and leave this chaos – you must be worn out in a way I can't fathom; clearing and ordering. What does it matter...' she stops, is quiet.

'But, I promised him,' I say slowly, unsure of the words as I speak them out, unsure if this is true, even, before then feeling as I utter them, that it is Kristján – in the final assessment – Kristján who fundamentally needs us to save him.

'What did you promise?' she cries, 'not even to publish them – just to gather all this up and destroy it, what point is there to it?' She stands up, vociferously smoking.

'We still have one more floor to open up –'

'It'll just be the same, weeks more now of his…glossolalia.'

'But, his system –'

'What system? Luce, you must realise, there is no system…'

'And,' I say, looking down, 'I must try and live on here, Jeanie. I have no city to return to, unlike you.'

There is a pause.

'Come with me, then.'

'No.'

'Come with me and you can act as secretary –'

I look up as the sun floods from behind a fast-moving cloud, lighting up Hafoc who leans smoking against the lighthouse wall.

'All right, perhaps not secretary,' she says, catching my expression, 'you'd find a place as an archaeologist –'

'Jeanie,' I say, 'come over here, right now. Just do as I say.'

She pauses for a moment and then, scrubbing out her cigarette comes toward me.

'Now stand here, next to me,' I pull her gently into place, 'look: where you were standing.'

If she reacts strongly, she holds it within, is self-contained. A mark, a growing mark like a moving mould stain is travelling up the lighthouse exterior like a rotted flower. Not quite an enlarged thumbprint, not quite a morphed labyrinth, it is dull and complex, starting from the base and spreading ten foot high on the corroded stone. Then, it seems to fall forward onto the ground and become absorbed by the earth of the island.

'A trick of the light,' says Jeanie, as the sun goes in.

'Watch,' I say, as it climbs the wall again. The atmosphere is thick with premonition, as if the island has slipped on the spectrum just a few degrees into monochrome and our actions and words seem slowed. Then, without knowing the origin of the thought or realisation, I speak: 'this is anamorphic,' I mutter, 'the island is a reversal…here is its distorted impression climbing the light-tower outer wall… the reflected island… a malformed map.'

XVI

THIS TINDER COURT HAS been waiting for us in a spherical silence. Again we split a lighthouse room apart. The upper-storey room is even more secure. It is like breaking into coffin-chambers, peeling darkness from the light. Hafoc's fingers, like talons, pull at the door joists, sawdust in her air. The wild call of wood being splintered… how objects have their own voices, objections, languages in their rattling percussion, in the daily handling of their physical possession.

This is the upper room of the lighthouse: the second that Kristján had locked and boarded up. Notes for the underworld: the air in the room has an almost religious tang, so that when Hafoc pauses, having broken open the door, panting, we wait at the threshold until the staleness has cleared like spirits escaping. We are too unnerved to smoke or speak, even. Hafoc still retains a hawk-like worry, an anxiety tipped in air as she hovers over going in, delaying. And so, I take the lead. The candle does its duty, throwing weird shadows all over the place; across the room's large objects which – for now – still hold their breath, it seems, as the flickering light moves over them, animating their bludgeoned forms.

I take stock of the time: it is eight in the morning.

*

Bar the day we discovered the lighthouse scrawling, neither of us has had much success in sleep: tossing and turning on the hardboard bed. We are continuously tired with the exhaustion of mild shock, and bewildered instincts, and each night the darkness lasts for many long hours. So now we try to sleep off our discoveries, like the contents of nightmare, sleep them off in a secondary phase of dream. Only, the content of this malign vision is just beginning its final manifestation.

Last night was such an example of fighting. Eventually, I got up at four. The milk had soured, left out by the fire, and I took my coffee black, like a tannin, like a tar or a bitter resin, poured it through my innards as I walked the bunk-room, back and forth among the paper piles, islands in a destitute sea. Hafoc turned in her sleep, with a muffled wail, and so I woke her, put her out of her dreaming misery. We have enough in our waking landscape to cope with – even fitful sleep seems the sole luxury of absence from it. Hafoc took the coffee cup I offered her with both hands as if holding a candle, its steam like smoke, pouncing sweat on her cheeks. Condensation of the dead. I watched her as she sat bolt upright in the slatted bunk, like a corpse sitting upright in its coffin, or a medieval sleeper woken for nocturnal socialising: sat very still as if a slim effigy of prayer itself, the steam rising in wet clouds around her.

*

Now, not quite fully awake, we stand shivering in this circular chamber, two living beings among several carved statues. The floor is covered in compacted sand which has seeped out from the room. Eight figures are arranged in a circle, facing inward. There is enough space around the periphery of the room to walk behind them. Strange markings are just discernible on the sand's surface, and around the edges of the room are the traces of footprints. Later that day, with the clarity of daylight, I see that Kristján had made holes in the ceiling and in the lantern room above so that moisture fills the room and the sand has continuously been kept slightly damp. The circular chamber is gyromantic, it seems, as I take in the direction of the footprints and esoteric lettering. I suspect Kristján had devised it as a magic circle. The light moves from blood to urine behind us as the dawn sky slowly lightens into day. The room's windows are small and I am grateful for the candle.

Hafoc has gone downstairs to return with a camera, a notepad and pencil. The camera seems ill-equipped for its subject, but – like all machines of light and air – gives a welcome level of control. It is as if the power of the statues is diminished, the more we record and document their presence, speaking to each other in low, intermittent voices.

'Like this?' she says softly and takes another photograph from below, from the base of a figurehead, working her way around the room like a mechanical clock figurine, moving through automated time. We stick to the edges of that room, but she leans into it as I grip her waist, to take aerial shots above the sand-drawn text. There are eight figures and a pile of ash, in it the charred remains of some writing, some documents. Hafoc photographs the paper fragments, and then I fish them out, sand spilling from the folds, co-mingled with flaking, blackened words. A title page is still legible, written in capitals: THE STAR-RAVAGED CO(R)PSE and some of the text is still in tact. In a sudden moment of illumination, I recognise this as part of Kristján's system; *is it?* Hafoc nods, passing it back. I kneel to taste a little of the ash. It is pure, like a birch ash, and burnt to a talcum-fine brilliant white. This was once another figurehead, now reduced to its terminal elements.

We plough through the sand, photographing, hunting. Each figure has an independent presence... here is the figurehead Kristján had named 'knightless' and he is positioned, sea-ravaged, to the east of the room.

Hafoc stands next to me for a moment, pausing in her efforts.

'I read yesterday,' she murmurs, 'that Kristján would mend his clay pipe with blood, prick the tip of a finger and use the blood to press a crack together... that there were four or five blood-sealed fractures he'd sealed up in this way...' she stops for a moment and then leans in toward the figurehead, bringing the flame close to the knight's rough face. His sea-worn eyes flicker with light and his pocked wooden skin is swarthy and flecked with gold in the small fire she wields. I watch, as she peers intently into his open mouth.

'Here,' she says and passing me the candle, instructs: 'bring it closer – that's it.'

She roots around in the small cavity of his mouth, for a moment, and then draws out a scroll of tightly rolled papers: a scroll once stuffed in the mouth of a sea-bound oracle.

'Tilt him forward,' she commands and I pass back the candle, before pushing the figurehead forward, using all my weight. Nothing more drops from between those carved lips and I return the knight to his upright position. He has the irreverence of statuary – an absolute indifference which places statues in a different category: in a class above feeling, above human emotion, where they carry the weight of the deific with a certain cold perfection. Even he, this sea-rolled figure, is marked with aloofness and Hafoc retreats with this paperwork, as if she now handles his passport and papers as tokens of entry to another world.

For my part, I turn to survey the room, to take it in: find meaning in the sinister arrangement of this standing circle of marine figures. I stand up and, taking the candle, approach the remaining figures, one by one.

*

The demon is made of driftwood or bog wood. Caledonian pine from night waters. Now I recall the small cuts to Kristján's hands, a few, slight lesions on his forearm. He'd slipped. The knife had spoken. How many figures had Kristján carved in the darkness up here when I was sleeping, in the months when I could not get to him? I walk around the circle of figureheads, slipping forward on the sand: There stands the lion, warped and twisted from long conversation with the ocean: an old one from the shoreline, and the knight with his sea-worn, cruel features – coffin cheeks in faded red paint, blistered by time. I trace a finger along the shoulders of the Gypsy torso, her bust splintered and gouged, trace the carved necklace around her throat. Next to her is the hermit with his folded arms. A proud and wounded centaur – an arrow stuck in his wooden ribs, charges into the sea in pain, and a sea-blenched wolf-like creature, so rough is the remaining wood with its dark-flanked stains.

Many of these figureheads are Kristján's own. I move through the sphere of effigies, feeling simultaneously watched and alone.

The demon is incomplete – I can see the waterlogged parts and the thickness or thinness of the pine's winter and summer growth. He'd found a face in the warped log. Unpainted, chiselled marks run down the demon's spine where Kristján had been hacking a figure out and there is a rough, uneven join between this spine and its skull. I remember, towards the middle of June, he had split his thumbnail hammering down the outhouses, he said. It was the same hand as was wounded on the rocks earlier that summer, which struck me as strange but I wrapped a wad of seaweed round the nail bed to help with the swelling and the injury calmed. Not angelic lettering... not marks from subterranean hawking: he'd missed the mark and his penknife had jounced, cutting his arm. Now this demon – a rough, whittled creature of blunt bones and hollows. An unlikely figure for a ship. Its shadow created dark shapes on the sand floor where no shapes should be, of jagged wooden ribs and gaunt pine hip bones. The last of his carvings is a strange one – a lone figure standing with two oars in its crossed arms. The oarsman, the ferryman.

*

When Hafoc returns, I show her my sheath of scrolls. Slowly, she comes to understand and takes them from me carefully, pounding down the metal stairs. Today she slips in and out of the room, wary, but a concentrated shadow of herself. I am startled, though, by the unusual behaviour of Varg who bares his teeth at the figureheads, backing away from the rough wolf-like image. He tracks across the sand, unheeding my protestations and then stops to sniff at the centre of the circle, scrabbling at the surface.

'Varg,' I command, but he takes no notice, working his way around this central pivot. I advance gingerly, stepping with care between Kristján's markings. Varg's fascination lies in a flat object, seething with sand, which I raise up as the dunes pour off it and clasp to my chest. At last: like a raised ship: Kristján's lost loggbok. Varg follows me dolefully and so I take him by the collar, irreverently kicking the unhinged door shut, and gently pull him downstairs where we both join Hafoc, standing like a navigator over her maps. It is a cartography of darkness.

I place the loggbok on the table where it disrupts her papers. 'I've found it,' I say with slow triumph. 'This might yield the answers to our questions.'

Carefully, Hafoc opens its battered cover. 'Now, I will need more time,' she says, her face pointed with tiredness.

*

This, then: not a book of hours, not a book of days, but a loggbok of sites. His maps and coastal awareness. His markings and revisions overlaying a wholly new topography onto the drafted landscape of Bàs island. The loggbok fuels our exhausted energies; the relief of ease and matching components evident in his rough handwriting. (The heart of the book of hours still beats faithfully, it seems). For the next day, Hafoc surveys the loggbok entries: how there are ten sites scattered across the island in which he has laid down a packet of papers and a personal possession.

'That's why I couldn't find most of his things. I had thought he might be wearing them when he drowned, when he left…' my voice trails off and we pay renewed attention to her explanation.

'These are the locations,' Hafoc says, reading out their names on his carefully inked map, 'and these are the places one of us will go to tomorrow and the day after, for whatever the length of time it takes –'

'While the other?' I interrupt her.

'While the other, and this could be myself, stays here to work out his schema, to make notes and understand, then – I hope – the link between figurehead and site, site and object, object and this, for example,' she now shows me several deciphered sheets typed up from Kristján's scrawled writing which he folded in the centaur figurehead's mouth:

*

1) I sperm this flame. A BURNING SCARECROW SCATTERS SEEDS. As sand is the subject for death, as corpse is the subject for blood, or defile. A SCHOLAR SKELETON MADE OF SAND, TRAMPLES A PUDDING MADE OF CORPSES. Saw panning for co(r)pse bones, sifting for co(r)pse matter: teeth and hair in the killer riverbed of regret. A MAN DRESSED AS DAYTIME SAWING UP SKULLS IN A POT OF WOOD, A SIEVE OF TRUNKS, A BRISTLING DOG ROLLS OVER A MUTILATED HARE, WEEPING WHICH MAKES A BED WET. Dead mirror waste. COLD GLASS DESERT. My body-flame numbing for accident. HEAVENLY BODIES CARVED IN ICE: THE MAN SLIPS. Now lightning reflects image-corpse fired in the fractured, dark, building in shocked panning of sphere-waterhole. DAYTIME: A THUNDER CLOUD MIRRORS THE PICTURE OF A BODY IN A CANON BREAKING THE DARKNESS OF BUILDING BLOCKS THAT SURROUND A ROUND WELL ON WHICH A DISH OF GRAIN LIES. Saw-seared dug cadaver, hazed into breath. A HOT KNIFE FALLS INTO A HOLE, MAKING A STINKING CLOUD. And reverse darkness consumed. DAYLIGHT EATEN BY A GOLDEN-HAIRED MAN: SOLAR. Sand-sucked is the darkness in which colour is numb. A PALLID INDIVIDUAL DRINKS A BEACH THROUGH A STRAW.

2) This has reversed breath:
the centaur, circling visions,
its hooves sink, sand-sucked.

3) Whose arrow-glossed tree is trust. YEW TREE RUSTING. Whose aim is dust. AN ARROW POINTING AT A MOUND OF POWDER. Whose heart is trampled sawdust. FEMALE DEER RUNNING IN THE CIRCUS. Bloodied flank; lodestone bloody. A HUMAN HIP ATTACHED TO BLEEDING COMPASS. Kolossos throws sperm, teeth, arrow. HUGE STATUE FLINGING

292

SEEDS, TOMBSTONES, A SPLINTER. Dust lines darkness and fighter is rough image and struck, whet jugular. Hanging rings on teeth. GALLOWS AND BELLS, ETCHED ON TOMBSTONES. Is water laughter. Arrow-seared. A BURNING BOW.

       4) Trampled blood juggler;
       bells, gallows, roughened walls,
       the heart runs sawdust.

5) Sand whines the building; trust aflame, yet itself throat-eats this squat nest of consumed human, the waste earth of colossean broken in his blood, silver turns, mud own dark heart – a blood-centaur sear. IN A SAND STORM A MINARET IS ON FIRE WHILE A PRIEST SINGS INTO A FAT NEST FILLED WITH A DEMOLISHED WORLD WHOSE EARTH IS MIXED WITH BLOOD, SILVER AND HEART MUSCLE – A SKINNED CENTAUR BRANDED WITH AN IRON. Scraped the circle dust, pierce-imagined centaur: the speech amphitheatre of stain's flowering. A CLEAN BONE RAKES THE GROUND ROTATIONALLY AROUND AN ARROW WHICH HOVERS ABOVE THE CENTAUR: A BAYING ROMAN CROWD'S SHOUTS PROCURE BLOOD, WHICH PRODUCES A ROSE. Hanging tryst, burnt has throat: jugular mansion streams soil. THE SCAFFOLD ROPE HANGS OVER TWO LOVERS EMBRACING, BLOOD SPRAYING FROM THEIR NECKS TO PRODUCE A HOUSE ON WET GROUND. A wet digit mirror by which laughter in quarantines is lame. A STEAMED REFLEXION OF FINGERS STUFFED INTO THE MOUTH OF A MAN ON CRUTCHES WITHIN A FENCE. The flame is clutched and in defiled spools. A SMALL LANTERN IS GRIPPED IN HIS OTHER HAND AND THE WAX POOLS ON DIRTY GROUND. Orator hens tower the house. A CHICKEN COOP OF CONVERSATIONAL BIRDS OVERSHADOWS THE SMALL MANSION. The sight mirror, end-trampled. A REFLECTIVE GLASS IS CRUSHED AND SHATTERED BY A BOOT ALONG ONE EDGE. A citadel of swabbed muscle. A CITY WHOSE EVERY WINDOW AND DOOR IS HUNG WITH RAW MEAT.

6) The contorting face –
bloodied nest in jet grasses –
is wristed in sorrow.

7) In memory river: ribboned corpse. THE RIVER LETHE
CONTAINS A BODY TIED WITH BOWS OF SILK.
The colossos pit, in end-lame grasses break in wristed clod.
IN THE COLOSSEUM, WILD CLUMPS OF GRASS
CLUTCHED IN THE HAND BRUSH THE WRIST OF
THE CENTAUR. I make the sawdust arrow-soul into
hunting; honey to coach colour-bone. AN ARROW OF
COMPACTED HONEY AND SAWDUST IS TAUGHT
TO HUNT A SPECTRUM SKELETON. Snow-numb,
sound marrow, flame-face circling water-skeletal madrigal.
A FROZEN SKELETON CHOIR WITH BURNING
TORCHES SINGS IN THE SNOW IN A CIRCLE.

8) The whole throat flowers,
madrigal of flame and dust,
then blooms into co(r)pse.

9) Last fighter galloped off and hazed in sphere. THE
RECEDING FORM OF A CENTAUR DISAPPEARS AS
IF IN FOG. The end centaur. WE SEE THE TAIL OF
THE VANISHING CREATURE. Hidden is the jet arrow.
AN OBSIDIAN ARROW HEAD GLINTS, HALF HID-
DEN IN SAND. Is of lens-thumbed colossus, made blench
in white. ON FINGER PRINTED GLASS SLIDES, THE
SUN BLEACHES PALE MAPS. Killer it away: cracked
dust, knotted arrow, sleeps against contorted amphitheatre
bleeds. Death throat is hair code is finger hooked. Quivering.
A WOMAN SHAKES A FRUIT TREE. Horoscopi in
bestiarum. THE ZODIAC SIGNS PEER FROM A ZOO-
LOGICAL GARDEN. Is hooped back from decision. A
WOMAN REMOVES CIRCULAR EARRINGS. Quarter,
half, full, century fathom. A CAKE INSCRIBED 'C' IS
CUT UNDERWATER. Book-licked tension. A MAN
AND WOMAN GLARE AT EACH OTHER WHILST
SIMULTANEOUSLY LICKING THE PAGES OF A
BOOK. Fruit falls from sight. APPLES, PEARS AND
PLUMS FALL FROM A WOMAN'S EYES. Wax of heart
encloses the honeycomb. A BEE'S NEST EMBEDDED

IN A WAX VENTRICLE. Black dew of honey-sealed sight. EYES CARVED FROM BEESWAX WEEP DARK TEARS. Do not slacken sight: teeth: tears: blood. A BLINDFOLD TIED AROUND THIS WAX CARVED HEAD IS BRIGHT RED AND STITCHED WITH TEARS AND TEETH. Sand of flame smeared on a heart for defile-sifting thicket. MARINE FIRE IMMOLATING A DEER/FOAL IN A WINDBLOWN COPSE.

1) A burning scarecrow scatters seeds. A scholar skeleton made of sand, tramples a pudding made of corpses. A man dressed as daytime sawing up skulls in a pot of wood, a sieve of trunks, a bristling dog rolls over a mutilated hare, weeping, which makes a bed wet. Dead mirror waste. Heavenly bodies carved in ice: the man slips. Daytime: a thunder cloud mirrors the picture of a body in a canon breaking the darkness of building blocks that surround a round well on which a dish of grain lies. A hot knife falls into a hole, making a stinking cloud. Daylight eaten by a golden-haired man: solar. A pallid individual drinks a beach through a straw.

2) The responding anamorphic IA focusses on reversals: breath (how can the action of breath be reversed for vision-making? Up/down, as opposed to in/out? No breath? Morbid breathlessness?) Here the IA manifests as anxious, bogged down, in assessing the act of prophecy. Perhaps circling suggests stasis or it could mean momentum. The omen is still warping.

3) Yew tree rusting. An arrow pointing at a mound of powder. Female deer running in the circus. A human hip attached to a bleeding compass. Huge statue flinging seeds, tombstones, a splinter. Gallows and bells, etched on tombstones. A burning bow.

4) The anamorphic IA here suggests cowardice in confronting and embarking on the act of envisioning, perhaps due to the difficult conditions or circumstances involved. Fear is at large.

5) In a sand storm, a minaret is on fire while a priest sings

into a fat nest filled with a demolished world whose earth is mixed with blood, silver and heart muscle – a skinned centaur branded with an iron. A clean bone rakes the ground rotationally around an arrow which hovers above the centaur: a baying Roman crowd's shouts procure blood, which produces a rose. The scaffold rope hangs over two lovers embracing, blood spraying from their necks to produce a house on wet ground. A steamed reflexion of fingers stuffed into the mouth of a man on crutches within a fence. A small lantern is gripped in his other hand and the wax pools on dirty ground. A chicken coop of conversational birds overshadows the small mansion. A reflective glass is crushed and shattered by a boot along one edge. A city whose every window and door is hung with raw meat.

6) The anamorphic IA is of the gateway into second seeing. The expression is anamorphic itself, contorted to accommodate the conditions of dream: bloody and full of upset.

7) The River Lethe contains a body tied with bows of silk. In the colosseum, wild clumps of grass clutched in the hand brush the wrist of the centaur. An arrow of compacted honey and sawdust is taught to hunt a spectrum skeleton. A frozen skeleton choir with burning torches sings in the snow in a circle.

8) The penultimate anamorphic IA in this sequence indicates a fully-blown vision: the recipient (myself) is subject to a violent, vocal blooming which climaxes in death. Whether this is a partial or full death, is not indicated.

9) The receding form of a centaur disappears as if in fog. We see the tail of the vanishing creature. An obsidian arrowhead glints, half hidden in sand. On fingerprinted glass slides, the sun bleaches pale maps. A woman shakes a fruit tree. The zodiac signs peer from a zoological garden. A woman removes circular earrings. A cake inscribed 'c' is cut underwater. A man and woman glare at each other whilst simultaneously licking the pages of a book. Apples, pears and plums fall from a woman's eyes. A bee's nest embedded in a wax ventricle. Eyes carved from beeswax

weep dark tears. A blindfold tied around this wax-carved head is scarlet and stitched with tears and teeth. Marine fire immolates a deer/foal in a windblown copse.

Diagnostic: Great courage will be required to undertake the conditions of dream: being in the custody of dream, in order to receive it but also to die to it/within it either wholly or partially. The risk for me is unknown in terms of whether the vision will subsume me or cause great and fatal risk as a condition of its undertaking.

CENTRAL TAGHAIRM IA

An arrow-struck centaur,
chafed by sawdust flowers,
stalks contorted dream.

*

'You must know, Luce, that he has perished somewhere: here or elsewhere, but somewhere.' Hafoc slowly turns the pages of his loggbok.

'Yes,' I respond, begrudging Hafoc her terminal thought, 'somewhere, lies his vanishing point. Perhaps not the act of death, though… perhaps… disappearance into an island mound. You know he was bound up for three nights in that sea cave on the southern tip?'

'You told me so… though, of course I didn't see it…' she eyes me, amber-set obsidian contracting, calculating, measuring the distance of truth.

'I will go out and find the things he has left at each place,' I say, 'I know the island. You and I will speak in the evenings and piece things together, bit by bit.'

'Yes,' she replies, without looking up. 'Though this may well not cohere, in the end.'

I say nothing and stare at Kristján's small island map on the table. Then the quiet revelation arises, shivering like a marine-

water mirage in the heat of intensive thought: 'Each site,' I say
slowly, nodding them in, 'each site is a station on his journey of
death. He lands here, on fire, in an old skiff. Incidentally washes
up on the beach. But his boat was bobbing in the small, aban-
doned harbour and there was clear reason for that – I had thought
it was just cast adrift as he waded the shallows, panicking. Quite
the opposite. He ensured the rowing boat met its destination,
even as he headed for the shoreline. In Kristján's mind he was
a death-bound pilgrim, sailing to Eilean a' Bhàis in a barque
filled with chthonic paperwork on memory. Look at the map:
Port nam Marbh – the Port of the Dead.'

STATION I

The Port of the Dead

(The Port of the Dead is where I wash up to travel the lines of death through this seawater fissure, blamed in fire, thirsted in salt. My books and papers comfort me still and I arise, a wrecked figurehead on the shores of the Isle of the Dead. Dysfunctional and forgotten, the architectural features of Bàs, such as the monastery and lighthouse, lie derelict. The only spirit guide present is myself, though other presences manifest on my death journey. Luce Moncrieff might be seen as a source of self-reflexion but she more mirrors my speculative self than guides me on my way, it seems. The Ferryman of death: self-propelled as I arrive at the Port nam Marbh, but shipwrecked in fire and saltwater. Laid out on the landing stone of the 'Eala', I consider this the stone of knowledge and transform my past. Transformation. The associative object is a helix of wind: my knitted yarn.)

LANDING ON THE SHORES of astonishment. What is this stone, but a stage or platform for corpse bundles to be honoured? And so, the Eala... the altar of dream, where the dead are placed to breathe the port air and mouth one word: O: into the blackness... here, the rusty rivets from galleys and barges can still be found, from the rotted coracles buried in peach-coloured sands... those vessels the shore turf thinly disguises.

Did he die lying asleep on the beach? Might he have been found dead on the sand? Perhaps he got into his half-burnt rowing boat, his papyrus skiff, and sat there until the wind blew the shore sands over him... or was he tied naked to the prow of a great fighting vessel that ran aground, secured like a tattered figurehead in knotted, sea-eaten ropes that the winds tugged at by night, his lifeless head lolling, his eyes pecked out by seabirds, his mouth open and his tongue caked in salt? Or perhaps he had a coffin built into the great arms of the pine tree where the saline planks and joists creak at night, wedged in its branches.

I have tracked the ancient port stones; the jetty and the harbour wall and eventually – finding these buried in the green-turfed mound – have dug up his mouldy knitting, enfolded in a scorched sheet of paper, to return to the lighthouse with this first, soiled package:

*

Flame-whelped, stick water. Hope salts my waterfall only to a fire-scattered love for bloods, soft the backs: vicious kelps and bleached string, lunar fishes cough-stamped still wild, mystery lichen. The howled stones, roan, crude my colours to the west. Crashed ruins, bluster keystones and the dry, a faded coffin that papers the eyes among. Buried coracles that attempted bodies, wind-filled rhetors, water-marked cliffs broil my seething moon. The path blaze-pitched and was high: the colour tang of hard rainbows. Calcified overcoat, light-drowned my sheer rearrangements earthed offshore. Most prows say oars, the figure in black barking himself, undying me, marking beach in burned charm and cinnamon. Lintels of the coffee beacon and a lava-stamping lifetime flecked me obsidian in surely mid-summer fields. Long moonlight, untimely, modest, dark speeches drown traditional salt. Ruins of her near out-wards outcrops, venerable winds, rubbed whirlpool of ocean. The mouth port flecked. Salt in seams for harsh cobalt grounds sphering sun throat, sandied on continu-ously buried buildings. These rolled deer edges... Minerals of the figure, sculled in floated embers I tomb upon boat squawking. Stitch the dead-shaved first dreams, in older saline a wax, urgent out in cries of the dead bog and ashen-stark, pink acts. Take sea and quick close its sat asleep hurt. Cobalt grounds note the sea saltwater. Packed wax, little rocks, exhausted the pyre as the dead rowed, released modest transformation solar-evaporated, palm upwards open tombs. Embers, offerings. All was touch alight. A still buffing recollection. Rumour-light, malefic tundra, the Marbh ink of the road and scrub birds stark-clamped to the pollen of ocean. Recall the grasses, pages, abandoned to forgetting libraries: bitumen seed and frightening, webbed nature. Longingly, volumes soaked, infeeding to water. A monastery-blown dram and times the boat herds for mariner to restore Hebridean wrecks that chink these in the road night with the storm badly, island's providing known sun-dank, washed solitary, were and into lots: totems: palaces: winds: pagan-reminds my massy books, I brought leaking buffeting. Fires, islands with stinking underworld too hot. Water-pale, nocturnal lettering staggered, rowed centuries, found world by the endless coffin. Congealing drowners. Whisky-walled heat. Morph heather and sandy bog. Flints stand with stars, water-hardened, pressed magic-knowledge large rocks, crafty sea water. At fire, my books. Drowner's tobacco, sun my mirror form, basalt-black ignition in the rune blush. Charred the ruin on rages. Saline hurt of derelict lungs. Wildlife's mortal stench.

*

The mourners poured their grief over the dead at the 'Eala' whose description has evaded the scholars: not the 'eala' used to define the swan; neither derived from the 'ealatrom' or coffin ('how strange,' I think, 'that this should remind me of the eutrom: another word for Kristján's Sluagh which I must have read in his notes') – no, the 'Eala' is the sepulchre, the tomb whose variant spellings are complex and numerous; some also suggest-ing raised fishing rocks or treasure troves… when a corpse was laid on the stone, the wet-eyed lamenters performed a deisiol three times sunwise in a clockwise motion around the 'Eala' as perhaps the Druids had done.

*

…because the skull and teeth play it equally: it is not a usual instrument, it must have human enamel and carti-lage factored into it and so is Ossian but also osseous, also ossified: a harp of clenched intonation, of determination, belonging to the human skull; mandible and lachrimal, the tears of bone marrow, all performed on a stone stage on an isle of the dead.

The notes of the harp or lyre purify and polish the mirror of dreams so that sleep may be charmed by its sound into submission. This is not the wild-winded sleep that is brought about by heavy silence. This is the carefully plucked dream notation: measured and successful.

STATION II

The Dead Lighthouse

(The Charred Arrow Shaft is the Lightning-struck Tower (tarot) and this tallies well on the map, being the site of a recently dead or out-of-use lighthouse. For me, the tower stands for a watchtower, but also the Dead Lighthouse is the anamorphic cylinder of the island which holds its chaos in a thumbprint or warped reflexion and whose inner life is a snuffed warning to those advancing toward this abandoned death port. It is also an arena of reversed play: an activation point and enables me to build my plans. The Bàs lighthouse embodies a much larger presence which I superimpose on the circular form of the colosseum so that it looms like a large lens, or eye. This sawdust or sand-filled arena provides the horizontal discus for imagination. In it, I perform back to the empty seats (a nod to Camillo's Memory Theatre) my own death rites as centaur – beast of my natal constellation. I created an interior arena on one floor of the lighthouse, covering the floorboards in sand I brought up in flour sacks from the beach. I placed each of the figureheads in a ring as an audience around the periphery of the room and made 'strange markings in the sand.' I worked anticlockwise in this place, whose central 'stone' (or 'Eala') might be perceived as the buried book. I see my own reflexion in the dead lighthouse which I have myself extinguished. This enables me to reflect on my predicament and how to escape it. Self-reflexion. The associative object is a warped coffin lid: my rectangular steel shaving mirror.)

HAD HE DECIDED THE lighthouse itself was a marooned figure-head, illuminated by his piles of books; a crustacean library, lined in salt? Deepwater thought? The vanished Norgé: philosopher of the hidden, shadowy notions, raging angels, familiar demons, sepulchral boats, fetches, sycophants, all lit up in the quick fire – the quickened fire of memory. And here lies the playing card of his birth: the wounded centaur, fallen to the ground: pierced by its own sagittal thought. I pick it up...it is faded and creased ...a fortune-telling card for the dialect of the future that speaks with a mouth full of bloody sand. With it, are his mirror and the long Sluagh tract: 'my darkest wounds, I heal with blood...', etc:

Wind-dared, light-tower. Murmuring smoke speak dumb-struck, heart pressed. I light disperse of wound. End of arrow-trowelled mortar. Nocking shot shadow drifts, one fingertip. In reflexion: steel: the tower has upstaged itself. The theatre is in reflexion cannibal. The arrow is back-fired to completion. My mirror flank is wet with dust. Ribboned in streams of soil. Panic herb. All masonry swabbed in destruction. The citadel crumbled and here, the light-tower: lightning struck, collapse. Ridiculous (dust) of obelisk. Not looped, language turned. Bitter in broken. The leopard hoop stands empty. Whose rubble – coins the fall? All collapsed brutal. Charged to heart and self. How is it earned again? Not to toil, but to back-stubble animal. All ruinous. Slipshod of humble. Lighting recollected. Revising and reversing. Brick stoney and flesh stoney and spirit stoney, nicked. Kolossos. Colosseum: mirror breaks in imagined fragments, fractured, the lame. Picture the systems rub. Shock the mud. The borne aim back trust, whole foundations – in these stones, sight-darkness is dead dust, whose rock bones off-voice, rubs rings. END. End of bricking with marrow. End of arrow-dug foundations. End of arrow-pierced stone, of stone amphitheatre – arrow-scraped graffito. Because tongues collapse, in swabbed aim systems, attitude bones. Because stone bitter breaks the precinct – broken-in flints with mortar ends humble toil-language. The ten disperse sleeps crumbled debris: derelict ash-framed fireplace. Custody of dream. How stone rings as circle reflects. End-flicked, broken mud, fractured, swabs with frame completion. Horse of these, stands in disperse leopard or lion or wolf or mule wound to burnt back. Charged stubble of lens back-hooped. This mirror-stubbed lightning, building collapse, atop indrifts of dust. The marrow sand. The smeared stone. The picture pierced, shot. The rank foundation muscle. Ribboned, wet-borne arrow, shocked convex, brutal. Colossos circle, mirror of sand-smeared muscle, reflects no subject. Lens of burnt murmur, (skeletal colosseum,) in the precinct sleeps.

*

Are the marks on the compact floor of his colosseum chamber – that weird tablature – possibly his hoofmarks of Christ the fool, and the footprints of his attendant crucifiers, this demiurge of smoke and mirrors? A pulped body in sacking and sand lies rotting in his inner vision – like the punctured body of the half-god: six quills piercing his right hand, vision like shattered glass... glass once sand, once sanguine. I feel relieved to have found his polished steel mirror: a warped inflection of his own hurts. He had clearly become irrevocably convinced by this presence of Monmhur; which was so obviously himself. The mirror sleeps in my hands: a pyrographic screed with a fragment of star code on the reverse side.

*

Therein lies the problem. The field, the room, the stanza, the place has become entirely squared and therefore mas-culine. The courts, the temples are squared. The lack of helix; anti-helix. Lack of the feminine. How to find the entangled undergrowth of the page. The act of writing is male doctrine. The positioning of the page, the square is the altar, the court. So writing becomes writhing; the river, the whirlpool – essentially circular, essentially oracular. The Colosseum in terms of the emptied skeleton, waiting to be filled with avid drama. I think of Camillo's Memory Theatre, banked up with seven rows of empty seats and the lone spectator – where the actor should be – who stands, look-ing up and witnesses the tiers as central to understanding. The lion gazing on the sand, like John Dee's lion having strayed into the ancient memory of the amphitheatre to kill and be killed again and again. This is ravaged memory. The bones of memory as ocular... seeing devices.

STATION III

The Old Coffin Road

(The Star-Ravaged Co(r)pse – the initial vision is of a
stellar body having passed through and in so doing, hav-
ing destroyed a wood or copse. It is a presence or atmo-
sphere of spirit which the body must progress through, as
a kind of aether, which ages the flesh. This ageing must
then be worn into death. It is the spirit which wearies and
acts upon the physical body of the individual advancing
through the spirit's presence in one's life. I envisage the
spirit as invisible but as an active agent that pools around
the person's body in a cloud or atmosphere. The spirit
can only be perceived through its effect which appears as
ageing in the flesh of the human by its own spirit. I pre-
sent this argument in the metaphoric image of the star
crashing through and so annihilating the undergrowth.
Whether I see the star as uniquely personified or attendant
to all who make such a temporal journey, is unclear except
for the fact that I align myself as poet to this trajectory.
The Old Coffin Road is the length of my dying thought
in tramping the trackways of devised amnesia: the full
length of sorrowful thought. Walking the star-destroyed
coffin road I contemplate 'meat spirit', my conditions as
poet and my life, and determine how to continue. Will.
The associative object is an osseous lyre: my jaw harp.)

THERE IS SCANT COFFIN wood on Eilean a' Bhàis. A copse of
worsted thorn trees tangles along the sea path and edges the
boulders of the Sraid nam Marbh, the old coffin road, but in
times past the islanders relied on driftwood and sometimes not
at all, laying their dead in the ground, tightly bound in linen.
For conveying the corpse to its grave, a dead bed or 'cro-leapa',
was used. The last cro-leapa was said to have been buried with
the body it carried. And, the last bier was said to have been
smashed against a thorn tree in island folklore of the Hebrides,
and irreparably damaged, to prevent the Sluagh nam Marbh

from later using it to convey the corpse away in its devouring currents...

A stand of pines and clusters of wild palm trees on the western side of the island, where the North Atlantic Drift brings in tropical currents, are all we have had to carpenter coffins, and so the Sraid nam Marbh is badly named. History has told of coffins rowed in from the mainland to be buried in our small island enclave, of strangers' corpses dug into the ground here to avoid wolves, and later bodysnatchers. I never saw a mortsafe in among the old marine graves or up at the kirkyard site, crouching like a surfaced mantrap over a tomb.

*

> Reversing the theme of the spirit contained within the body
> and considering the body or meat as having to move through
> the spirit – in the way that we alter time through existing.
> So, in this sense the spirit ages the body – it is a spirit
> field or emanated area but it is also a conceit, because it is
> linked to time itself.

*

Now, stramping the rough track in the early cold of a late January morning with breath rising like a familiar ghost, my oil lamp casts strange shadows across trees bent and flattened with the storms. Somehow the accident has made me stronger. In my pocket is the folded scrap of paper I at last found in the figurehead room he'd filled with sand on the third floor of the lighthouse. It was only a few days ago that we found them standing in their odd circle – some that were washed up, dragged from the old marine garden; others he had carved on his own. Until then, nothing was known. How some things are always close to being lost. How Kristján might have hidden this from me, in the end. I could easily have drawn together his other notes and writings, tried to find a willing small press, independently published them. Now, all that has changed. I have been up all night,

307

reading and everything I have discovered in the past three weeks either pales into insignificance or is only important in relation to this. All those disjointed ramblings about memory and the colosseum... that sand-filled circular room... his three day vanishing. I think it is a test – perhaps if I play the game, he will return. Perhaps he is hiding. Perhaps he is watching.

I sit by the lighthouse fire, as usual and read it again, then sift through his other instructions – impressed by their clarity. Here is his strange celestial metre, or starn metre, distilled from fragments of constellation..

There were yet more lists and these are what led me on the bier road this morning, thinking to take Kristján at his word:

THE CONDITION

The star or meteoric body that has passed through the first page, close to the ground, causing the wooded place or forest it has moved through to evidence its path; broken-twigged, mud-screeded, nest-burnt. Perhaps smoking from a corpus of fire-scarred and coalish underwood. This is evidence of the first night. This is a track, rather than a pattern poem. The contents of a ravaged passing.

THE RESIDUE

The exploded part of the 'doodwegen'; the medieval Dutch death road and the 'Geisterwegen'; the old Germanic ghost road. This is a poetic ley line along which we track. A melted wax tablet.

THE MEANING

Inclusion of words as if recipe ingredients through the impact of their etymologies, less their sounds (though both are intrinsically linked). Scale.

*

And so now I am here, a living body on a dead coffin road, trudging up to the monastery. And as dawn illustrates itself in shot pink and azure, I catch my breath – as always I do – at the sheer beauty of Bàs, whose thorn trees are spangled with thick, wet cobwebs hung with the evidence of the night's dampness and already heavily rippling with a firm breeze that tells me the wind will be here again. I whistle for Varg and he comes racing, too lively a beast for the underworld's taking.

The corpse road isn't long: about a mile or so, but in the curdling mist even the trees are obscured and I am hunting for his oxidised jaw harp. The old cloot trees would be covered in laces and rags, tied on as offerings and prayers. One harp hung in a thorny bank. Then I remember the single thorn, half a mile along the road, within sight of the old monastery. It stands in its own shadow as a wild thing, blackly and densely, and has seen many a coffin pass, raised on aching shoulders. Bent and blown nearly double, the thorn's rootwork is knotted and raised. I go up to the gnarled bark and trace the moss on the trunk. The light is a clear grey now and looking up, I spy something dangling in the lower branches – the rusty hoop of his jaw harp, with that strange twang, wrapped in another burnt sheet of paper:

*

And then, burnt, than splintered smoking, I pathed this memory-broken forest: which moved: coalish night of shattered, wooded, nest-corpus. Scarred passing-fire seemed deepest thicket or twigged falter. A co(r)pse. This perhaps THEN faltered page evidence. Lost. Within the from-first place, thought close and ill, point-scored underwood, evidenced ground in track-ravaged contents; defined pattern, first-form screeded. Human-pooled, the passing of the insistence-person be: X D E O: Neolithic spirit contents. THIS presence, old to the time-too symbol – X body – a passing form operated around which through the human. In arable time through, but immolation-person, kind land-marked-told. Co-physical aged prayer, belief been star-ravaged, subjects perform of only merely the grove spirit, lie with metaphor. The in-anatomy kind, as made pooled of have, signifies the body question/place: time: fiery-cause starlife ritual, which represents/whorls the individual. Anamorphic, wheat-worn turnstile. Dead and tears. No violence-tract outcrops footing of tang-print woodland marauders at very north, while you shoot-copse road, looking like matter beaten. Now you rill dusk, molar-gentle. You – pass: dusk, molar-gentle. X you pass: no late skills. Everything in disarray: dead horses, dangerous guess femurs sawed into materials but no wood mutilated. You: a coffin poet, repulsed on singing winds, yes – vigorously travelled. Thirst, yes. Devastated, dead gentle in woodland. Guesses and violence. A guess shade. A co(r)pse that through-warped nothing, obliged. Wood of courage, art thou dead? Low-processed guesses halt my procedure. Shadow. There is a wood-snapped currency filtered through bone-kept sound. I am an osseous lyre. What the drum bones destroy in troubadour alone, is by no means musical. Lost tibiae garden songs. Some furred, mating with sound. A drum abjured becomes knees, warped femurs. Present country breath is saint honour; the poet there myself for leave, sang. On small trace burring is a bark. The damage-lyre, the thought-box, has been heat at the wind's direction and is now all river's impulsed in wick-scattering and the wood-own has a digit thirst of skeletons, warping in the find-summoned night. And shoulders to such savage fatigue. Water range waxes hoarse. Winter lithic. Haunted tongue is young Medieval at first. Jurisprudence. Then, torn, mimics watching l and comes circlet-quick to healing, skull kneels in reverent prayer to other, Neolithic recollection. Have there those earliest survivors of tongue-bait: X D E O S P H Z. The skull waits time. DEO seen in darkness; back-remembrance. Summon-taut my bones, warped springs fading through spirit-looking. I think me bone-provoked, beaten. Gentle in beast, a poet body, disarrayed wood-song, lurching at some essence-shoot, outside embrace, ravaged.

*

I see a meteoric body, a star or something star-like, passing through a copse, a wood, and leaving complete destruction behind it. In my mind's eye, the trail is all that's left. And

I think this is the body, travelling through the spirit. And I think this is the co(r)pse: the body in the wood. And then I came across a co(r)pse of ill-defined wood in which the tree forms seemed shattered, splintered and burnt. The star or meteoric body has passed through this first page, close to the ground, causing the wooded place or forest it has moved through to evidence its path; broken-twigged, mud-screeded, nest-burnt. Perhaps smoking from a corpus of fire-scarred and coalish underwood. This is evidence of the first night. This is a track, rather than a pattern. The contents of a ravaged passing. The deepest point in the thicket is thought. The co(r)pse is merely a metaphor. It represents the body. An individual's body is aged by passing through the contents of the spirit. It is the spirit, which operates as a kind of pooled presence around the physical form of a human, that subjects the anatomy of the person to the ravages of time. This time is the lifetime of the person in question.

It is the body of the star, passing through the presence of the wood. We might make the body of the star abstract: already a conflagration of fading dust. We might make the self or the presence or the animating spirit the wood, webbed with all woods. And so the human body, the animal body, passes through the presence of self. Not that the self or soul inhabits temporarily or passes through the body.

> Webbed with all woods –
> silver nest in jet grass –
> stood, concomitant,
> yet aflame.

> In the pores of heart
> burnt a history of.

Star in the undergrowth (not a moon) – the meat of the body as aged by its passing through the terrain of spirit; the spirit as terrain.

STATION IV

The Ruined Lunar Mansion

(The Ruined Lunar Mansion is where the lion purges fear from my innermost being, like sweat, and is a place of keen reckoning. This not a demon-haunted quarter, this is a slipping recognition of selves, all similar, all different, in wrecked fireplaces and slipped masonry. The shadow allotment of stars. Al Jab'Hah – here we have the ruined mansion standing for Lunar Mansion X in the Arabic system, (my mansion of birth), filled with lions. The Arabic mansion name, Al Jab'Hah, refers to the forehead of the lion and this is used as a seeing or scrying device, subsequently referencing the Neolithic remains of cave lions used in prehistoric mark making. I also worked in relation to lunar mansion sonics which, in the Arabic tradition, were sounded as the twenty-eight models of spoken letters: Mansion X sound is 'sh'. I identified leonine presences as lurking shadows of my own selfhood and perceived the outside structure of this mansion as decayed, derelict and abandoned. This of course, the site where I built an enclosure for the young lion I found washed up in a circus freight. Lunar Mansion X, the house of my birth, stands in ruins but is overrun by lions who govern my human heart, my forehead of instinct, but also the back of my head – the occiput – in sensing, and can be confused as merely skins. Inspiration. The associative object is a lion skin wristband: real in both existences.)

LUNAR MANSION 10, AL-JAB'HAH (The Forehead)
25° 42′ 51″ Cancer – 8° 34 17″ Leo
Agrippa: It strengthens buildings, yields love, benevolence and help against enemies.
Volguine: Considered a favourable factor in social elevation, particularly where due to the native's own efforts.
Volguine: Indicates a broad field of activity and is believed to exert a favourable influence from a spiritual aspect.
Ashmole 396: When the Moon is in this Mansion, make

weddings. Take no journey. Borrow not. Wear no new clothes, apparel not your wife. <u>Build, for it shall be durable.</u> Take fellowship, for it is good. Beware of seizing for long imprisonment.

Volguine: Indicates a mixture of kindness and calculation.

Volguine: Considered very favourable from all aspects, for studies as well as for earnings, for professional success as well as for love; but often makes the native very sensitive to the feelings of others and inclines him to abuse of drugs and medications.

Lions pad among the mansion ruins. If the wood is Dante's, then prudence and Medieval aspects of mnemotechnics must be seen also as his. The leopard, the she-wolf, the lion. I have tried dissecting Canto I, to see its guts. A kind of paper haruspicy. What I hope to find are the prehistoric animals of the earliest self... the infant that is lion. Perhaps then the Neolithic lettering which survives, the Z, H, P, S, X, D, E, O, and these letters are the X of the tenth lunar mansion – the forehead of the lion, lEO and the D – the half-moon – of 500 Arabic units in Roman calculation. This, from Dante: 'Day was departing, and the embrowned air/released the animals that are on earth from their fatigues...' and then the embrowned brow of the Neolithic cave lion, the lunar mansion X. Day – and dormancy – left this lion behind and the clarity and alertness of nocturnal vision ensued. What kind of pit would double as a lion pit and a lunar pit? What kind of pit mirror holds the death of a lion and the position of the moon. These are the sinews of my thinking... the lunar sinews.

And the land of stones turned in my tongue. And the land of stones tuned my tongue. In the wind
swept places there were none and fire
turned on fire.

Whose is the name?
Whose is the name without calling is fire,
sweet to sound. All ravage.
All ravage done in desert conflagration.
I poured fire into it until it turned.

*

And so, I note, when outlining the appearance of the lunar mansion (as Kristján would have it), the symbolic descriptions are not to be taken at face value but actually delineate the spatial relationships between the archaeoastronomy of the site: between windows and doors: the rooms' length and height: the elevation of what once was the roof. Of course, this is now a ruined stellar site: all such measurements can still be perceived but are no longer robust – the length of a wall which has a portion missing can no longer be measured as a whole but must have the missing part accounted for, even though it is the ghost or trace of that measurement and could otherwise be used in attaining a figure. Now, this is not the case. I pad around myself in the loping shadows and hunt for the next package... it is there, placed in an empty hearth: a strip of lion skin curled at the centre of his folded writing:

*

Lion carcase saith me: fire. Stroketh fat, seemeth to lick. Come dead, stroketh. Now putteth me in word and, seemeth to lick me, became principal hair for bush. Saith wilderness. The earth, dead lean. Flags be dead. And taketh stones and earth. The wordstone again. Now, wintertime disperseth. Saith wilderness. The altar is fascinated by bone. First diggeth the senses. Take the fair tail. Putteth out comfort and bramble up. The amnesiac bone is wilderness-carcase. All rugged bone. Stroketh leaves. No–not pride: courage. Only one. Hunger-mad with young courage. Wood-snapped. Death, which men water-planted, piteously lasted a short gaze. Embrowned. Inconsolable. Harassed heart. Hungerings of air. Not uplifted, hoarse fire. Comes before me: dark forehead. Save downward things be answered, I am ravenous. Bitter, abroad animals. Thrust lofty – thou fear a good skin – was said. Lion forehead spores, glimmering. Abandon breath of things air-bitter. Wood amnesiac. First, colour ruthless. Beast senses to grey of fire, rugged waxes. Spoor smaller –

transverse and dead dark. Disperseth skin leaves. Deserted tools. Stones of fear. Moonwort and coppice. No brush-word presents crumpled lovebreath. Hungerings carinated, spalling to person, piteously smoke. The skull mansion breathes in crybounded heat, paused, estranging and frame-up-to-time. DERELICT SH of time. Blink darkness steps stellar-sound. Whets the pillars in moonlight, – derelict within the SH. Trapped longer it has a hush; fizzed where pressure desiccates and in glimmers stand lions slipsweating, lions who flicker back. Sound only dints bone as dazed, one lion's outer fire, solemnly thirsty, still in images comes, movements roiling. My crumbling air turns footfire slowly, shadowy stonebreath on head bone as body CLEARS the flies… and lions of decided, destroyed colour, disappear, limbless. The walls more trick, old-touch, wilderness great smoke – den sealed smoke in old-responding mansion – star-panting seals up my face. All lions air-mirror. Steeled smoke. All growing shifty on dusk, new-wet pads dried – place in motion, back-roiling bone, dusky roar-rivering mansion. Wilderness hock. A shuffle of musk showing in the new-hinted night. Of not, they pace where and face its frame, but wooded and stand clear, as had those walls touched leonine backslipping form. I, bruised with sweat-ing, would shadow dusk, holding stellar the stir. Fire, it's all their wonder, the like-realised breathes in, skull-to and for its abandoned, dried-plodding cry, realises lion-parched images. Parched, thirsty clouds, a lion's foot. I desiccate metal into a moment-mansion. Dinted. Trapped, navigate, so stand and contained eyes. Then air-ravaged, stock, musk, moonlight heart. Blink-roiling: derelict in dusk. Air den, dusk, smoke and themselves mid-vision, roar-flickered out, I in entranceway HAD bone, did the responding between solemn pack-panting – respond limbless on river wilder-ness toward dead-looked and I CLEAR me: come of swift which great-made lions have, as crystalline grows the band. I have new light, star in place-movement of cry, so move-ment – something air-held – pressure-lowering motion toward sound-mirror, on turn of breath. Within glimmer-pads: fire as torso. Wet-crumbling movements fizzed-in and am first hardened, have in darkness. Pillars are with face-up, fixed steps, release an oily tang. My stillness: bounded-caught as estranging tears. If place-hush they destroy, comes old courage in columns. Holding cry: skull-band of disappearing body pressure, a fainter heat, I face a place utterly flies and for air – bruised eyes responding stench and its tears – step onto crumbling-shone occiput.

STATION V

The Gate of the Ford of the Dead

(Sequences for A Tariff – at the ford of the gate of the
dead stands a wolf and I must pay a numinous tariff in
order to pass. Though I have already landed, or been
landed on the shores of the derelict Port nam Marbh, I
have not yet paid my dues to make the necessary crossing.
At the Gate of the Ford of the Dead, I must forfeit tariffs
of self-awareness to continue. I must give up offerings of
denial, pride, hope. Melancholy. The associative object is
a withered wheat stem: my walking stick.)

'VARG IS NOT WHOLLY a wolf, but is defined by the strength
of wolfishness within him,' Kristján had observed one day as he
walked toward the summer ford: a floor of corrugated dust with
cracked alphabets and scores of the river's histories. A burn of
the dead.

'You,' he continued, 'are not quite human, as shown by the
level of lucidity found in your blood. You have an uncanny light
about you. And,' he added, squatting in the shallows that now
had vanished, 'you have the ability to appear and disappear at
will and very swiftly. Most certainly a mark of the otherworld.
This is strange,' he said and raised a small object to his lips to
taste it. 'It is a fragment of bone but not human… and significant.
A mandible.' He pocketed it. 'Alexander lost his voice when
drinking from the river of death. I wonder what this river lost
through being sampled – Varg!' he bellowed. 'Something has
caused it to dry up.'

'It happens every year.'

'Yes, the heat has taken it, the sun has drunk from the river's
peat water and found it so sweet, thought she would finish it –
not to mention the moon, who must be parched for milk and
finds the liquid silver under her own influence. What offerings
do the sun and moon leave as tariffs for their interference, as

317

they sink down, drowning into the river's currents? There is burnish to consider, and heat and the pull and push of nocturnal elements… but do they drawn in drownings: such as this wolf? Here –' he passed me the jawbone.

'That is from a female skull,' he said. 'I think perhaps the wolf was an offering that the moon laid down into the water in order that she may quench her thirst. Perhaps there are packs and packs of wolves lying curled on the riverbed, their bodies indenting the soft peat soil. This one, at any rate, is our tariff for deciphering this language of the dead.'

He crouched on his haunches again and for a moment, the sun in my eyes, when he looked at me – me standing a little way off, not really listening to what he said, wondering if the blackberries would soon be in season, turned when he paused and saw him as a wolf. Then Varg had come and stood on the other side of the dried-up ford and the air was very still; shimmering. When I looked back at the bushes again, I saw Varg scampering toward me, tongue lolling and could not fathom how he'd made the distance, but Kristján was already off, before I could question him, wielding his staff like an underworld gondolier whose vessel was the split and chalky riverbed: he walked it like the length of a spine.

*

Remarking or observing the dried riverbed – observances on a dried riverbed. Parched hieroglyphs. The river water leaves desiccated traces. The water-poet. Burn-carrier; water bearer. The riverbed is incendiary, ignited, a dry riverbed on fire, awash with flame, watermarked in flame. Rivers of fire. The spirit becomes more complex as a substance. The dry riverbed ignites under certain conditions of wind; or a specific incendiary wind, blowing across its dry and hieroglyphic surface. A condition of self. Wind-watered selfhood, immolated rivers. And the water became as fire. The riverbed as scorched and blackened by currents of rose-coloured flame.

Perhaps the 'Sequences for a Tariff' are the metonymic

objects: the occiput bone of the lion skull, represents all of the lion's observance in reverse... the back of the head... a fragment of lion fur, of skull, representing the whole of the lion's experience, or leonine experience, or hunting experience.

Dante's mnemonics embedded in the presence of one, metonymic and Neolithic element. The drowned lion in the wood, in the waterfall, in the cave, on fire with the sea, scorched with the sea. At the very centre of recollection: the drowned lions' den. This is the image. It all leads back to the crashed banquet. And yet, is this simply a system for forgetting? The imprint that repeats and repeats and then is catalysed by other elements: rogue imagines... the turn of a heel, the colour of a sheet, the tone of a voice, the back of a head that looks as if it should belong to a certain person, a certain figure, but doesn't. Everyday imagines. And then returning to the place, the locus, over and over. Or when loci suddenly turn into cruel theatres of memory – instantaneously and in the flesh, not imagined places constructed in the mind's eye.

*

Now, the ford is swollen and I cannot think he stashed the packet of writing with his walking stick here... Varg scuttles around as rain begins to fall. I look under the wet stones of the bridge among the ferns and mosses, near the lichen-covered trees and see a branch or something upright stuck in the mud. It is Kristján's staff with the paper package tied to it, sticking out of the fast-flowing water. Varg watches me from the bank and then, as if to assist my will, plunges in and retrieves the wooden staff in his mouth. I pat him down and grasp the marker: this water register with the level marked and its soaked bundle looped with string and scored with pencil, this tariff, this offering:

*

Speak into cries. Rushing, turned wolf. Dead, vulnerary dark. The very desert entered hooves: crumpled. Lamentations underfoot. Ruthless pathway. Took hunger of love, seemed to look. The hope beast cry. Still way wood. Abandon will, who that pass breath. Howl stools thrust apart, answer the wordbone process. The cry, not freshly made, digs into rugged colour. Glimmers in fatly wild on lamp moon. Young, my squalor wolfish thumbed the light star sweat nervous back. Copulates half-baseless heart, time with wolf chamber: secret, stolen a heart. The bone which there lies dead to courage. Skin leaves, such sherd. Thicket-heart, thickening. Rubble-heart, digit pit: a broken digit of thickening heart. Sacrifice in the thicket – hunting. Vellum field. Pumiced hope finger. Wolf losses, heavy and turbu-lence. Dark comes in sense ritual that stains and moments the trial. Accusations spin on air-heavy waiting. Betrayal: scarlet comes up hours. Not jewel-wasted, the show in contempt: wheedled, ribbed, oiled roots. All lines shadow, wastrel leg and carcass-brindled. The whine, paralytic, tricks the creaks. Grim flesh cues, baseless star-awakening – come waterhole wolf, flanged of whip, of drawn dark-ness. The spin only now sweats weeds, intense. One small pulped, always survived. Lupine chattered, night-charred. And somewhere watered, sense blood in spoken, bewildered, prepared stamp thing. On secret air, ritual falls into tariff-housed presence pack.

STATION VI

The Derelict Monastery

(The Derelict Monastery is a flagged league of flattened stars whose mineral floor rings out with the single stirrup of a vanished knight: or a single stirrup that scrapes the length of the choir in a jagged cry. Here, the honour of death is abandoned for show. Knightless – is the knight reversed who, having progressed on his grim journey along the Bàs old coffin road, finds no place of rest in the monastery ruins and is now outcast. Its symbolism may refer to one missing blade, or one representing the sum of many. For me, it embodied the power to whittle those figureheads of my own making. There is only one sword. In the derelict monastery, I am not allowed to rest: a false burial ground as I have been 'knightless' and so this is a false station. Acumen. The associative object is a rusted sword: my penknife.)

HERE, WHERE THE NORWEGIANS kept the island for over 400 years, lies a rusted sword in the lichens. Fierce in this place: they possessed the island under its blade and they possessed the time; four harsh centuries, under its tang. Time and place. This unsheathed, mouldery weapon quietly remains next to the bones of its owner warrior. Both are vulnerable to the elements but as much to history. History will ravage their meaning, galloping away on a stolen horse.

He writes about the glinting sword of a sleeping Viking, coruscating in sunlit messages a revelation to any murderous watcher. There, the Viking warrior and his horse sleep beneath the earth, their throats slit, betrayed by light.

'There are those,' writes Kristján, 'who have met their goal in fire or water, but there are also those who, beneath the ground, are buried in their belief; who have found their death goal within the earth and turn among the shining stones.'

Here are remains – standing stones – cairns – burial mounds

– knowing stones – gallows stones – druid circles – all seeming-
ly irradiant from the sallow-earthed monastery ruins. But time
would make this a false arrangement: we cannot know the heart
of the dust unless we have tasted it ourselves, for the cairns and
the standers, the druids and the knowers are all older by far than
this blessed rubble whose heaped tombs show the usual skull
and crossbones (those corporate images of death) but are carved
out with other motifs: tinkler headstones all now overgrown with
milk vetch.

It is still possible to see Kristján as 'sword' – as his own morbid
instrument? Who will divvy up the stones with this tarnished
blade and present a miracle of his future?

His own, glinting blade glances out of my fingers and when I
pick it up it flashes in the sun: a pointed glare. Around the blade:
sheathing its length is the usual tract – his penned note from the
wind. His desperate collaboration:

*

Corpse-panning. Body in a sieve. Of its way, like pouch,
water insistent. Spirit-smoked dint stirrups. I midway me
untie, in upheld river storms. Air the shivering water, hands
picking, I reveal among more gold twigs. And only still
dip-flit banked decipher figure, mount together, as lower
fire alike, burn I for river and of it glowing dark, sink like
snow, dowsing bundles. Unsure myself, hold dying shal-
lows, thing-silence: anything kept through. The sun only
circle returns until bringing ground river up, walks nights
and day, becomes knees around mine and rises in the
sphere of sun and I, bending, reach deadhorse – a shake-
stepping, pulled travel, bronze. Then, because precarious
(uplipped stone over white divining bloated, black ground),
I am the mind in rings. Unlacing, find the golden imprint
upward the hours, the one watched, this to out eye-river.
I reflect on a strip then, for everywhere proper, half into
riverbed heavy my breaking, when horizon into light swollen,
heat of hold and light rocks or strange-quivered water
slowly turns. I slip, steady. Birds come to every scraped
neck. Myself tumble thin water to growing, pulling swifter

disappear, realising within branches – fingers – running long visions, dragging the water, heart-time middle water, like a boy that grows a month and tethered in trees against the mouth afterwards… branches underfailed kindness, way turned of that… In the turn: walking, weighing, dissolving my solid surface; the water flecks sitting, the stones had mid-soaking clothes soaked, baptised skin shallow. Another bright, else written water, lodged out wet first rods. So softening my undercurrent is only each branch, water to my horse on light, whether – as wind the worked leather – the watching rose, and outsifting words I silt-tongue the move. Slow the lifting bird deeds the muddy retract of foot here, like lack in scoop, in rocks. Water on darkened gold held in sump. I tree, my pulled leaving, and branches inside me and carefully to the rock larger at the form in aqua for packed pouch the clothing to fetched bank rising, using my sliding skin, uploosened from corpse-panning fine to hands, panning with patiently. Abandon money and flints of air-bitter birds – rugged colours fail.

STATION VII

The Wild Hawthorn Field

(The Wild Hawthorn Field is where my grave is dug by the Travailers and awaits me, as if I were the body language of a freshly dug poem falling into the plot as an augur of bitter histories: for is it not so that we need the past predicted as much as the future, which is memory's own desire. Sump represents a sacrificial field with a rectangular dugout grave which, in my mind, can be roughly transformed into the stanza on the blank field of the page. Around the pit, Travailers camp. This is a hawthorn or fairy field, variously occupied by Summer Walkers or Travellers who fished for pearls and spoke an old Gaelic. The pit may also be a firepit for visions, or a stage – possibly cut into the grass (or roughly built up, which leaves a flattened impression on the lawny surface) – on which a stage has left an impression. Here, the daughter of the wind, named for a wild, windblown, anemone greets me as the mysterious embodiment of no one, enabling her to move between worlds unnoticed. Now, hope grows wild with the promises of portent. What sacrifices should be made in the wild hawthorn field? Intuition. The associative object is a hole-cut cloth: my hunter's hat.)

IN KRISTJÁN'S BOOK ARE pictured the jongleurs and troubadours, the wandering minstrels and performers of mysteries and miracle plays, the tinklers and pedlars and Travailers, the motion-men with their marionettes and transparencies. They tell weirds, deaths and fortunes. Pilgrim strangers: peregrini mercatores, the farandman, the dustyfoots, caerds and bards, fools and players of the Fante-følge: the Scandinavian troupe of travelling harlequins. Dancers, tumblers, mimes, puppeteers moving on foot or by cart in their roving theatres. Hunters and trappers of laughter and tears. Violins, bagpipes, tin flutes, Carvers of horn spoons and woodenware, menders of tin. Sellers of salves and tinctures and remedies for the future. The Travailers speak an aristocratic Gaelic cant laced with Latin and French and their cover tongue is named *Beurla Reagaird*. Smokeborne laughter and laments among the tombs. Here one Travailer company will perform for us *The Fall of Kristján Norge: A Faustian Demonstration*, a dance of death staged in the Hawthorn Field:

FAA: 'He stands, face whitened in lead with cherry cheeks and a Fool's cap of otter skin. Who will find the otter stone?'

THE MOON: 'What do the Travailers want?'

FAA: 'Laughter in the fields.'

THE MOON: 'And what of their stoneground monuments?'

FAA: An ancient flour for estranged bread. A dough that rises into the moon's full face. An otter stone, puckered and floury. A Fool's features, pale and grainy with moon-struck flour.'

THE MOON: 'Faa, Faa and away! He will be pale with the devil's work, young Norge!'

FAA: 'We have daubed him foul and fair, given him a tide of mercies, ridden him into the wild sedges, covered him in tinkling bells.'

THE MOON: 'And still he dances with the horned one...'

FAA: 'Fear breeds in multitudes, the inner linings of his face. He is a silver nest in jet grasses, a buffoon who longs for release. Travails of the spirit-ravaged skeleton!'

THE MOON: 'Let me enlighten you, my friend. He keeps court with two women, a lion, a wolf, a boatman, his own reflexion, a donkey, a young wandering woman, himself alone, and the leader of the winds.

FAA: 'Who are these?'

MOON: 'All are beleaguered aspects of himself; all are the presence of poesis, the making of that encrazed art.

FAA: 'How indeed, does this fall out?'

MOON: 'Let our players reveal it to you. First we have the donkey, Asan.'

ASAN: 'I am half of the twin ass, the double fool, I bow and my brother dies: the limb of the birch took him to death. Now I come to you as Norge's vision – see, here is a second player come:'

GABRIEL: 'I am the lion of inspiration, whose courage is linked to the donkey's foolish vision. I roar and inspiring falls from the heavens – see, here is a third player come:'

DAUGHTER OF THE WIND: 'I am the softness of intuition who travels alongside, apace with breath, apace with visionary inspiration – see, here is a fourth player come:'

SLANE: 'I am the ferryman, the point of transition between all these elements and conditions of poesis – see, here is a fifth player come:'

VARG: 'I am the wolf of melancholy slipping around the legs of reason – see, here is a sixth player come:'

LUCIA: 'I am the bearer of light, of selfillumination, casting light on areas of difficulty, of darkness – see, here is a seventh player come:'

THE HAWK: 'I am the raptor of doubt throwing a shadow across small things from a height – see, here is a eighth player come:'

THE NORTHERNER: 'I am the wandering intellect, contributor to my companions – see, here is a ninth player come:'

SGRÒB: 'I am the presence of acumen, the unchivalric shrewdness – see, here is a tenth player come:'

MONMHUR: 'I am self-reflexion, the holstered mirror polished with illusion, the final player in our small exhibition.'

*

Daughter of the Wind... she has slight, capable hands and a cadence to her voice and fine, light brown hair that lifts in the breeze like topographies of smoke around her beau-

326

tiful, clear-eyed face... her stance is contrapposto, mostly, standing with her young brown-eyed son on her hip like a basket of pollen or a tinderwood bundle, as his small fingers grasp her hair like unstranded silks. The Daughter of the Wind steps forward into my mirror, alights behind my reflexion, and speaks to me in light currents of air: 'they will dig a pit of fire for you.' she says and the mirror surface ripples vibrantly; 'and they will lower your old voice into it and you shall writhe there like a song, a charm, a prayer, and your poem shall then become an altar and we shall drink to wine to it and rake the coals over as we dance softly with bone tambourines: see us now – the intent, fire-flecked faces, hands of chalk and eyes of rubbed gold with knowledge in our fingertips of reversals and hazards, retentions and submissions. We draw a circle wide in the mud, in the sand, in the mineral core, and light the peri-meter with torches that flare and spark in the fragrant darkness as our song weeps lower than blood and blows across the night sea of love, dispersals in the hedges, dis-persals in the copses, dispersal in the bracken, brushwood and boscage, when all our ancestors came upon us, rubbing seeds from the soft lawn of knowledge; rubbing time from the hindsight of the stars, rubbing hope from the broken land. One way, then, for the field verse to become a tomb. The second is an altar – not a pit, but an altar and on this you shall then be raised up in song and wine and made to perform, to dance on a chain. And this, shall be the nature of the poem. This is the stopping place: the pause: the rest in the thought as you traverse your island of empty rooms: these are the parameters of your living thought, ignited in blood, watermarked in flame.

*

Now to wear the hunter's hat, hung in the field on a wild haw-thorn...in it scrolled his message from the dead like a long prayer, a hint, a summons. Bewilderment stuns the heart, the hands... (I daren't put the hat on) and when you swallow, you swallow the bird of the heart... the rigid bird that scrapes the innards... and here, his unscrolled penitence, here, his writing, on its knees:

*

My raptor cloth on, carvers of moon. Sedges, hawk grasses, flute staged: wind's bird-bundle song. Silver-floury, my light. Full birch as daubed illu-mination, impression of court chain, hands casting dispersals, mirror work. I hold the penitence horn, does took conditions, mimed prayer twin, violin. Smoked prayer. Minstrels breed you in slip-ping brushwood, skeletons en-crazed us: breeze, bells, poems. One, final rubbing draws charm. There, grinning, your caravan dead. Lodestone squalor, losses feign to code silk glimmer. Vibrantly stranded darkness. Beer theatres, chalk anemone, tum-blers, woodenware. The mineral shall come a-wandering in a Gaelic of silks. Thread-borne, baskets, rakes. Alight young corpses, donkey hunter's stage perform a hawthorn from his to field, intellect is puppeteer to keep the dead player up. Wandering shadow-second in pale cherry voice. I sing fourth laughter, fished shrewdness pearls and the light fire players. His stone, moonstruck aspects swallow. Bread eyes of the foot, the fair man light and daughter, dance you the perimeter. Cheek tambour-ines fortune: they and stone? The boscage air, player by the coals. He roughs on a donkey, companions in the hope. Sump love dances mirror-rectangular of your pollen, your field. Tinted fire and the flammable moon, ancient land wandering unnoticed, the blood troubadour. Wide hat jon-gleurs own ninth the hawthorn. Double harlequin scrapes the altar, motion made from otter bewilderment. Darkness performers: tinderwood, woodenware. Half-presence, courage. All you, foolish heart roar, holstered mirror, blood with face. Daughter laced in deaths, strangers wind but the moon put visionary features and whitened summer-hole: see, beautiful. Bird traverse pilgrim, unnoticed sell-ers whose tinctures fire the flame. Birds traverse the pil-grim, the dough heavens. Buffoon spoons, tinkling coffin carts, writhe vision-walkers.

STATION VIII

The Old Whaling Station

(The Old Whaling Station is the wrecked interior: no longer hunting itself, the cavity of demon lies fallow. Self-preservation is turned to wax plugs: plugging oracle, ventricle, cochlea, nostril, anus, tear duct, meatus, larynx: this last that muscular cat, related to panthera leo, who haunts the vicissitudes of emotion. Of whaling see another man's curse. Meat Spirit – here lies the old whaling station where the vast, waiting bones creak and rub at night. Apparently a demon-haunted quarter where malignity lingers within the rusty-hinged outbuildings, the old whaling station draws me back to my own roots. Dangerous to have become subterranean. Underground necropoli, occluded and occult activities, graves dug. The pit of the whale carcass – monstrous. Doubt. The associative object is a Neolithic painter's belt: my belt.)

THE SOUTHERN PORTION OF the island is run wild, overgrown with Sea Maram and Sea Sedge whose roots bind the sand. Here and there a stand of willows; some shrubby elders. The soil is very thin; there is hardly enough to dig a grave and the dyke wall is supported by embedded whale skulls. In previous times, when there was a big cull, the islanders used the blubber and flesh for lamp oil, bootlaces, leather and manure and the bones for carved knitting needles, scoops and spoons... when a large herd of whales was beached the men would carve their initials into the skin which bled brightly in the sea air: a cruel lettering. Still, it was once the island vocation. A man denied work on a whaler had his mother curse the whales with a thimble buried in the surf and not a creature was caught or landed for over a year... such was the witch's curse. Now the rusted chimney stands like a marigold-coloured obelisk.

His mother and father had met on Shetland, Kristján told me; his father was captain of a Norwegian whaler and his mother the daughter of the shore-station owner. He was at home here, in the old whaling station, where I have not been since he vacated the island. I need it now as if it were his death mask – as if it were a way of tracing his contours in the wood-filtered light. It smells of kerosene and stale paper. A bird has died near the window, clawed feet curled like ribbons. I realise I have been moving for a month as if in water. That the exhaustion of his disappearance has made me feel as if I were pushing against the air like a strong current. All those tracks we make pushing across the unenvisioned expanses of shore and wood, moorland and shoreline. Most of it done in sleep. All the prints in air of hand and foot ploughing down to floorboards, concrete, rock. My tracks were weighted with the sea, with the black peat of the island, with the wind: with the voices.

I move the sunlamp in here – find an old print, a photograph: the water darkened behind him, as he plunged ankle deep into the near-water of the sea. No, I thought, looking at the image, it was the wet plunge of the sand filling as fast as his foot had left. It filled in again like desert sands, indifferent to the tide. He died, I thought, as he lived, in the desert. Black plunge holes in the sea floor. A merman taking his first steps after losing his tail. A man walking on a marine moon. A man tracking the soft dust of his own memory. A man having his trace filled and refilled as he made it. A man walking into the earth whilst sinking into his shadow. Some ice is kept hot by extreme cold. Some is kept frozen by extreme heat. I never knew which and he enforced his charge in the smallness of everyday actions so that it was never traceable, never quite replete. Picture: a moment in a man when beauty passes through him. People talk of ghosts of the deceased. He was occupied by shades of his own making. Who stalked that face... all passing through... I put the photograph down. This image pales to vanishing under the blue ray of UV. It looks like a smudge of carbon on sunbleached snow. I pin it up in the whaling shed and watch it into blackness as the sun goes down outside. I finger the piece of baling twine: his Neolithic painter's belt wrapped, then loosened from this screed of writing:

Hot darkness, squibbing, flushed white. Stars occur higher up the body tranquil ribs. Lurking pallor-works thresh. Last visible cooking stage. Imagined spirit, I bore vision-images: occupied the wood, a wound-house reversed. Spirit is out-with, I age as meat pushing through my own spiritude. The down acts razed my scrubmeat, but pushing Spirit-ravaged mansion, time repeats regret, star-like things burnt. Housed in some to the body's mansion stars me, occupied by signs. Memory's for age. Through me, lurking old are no scabrous demons. Memories of seeing spirits, statuettes by art outside my own, mine cetus. Not of Time: forgetfulness stolen. Smoke some motif, heal starlight bone. These the signs – spiritude as smoke. Wounds smoke forget-fulness. Sequences say not, the move this passing body's burns. Memory's scrubwood of bored planks. Burns meat: in repeated, stolen sequences. Bone stars, pushing picture vision. that the larynx related haunts longer last of muscu-lar of wrecked turned interior see curse hunting meatus ventricle emotion vicissitudes itself this no oracle-tear. Nostril, fallow, plugs preservation-cochlea another whaling cavity. Black my dyed skulls, old tide whaling. Hair is deceased, is ploughing the line and old flesh.

*

There is a harsh wind that whips the hair into my mouth as I trudge back along the shoreline: whipped in to silence me.

You don't know how, but doubt becomes pure, as if your ghost – if such a thing concurrently exists – might only be an emotion. I know I will haunt Jeanie first with light and then with consternation – but I don't know that it will be me to go on without her. Whatever should have killed me lets me live. So I am survived and walk the beach and the water until I find out what Kristján wants. What he is trying to tell me. Then I need Hafoc stunningly and run hard through the bitter darkness. I return to find her sleeping, a small burnished living being bundled up in an old overcoat. I touch the nicotine-stained fingers of her hand and she stirs and turns, lemon-gold hair printed to her cheek like a shining hieroglyph. We sit together watching, watching in, the last parts of night.

STATION IX

The Cave Behind the Waterfall

(The Waterfall of the Blood is a premonition or knowledge of my death and how it may be acquired as a roaring and sentient knowledge, when bundled up in the tariff offering of an old, bewildered overcoat. This skin contains morbid knowledge and demonic forgetting when fermented in a frenzy of vision. Taghairm – the wounded centaur is, for me, the dying centaur (another reference to my birth date as aligned to the archer in Western star sign systems) who is the slain self and undergoes the ritual of the 'taghairm', wrapped in a steaming animal skin, to gain a vision. Here is the part-beast figure of the demi-god, perhaps. In most accounts the skin belongs to a bull, but I previously used the stag and now draw on the wounded centaur – partially as the crucified and foolish ass of the Roman graffito, partly as the classical arrow-slain mythic figure. In the cave I have a vision of my own damaged appearance, or skin, as a pointer for recollection of what lies beneath. An anatomy of memory. Vision. The associative object is a woven breastplate: my overcoat, which represents a flayed skin.)

HERE I AM IN the cavernous chamber behind 'Eas na Fola': waterfall of the blood, with its whetstone (or altar: perhaps this sea cave, like so many, was used for formal Christian worship). Pottery shards and arrowheads scatter the cave floor around the old whetstone. These inner recesses are reached through a narrow corridor of rock named 'the narrows of confusion' by the islanders of the past and this inner chamber is as silent as the centre of a seed. On the walls are Neolithic rock paintings of deer. The outer, wetter cavity of the cave has a natural spout in the rock-ribbed ceiling: when the tide is high water sprays water the hole like a leviathan, creating a spurting fountain in the turf above like a spring. Rock doves flit in and out whose calls create a web of noise just about discernible in the narrows of confusion.

Then silence falls.

The taghairm: is the sound of the touch by echo; a spiritual quarantine. 'TA' & 'GHAIRM'. Here are its roots in place, house, weapons, exhortation: to select or choose – a summons and an echo. A spirit cry. None touch the dead. And the wearer is bound up, it seems...tied at the ankles, wrists and waist (though some say the neck) called the binding of the narrows: ceungul nun tri chaol. I can say I was bound by the throat and in the throat and that no choked echo emerged from my larynx, bound as I was by Monmhur in my overcoat... a wax-dipped garment. I can now ignite it at will and it flares wildly in varying luni-solar colours. I would like to pour moonlight through these seams of salt, sipped at by an old sea, seething with magic. This will be tomb garb for departure to the under-world: it has a collar of wicks at the throat and wick cuffs at the wrists for a wearable 'fireoglyph': a flaring needfire of a winding sheet or wax-shroud. Monmhur will bind me up in it, with pledgets for my bleeding eyes.

*

Returning here is a strange sensation: I half-expect to see Kristján bundled on the altar, wild-eyed and catatonic and am suddenly frightened when I perceive a mound in the darkness, wave my candle light across it... my blood pumping fear into my vision... approach it with great care and find it is his overcoat, folded up and on it is pinned a drawing. And here the donkey comes, from the executed philosopher Giordano Bruno no doubt, but also from Kristján's old print of a Roman mockery. I lift it up to the candlelight. It is a black and white hand-drawn copy of a graffito, a horse or donkey-headed man being crucified. His arms are spread like wings.

'The fool,' he has written on the back of the image, 'is the crucified horse – no: the crucified donkey, the foolish ass. And his cap is thick with thorns: in that tradition and swirls with the endless dance, in another tradition. Or the stag with his

readymade crown. Or the hind: rearward: posterior. A reversed
centaur':

*

I sperm this flame. As sand is the subject for death. As
corpse is the subject for blood, or defile. Vision body-
flame numbing for accident. Lightning reflects image-
corpse fired in the fractured dark, shocked sphere. Saw-
seared dug cadaver, hazed into breath. And reverse dark-
ness consumed. Sand-sucked is the darkness in which
colour is numb. Whose arrow-glossed is trust. Whose aim
is dust. Whose heart is trampled sawdust. Bloodied flank;
lodestone bloody. Throws sperm, teeth, arrow. Dust lines
darkness and seer is rough image and struck, whet jugular.
Hanging rings on teeth. Is water laughter. Arrow-seared.
Sand whines; trust aflame, yet itself throat-eats this squat
nest of consumed cave, the waste earth of colossean broken
in his blood, silver turns, mud own dark heart – a blood-
centaur sear. Scraped the circle dust, pierce-imagined cen-
taur: the speech of stain's flowering. Hanging tryst, burnt
has throat: jugular mansion streams soil. A wet digit mirror
by which laughter in quarantines is lame. The flame is
clutched and in defiled spools. Orator hens tower the house.
The sight mirror, end-trampled. A citadel of swabbed
muscle. In memory river: ribboned corpse. The pit, in
end-lame grasses break in wristed clod. I make the sawdust
arrow-soul into hunting; honey to coach colour-bone. Snow-
numb, sound marrow, flame-face circling water-skeletal
madrigal. Last fighter galloped off and hazed in sphere.
The end centaur. Hidden is the jet arrow. Is of lens-
thumbed, made blench in white. Killer it away: cracked
dust, knotted arrow, sleeps against contorted amphitheatre
bleeds. Death throat is hair code is finger hooked. Quivering.
Horoscopi in bestiarum. Is hooped back from decision.
Quarter, half, full, century fathom. Book-licked tension.
Fruit falls from sight. Wax of heart encloses the honey-
comb. Black dew of honey-sealed sight. Do not slacken
sight: teeth: tears: blood. Sand of flame smeared on a heart
for defile-sifting thicket.

*

335

'Was Kristján's wax-melting to create this cerecloth or wax-dipped shroud of his overcoat?' I ask Jeanie, unfolding its stiff and whitened wax seams.

It was as if he were last of the graveyard watch – the 'faire chlaidh' – with three thousand of the dead summoned, traiking out to the fields in those thousands, incanted over by the language of birds.

She looks at me solemnly with those thought-burning eyes; 'it was his apparatus, his dress for the afterlife,' she says, 'he has been on a journey to *our* underworld.'

*

No, it was the water that talked and roared like a summons, like Columba roaring his prayers as a lion and his blessings as a thunderstorm. The demon that came…was Monmhur …was myself…was my gagging and choked reflex: my guttural reflexion… my mirror of falling water, like a single, roaring note.

Then there is the bumping the buffeting of the hips of a person on the banks of a boundary river – to agitate, I think, to knock the bone and musculature sideways, sluice the blood back and forth and then procure from this profound unsettlement a frenzy of visions. Or pounded with a birch branch or baton… a wooden wand for this disturbing of sense…

*

I now recall Jeanie's dream: the irradiating birch canoe balanced on the waterfall – his nautical library; reams of birch paperwork scrolls scrieved under a boatlike new moon; the birch tinderwood bundle of the lunar fool on his peregrinations singing to the high and dark, avid night sky; and the birch branch that killed Asan, the smaller donkey, the sacred ass, and the painted stags dance before my eyes in the flickering candlelight, bobbing and tilting in a Neolithic cinema of dreaming.

But here, pinned to the waxy lapel is a withered stem… a

personal clan badge made detrimental... a poet's twig and it is the rowan for demon-beating and the framework of visionary mattresses, on it the freshly-skinned hide was spread – Kristján's hide: his overcoat, his cerement, and I am overwhelmed by knowledge so that I grasp his wax-coated garment, the scrawling and the photograph and bewildered by memory, stagger out of the cave mouth.

STATION X

The Walled Monastery Garden

(The Walled Monastery Garden is overgrown with branches, grasses and rubble; its outer boundary wall tumbled down, scattered with bonfire remnants and rotted planks: walkways among the tombs. Here is the death and smoking pyre of religion, whose belief rises into dusk. Here the wounded angel gathers up the broken and smoking kindling of religion in allusion to the star-ravaged wood of the third sequence. This is a site of hermitage, where, chained to a wild plum tree, the angel figurehead stands – washed up from a wrecked ship whose wife and son of the captain drowned. The old mariner tombs are here, overgrown by nettles among the barren fruit trees. For me, this is a hermetic bewilderment of blue flame: a contained and diminished illumination. As now self-aware, I am still the fallen angel trying to rescue its own image reduced to the behaviour of a scavenger, vulture-like as the image burns. Redemption may be possible. Illumination. This is the final stage of my deathly procession. The associative object is a smoke-filled bone: my tobacco pipe.)

THE TOMBSTONES STILL SPELL out messages in worn lettering like so many children's blackboards, sitting upright in the turf, with strange spelling and coded meanings: D E O...

Perhaps this is where Kristján got his idea of Neolithic letters from, wandering among the skull-carved tombs, making rubbings of the inscriptions. *Neolithic lettering from the mariner tombs: Z, H, P, S, X, D, E, O: Zachariah, Hector, Phail...*

Here is his stone coffin lid, slightly ajar to reveal the depths of blackness within...

> where the lettering falls the thickest in deranged scratching: less glyphic than febrile evidence of desperate escape. To be locked into the tomb alive and petition in bloody fingertips, as a frenzied scribe, the rights to one's own escape. Or the lid as the blade of the scythe, glinting in

deathly fields of lunar corn, the mirror as the axe head, the maiden blade, scored with the lettering of execution.

The deepest point in the thicket is thought. Religion, relegere – the latter thought to originate from picking up or collecting wood. Enheduanna, lunar priestess with prayer poems to the moon. The moon, to measure (etymology) and connected to 'me', to cut down grass or grain and this can be connected to one man and his dog, went to mow a meadow and the man in the moon who carries a bundle of thorn (legere – also to cut or strike down) and religion, the bundle of twigs.

Caesura comes from the Latin 'caedere' to cut down, which is evolved from the root word 'kaedid', meaning to strike. From this root word various evolutions include: avicide: 'slaughter of birds' gives us: 'chisel, decide, circumcise, precision, scissors, suicide'. The Celtic calendar with equivalent Ogham strikes for the relevant letter plants. Perhaps, related to its etymology, caesurae could be read as trees cut down? Starting with spring, here we have the beithe, luis, nuin – the first three letters of the Gaelic alphabet: birch, rowan and ash: I II III.

The Cabbalistic alphabet was given by god who taught its wisdom to the angels. They in turn were commanded to tutor Adam so that he might be enabled to rise up from his fall (cadere). Enoch was given the position of scribe and while God still walked the gardens of Eden, Enoch recorded all the comings and goings of both men and gods in the precincts of the garden He was rewarded for his work by deification and is now considered the fundamental and archetypal influence on the Egyptian Thoth and both Mercury and Hermes in the classical myths. This triumvirate persona enabled the Renaissance manifestation of Hermes Trismegistus, the founder of Hermetic science to the great Medieval and Renaissance alchemists who suffumigated mirrors for esoteric messaging.

*

The night air here is tinted like smoke; a mirror wiped by time. Nocturnal fusions of the tinctures of the stars: those of illumination and power: those which create a seed of scent. Here the tindersticks are perfumed with bitterness and burning, suffumigated in sorrow and wisdom and piled up in pyres of intent. We see their smokes rising, co-mingling with fragrant sense. Here, the wounded angel, in sacrifice and sentiment, has curses pronounced over her decaying head. I have found the smoke-filled bone – his tobacco pipe – and the last tract of writing wrapped around it, along with the familiar scroll, pushed into the tongueless hollow of the angel's mouth:

*

Collecting wood of the word: ruminate. My wood has bitterness. The taciturn forest. Roiled and scabrous. Statues of tree substance: is tree, is forest. Sweet woods, tasted by the eyes, blenched and outpouring. In my moon of words, burns the sun. In my words of wood, burns the moon. In my word of moons, burns the sun. It is done, the reckoning, grained legere. This twig is wine, this twig bread, this twig beer, this twig meat, this twig fruit, this twig honey, this twig water. Horoscopi: timewatchers. Cuts the teeth of my senses. Gather, collect, cremated bones. Reads: mirror wood. Wood burns: my pelt. Clean the senses in this lion tree: wood, sun, taciturn moons, words, eyes, blenched honey, word-cremated wine skin. The fruit-greased twig: twig-tasted watchers' time. In smooth thirst, horoscopi bread, finely ground. Gather bitterness, shave my words, water-centaur, meat statue. These bones and pouring skin, this cleaned word. My wood cuts: legere, moon burns cylindrical and smooth in forest stone, rolled. Sweet, this teeth-grained moon is twig unborn – Pumice-shaved water, stone burns my moon. Flat colour burns vellum – stone is time-rolled putridness and smoothed, my eyes wash word-blasted statues. Retrieving animal sense: colour in the raised roughage of co(r)pse, I swell on time. Star-blasted kindling, wood senses stand broken, ravaged.

*

I pocket the smoky paper and pipe and light a cigarette. Dusk is falling, perhaps to rise again tomorrow like the fallen angels, perhaps not. Here is a last assignation defined in Kristján's uneven hand, a rogue scrap from the mound of papers that lie at my feet; I pull off my other glove to read it:

*

Now, the bonfire is nearly built and the dry weather this past week has helped. She has barrows of paper lying in piles: each kept in place by the weight of a stone like the stone placed on the stomach of the night-composing bards of old. The wheelbarrow will have one more journey or so left, from the old walled garden up to the lighthouse steps, and then she will bring the figureheads down. Or perhaps they will drown them, as Hafoc might suggest. Luce could wish for more kindling, though, and bends a branch on the wild plum tree: tuning fork of my desires. It is rotten. Now for the shovel work to cut out its roots and then she takes the axe to it as the sun bleaches the grey early afternoon, only to find the rusted chain ploughing underground – tethering the weatherbeaten angel. Her impatience startles me as she chops the rusty links and tilts the angel onto her back. She is dry underneath and leaves a sacred, arid patch with nothing but insects to moisten the earth. Her dense heavy measure, the massy weight of her will help: she will be my angel of the bonfire. Now the pyre is built high with freshly hacked plum wood and Luce heaves her on top, like a lifeless Jeanne d'Arc. She slots my papers like sheaths into the gaps and lights the bottom tier of this five foot stack of kindling, wood and scraps... it will be many more hours before it takes and so she'll wheel the barrow back toward the lighthouse as the angel, unchained, watches Luce go, though her eyes are sightless and her wings pocked with holes. What can now communicate my deepest sorrow?

III

THE NARROWS OF CONFUSION

XVII

FIND ME IN THE old monastery garden, stoking a bonfire. The wild plum tree has at last decayed enough for me to hack at its roots and cut out more fuel. Fire crystals turn as I rake over the glowing ashes, mingled with flakes of snow. Varg sits on his haunches watching me, eyes glittering, utterly still. I have the last barrow of Kristján's papers and the correspondence card from Hafoc flits into the air as I tip the pile onto the fire. That small card of her undertaking to visit, to sail across to the island on Slane's boat. Turning to uproot the plum tree again, my spade hits metal, and I pull up a rusty chain… the angel figurehead. Without her tether, she falls forward, but the blighted tree is now dug up. I pause for a moment, my breath clouding the frozen air, and hobble around her, contemplating. The base is rotted away. Unsalvageable.

There is no more time. The stitches in my thigh have slowly become infected and I must return to the mainland for treatment. However, Hafoc tells me she has finally pieced together Kristján's instincts and that she will fill me in this evening on his system, once I have prepared the bonfire.

Strewn across the ground are various timbers: the birchwood branch that killed Asan, diced; an old pair of split wooden clogs and a small door made from a coffin lid, fitted to the whaling station outhouse that was blown off last summer by the storm. I couldn't get it to fit the privy frame again and wheeled it down here when I remembered it stashed with the winter fuel supply in the station log stack. Here too, are the small, split oak beams salvaged from the ruined mansion; a collapsed child's desk with its strange ink stains, an old ripped kite with a picture of a stag printed on it like a heraldic shield, and a pile of moth-eaten blankets from the storeroom. All these feed the fire I'll tend, along with the carcass of the lion which Hafoc and I carefully lifted from its small lighthouse tomb and wheeled along the coffin road.

I survey these assorted fragments looking like disarrayed parts from a blueprint for a sepulchral barque. Then I load them up, sweating in the late afternoon sea mist that wraiths the damp holly bushes. Lux of gilt: halcyon lux: auric. The sun's fire-eye ignites the brume in clouds of gold, so fiercely blonde, I shade my sight. In this fire-gold atmosphere, the sea beating like a dream against the shores of my task, I perform the final touch: I pull off my gloves and drag the angel on her chain onto the bonfire apex where she lies in a cradle of smoke. She is much lighter in my arms than I would have thought, and I mount the ladder like a steeplejack raising a fallen angel to god. Blue smudges the gold in rising smoke, but it will be a good few hours before the stacked pyre takes and the flames lick around her.

I painfully climb down the rungs and leave the kindling to smoulder in the snowy, darkening air which turns mallow as the sun sinks putridly into the harsh sea as a wan moon rises, and stump away with the empty barrow, wheeling it along the old coffin road before darkness envelopes us both. Tomorrow will be the burning of the other effigies, I think to myself, as Varg slips, a shadow among shadows, toward the monastery bell and then back to me again. How the wheelbarrow lends a rhythmic creak to the dusk, how a small, leafy scrap of correspondence lifts in the wind, taking Kristján's words with it, his last annotations of summer and smoke and disturbance.

*

The skin of the star and then, its underlying structure, is the stuff of my enquiry. Etymological cosmos-making. There is 'stiff', or 'stark' and then there is 'sterphos: hide, or skin'. Though themselves post-mortem, the linguistic soil which 'star' is buried in holds crazy richness. I want to flay the hides or skins of these figures, to reveal their underlying syntax. Constellar anatomy. In these 'stark' moments, far from feeling myself 'ravaged', my atlas is a friend and we go out hunting together, in the dark, through stippled skies... reams and reams of stellagraphia issuing from my thoughts, compelled to undergo the trials of star-craft. For wounding (or ravaging), I must stick variant starn clusters together and allow them to be reversed as metrical lines. Centauri and Sagittarius and Sagitta, the arrow, can all morph under the skin of the poem in a prosthetic physiognomy, a sack of stellar bones and muscle giving rough and strange shape to the appearance, body language and appearance of the centaur. As in the 'Star-Ravaged Co(r)pse' these stars ravage their own physical environment as they pass through their self-perception. My true aim is flayed galactic verse. Like a star, I am clothed in an image which means my underlying pattern can be recognised and learned... but the outer image: of a worn-down, reclusive poet, is no longer needed. The configuration 'centaurus' has no need of a centaur. What use is a half-man/half-horse to a constellated syntax of expired cosmic radiance? The centaur is only of use to the meaning, to the recollection of those stippled groupings. What use is Ophiuchus? Unless the stars died to procure the myths, sacrificed on the great storytelling ground of every culture. And so, my celestial metre shapes the skin of the image by arranging fragmented, constellar anatomies beneath the surface of poetry. What is really meant, has nothing to do with the metaphor, the allegory, the simile... what is really important is the bludgeoning presence of starcraft beneath, fading to give the image light.

XVIII

WHEN I RETURN, HAIR thick with woodsmoke, fingers ashy and numb, I find the lighthouse empty – I think. Something hollow in the air. I trudge up to the second floor after pulling my boots off and pause for a moment, listening. There is a faint fluttering and I remove a glove to help the small bird that flits against a stairwell pane, take it up to the lantern room, draw back the screen and release it into the darkness from the balcony, off into the snowy gloom. Then, turning inward, I descend the steps again – 'Jeanie?' I call and shunt the fourth floor door open… it is heavy with obstruction. For a moment I see nothing in the darkened room but then, of course, Hafoc is there. She turns toward me, silhouetted in the small candle flame, and I instantly know something is wrong.

'What are you doing?'

She speaks feverishly in gutturals, in uneven tones, 'I can bring him back, Luce, I can bring him back,' she keeps repeating, down on the floor on her knees, scraping together the mound of ash into a sticky sort of form. I look at her, aghast.

'Stop it, Jeanie,'

'I can bring him back, Luce – Kristján – you don't understand.'

'Well, tell me then, tell me. This will keep.'

She stands up, clutching her paste effigy, gazing at me, wildly.

'Stay there, then,' I say and go down the stairs to get a couple of oil lamps, swinging them up again with a huge light flaring up the metal stairwell. I approach the room of paperwork and going in, set down the lamps and stand at the desk for a while, smoking. Hafoc has arranged the sequences in some kind of chronology and laid Kristján's notes alongside. Surveying drawings and diagrams he'd made of the circular room with its figure-heads, I tip the ash in my hand for want of an ashtray and leaf through the sheets, turning them over.

*

This ash perturbs me the most. If I could be regrown from the ashes of myself in some sort of receptacle: encouraged to emerge from the starting point of an ashwater paste, then all of this – if reduced to char – might evolve into voice and bring to bear a proxy, a stand-in. With this, the Sluagh could be assuaged: the wind of voices that draws out terror from my blood. I did not know the depth charge of fear I carried within me: that I only needed to hear the night-call for a resounding answer thumped out in messages from my heart-bludgeoned blood. This wind carries the dust of death: the teine sith: the flickering, blue light: the rising, cobalt cloud of dust. All this in the heart of the blue flame: the heart's fear turned to blood. This can be mixed with idolatrous ash.

*

Then, I get down to the roach and I scrub it out under my heel and take up the lamps. I'd get down to the rest later – and ask Hafoc what her feelings are. My shadow blooms violently up the inner walls as I mount the circular staircase, walking slowly. I am tired and I feel volatile. Time oscillates between us, Hafoc and I. Sometimes she seems to hold the wand of time and it is torpid, the turning. At other moments, I am passed this wand and time seems to leap from point to point without allowing us to take in the sequences between. Just at this moment, I am exhausted, cold and dirty. In a flash, I realise a whisky will cure me. I'll lure Hafoc out with the promise of a dram. If I am overdone, she is probably worse by now: unwell or strung out. Tomorrow it will all be done: the fire stoked, the remaining papers brought down and the figureheads wheeled to the old monastery garden for a ceremonial burning. Then, through Slane, I can have the lighthouse lantern fixed – get someone from the mainland – and Jeanie can stay a while longer, or return to Edinburgh and get away from all this endless hardship. Later, I think, after all this is over, we will have a drink together at the World's End and mark the time we spent recovering Kristján's work and honouring his wishes by destroying it.

349

I nudge the door open with my foot and the lantern light swells in the room offsetting Jeanie's estranged and enlarged features. I cannot quite accommodate the change that has taken place in her during the short while I was downstairs, as she now assumes a defensive position, gripping the figure in her arms. Even Varg, who stands behind her, snarls.

'What's this?' I say.

'You're not to take it away,' she replies in a raw voice.

I look at her, not understanding.

'What have you done, here, Jeanie?'

She gazes at me, through me, a moment longer. I pass her a cigarette and she takes it between trembling fingers, kneeling on the sand.

'I think you had better tell me, now. Take your time, have a bit more of your cigarette.' She nods slowly, like a child, and lets the figure slip into her lap. I squat beside her, tuck a strand of hair behind her ear.

'It is the ash,' she says, presently. 'I realised that his statue had got burnt. Only the papers with that part of the system survived: his system for forgetting. He is number III and that sequence is number III. So, I thought I would bring him back: if I made the statue from its ash...'

'A Roman concrete,' I suggest, not really following.

She nods in assent, 'yes, well, it's just a paste really.'

'May I have a look?' I ask, keen to get her to relinquish the object. She gets up, gathering herself.

'Yes, of course,' she says, 'here.' She passes it over and stands smoking, much restored. The scene is beginning to accrue a tang of the absurd as I examine the slippery effigy.

'It'll need to dry out, of course,' Hafoc explains to me, exhaling, 'I thought if the weather was fine tomorrow, it could go outside for a while. . . '

'Yes,' I say, 'but what is its purpose, Jeanie? Why have you created it?'

'I've already told you,' she replies, astonished. 'To bring him back. And we must recover his papers from the bonfire you've built. The whole thing can be reversed.'

'Reversed?' I say, suddenly very tired.

'We can bring him back,' she says evenly, squaring up to me, 'if we remake his burnt figurehead. It's all in the notes.'

'Jeanie,' I begin, 'you're worn out, the whole thing here has been an increasing strain. We are nearly finished – you could go home as early as the day after tomorrow – when Slane arrives, weather permitting...'

'To Edinburgh?' She laughs and her features look suddenly harsh, 'oh no, I'll need to be here when Kristján returns. You realise that, of course.'

'Kristján isn't going to return. I think you need to come down now and get some rest and tomorrow we can discuss it.'

She turns sharply, those hunting features exaggerated in the weird light cast upward from the oil lamps, and her shadow spreads rapidly across the ceiling. I involuntarily step back as she seizes a lantern and stands, staring at me. The atmosphere thickens.

'Well then, what?' I remark, slightly shaken, but speaking with a calm deliberation in order to break the tension. 'If you come down,' I repeat, 'we can have some coffee, whisky and talk it through now, tonight.' I step forward, as if to take her arm.

'You don't want him here,' she hisses, recoiling, 'you don't want to make him return.'

'Jeanie, I promised Kristján – he insisted we destroy his work. I have had my doubts, too, but it was what he wanted; he was quite emphatic about that.'

She draws herself up and stares at me. 'It is more than that,' she mutters, as if to herself, 'we are a part of Kristján's system. If we destroy it, we destroy ourselves.'

All the while, doubts are running like dry sand through my brain: why not draw all his considerable output together, there must be an archive somewhere that would want it...it is morally and artistically corrupt to eradicate... to ravage... his work. I can retain and measure the philosophic part of her argument:

351

we have, indeed, become a little subsumed, but that was inevitable, given the nature of the recovery. In this, as in all things, Kristján has demanded absolute focus, absolute concentration. Hafoc has broken under the strain. Kristján's will must be carried out – those were his final wishes.

'Tomorrow I will be removing the last of these things for the fire, but for now I am going down to warm up; I'm stiff and I'm tired and I need a good night's sleep and I suggest that you do the same. I'm going to need you, Jeanie. We have to take these figureheads down tomorrow, clear out the sand.'

I have already turned to go, with the statuette of Kristján still propped under my arm, when she lunges forward.

'You are not listening,' she says heatedly, 'we are not just a part of his system, we are aspects of Kristján himself.'

'No, Jeanie,' I reply, now putting the crude effigy down. I take her firmly by the shoulders. 'This is the end of it now.'

'Tyrant,' she says, in an abrupt shout, and frees herself violently from my grasp.

The rest is difficult to explain…somehow, in a single gesture, she'd knocked one of the standing figureheads which had toppled and then fallen. I saw in an instant that it was the demon as its head rolled across the sandy floor to rest at my feet, like the apple that had first rolled toward me when she stood on the shore and I stood in its thrall for a moment before realising that Hafoc herself had slipped and went toward her, Varg snarling, and grasped her again by the forearm.

It was then I saw she was quite dead and that her head had become severed from her compact body and I saw that I was now standing in a darkening pool of blood which Varg lapped up gently, almost tenderly, in the presence of my scream.

XIX

AT SUCH TIMES, OLDER instincts favour human anatomy: only the corpse is in control and you find yourself at defined moments becoming lucid within a series of physical actions. That is when you realise the cadaver allows the will, the soul, the spirit, the personality, to ride it out, until – when there is pure crisis – only the flesh rules and the other inhabiters take on the sole status of occupant: of ghost. Not borrowed time, but borrowed sense. At least, this is what I feel as I find myself now standing by the telephone, attempting to contact the mainland, in the keen understanding that I must have descended the stairs and that my seeing fingers and grasping eyes are leading all other attendant forces.

Whatever had transcended my everyday experience, up there, in the room above, must stay there for now, this anchor, my spiralling thought understands. I replace the receiver: the line is dead. Slowly, the assertion comes: I will telephone again in the morning. All else now, is a storm of colluding information: rapid-fire hunting: radical deduction: accurate stabs in an encompassing oblivion. What I need, I have – a sudden acumen of fierce and penetrating light. The circumstances are paused, it seems, in order to allow me to apply that enlightenment.

With that, there is a slow-passing flash across the window pane which cuts the outer darkness and I pause, disbelieving, waiting for the second pass. When it comes, I realise the lighthouse lantern is functioning again. Light crosses the room in a long sweep that raises strange shadows, but it is for a moment comforting: a searchlight, like my own inner questioning, and it breaks the monotony of the dark. I have a sudden and unwanted vision of the scene upstairs: Varg's bloodthirsty licking as the lighthouse beacon illuminates the blood-soaked sand; of Hafoc's head still issuing blood: the walls spurted and running: the figures monotone, then garish, in the lamplight... and think of the island as a living tomb.

This watchpoint increases my fear again, and I shudder. But, the districts of sleep, of dream, of distended and pooling time, now surge in, occluded by nightmarish torsion, the seething nausea of horror, as the vault-like chamber above rehearses its scene over and over. And so, I get hold of the bottle of whisky and take a long drink, then I manage to get a cigarette lit and smoke it down to the root, all the time swigging without feeling drunk, and after lighting a second cigarette, take a seat to witness what Hafoc had witnessed in Kristján's paperwork: to see what she had seen:

*

What, then, is a fallen angel – a demon? I now know it is the moving image within universal memory of a fallen angel. I am the image of a poet who considers himself 'fallen' – an IA or image with agency to catalyse a memory of myself in the mind of god. All contaminant parts are with me: the women, the wolf, the lion, the boatman... all parts of this diabolic mnemonic image. They are merely parts of my poetic presence. I am the image of a fallen angel who thought himself a poet who is merely a memory image in the mind of God, who himself is a mnemonic device, a stimulant, through his vanished son – Christ the poet, to a greater universal recollection. And so, this is what it is to be divine, to be damned. As an angel, I shall fall through the plight of memory's mere recollection and forget how to rise again. It is done.

*

At some point during this nocturnal study, I nervously get up. Outside, the wind is flickering and a small, strained draft bends the candleflame and uprights it again in the lantern prism. I trudge upstairs, too tired for nerves, to assess Hafoc's body and make a decision on the next day's actions. I can only put it down to a kind of psychic suicide, or that she'd fallen on something buried in the sand, some sort of blade, or that there must exist certain angles in the flesh and bone that, when force and speed are applied, cause severance. Such things cannot be unknown.

Varg's eyes in the dark are frightening as they catch the lamp-light: and I think for a moment he might attack me. He cowers, growling and then, as I speak his name, shoots out through the gap in the door and clatters down the lighthouse stair-frame. He will be cooped up in the base of the lighthouse until I can get to him, but first I need to inspect the corpse. The compact sand glitters on either side of my shadow as I hold the lamp higher up and let its globed light tell the truth of the room. When the heart stalls, it is not always in shock. There are times when the heart stops because it knows and, in the moment of recognition, has to right itself in alignment with this confirmed knowledge. Such is the condition of my heart and breath in that single instant: Hafoc's body is gone.

XX

SNOW BEGINS TO FALL in a sky newly emblazoned turquoise
and gold. Dawn is an armoury of burnished metal, mother-of-
pearl, and iridescent scarlet. The bare room glows. Shiveringly,
I put on Kristján's waxy old coat – the one folded up for burn-
ing. In my mouth, soured whisky and nicotine: I am wearing
exhaustion and nausea to face the dawn, slowly emerging into
recognition. And so equipped, I continue reading:

1 Port of the Dead	Port nam Marbh	Wounded Ferryman	Boatman	Transformation
2 Dead Lighthouse	Charred Arrow Shaft	Wounded Hermit	Monmhur	Self-reflexion
3 Old Coffin Road	Star-Ravaged Co(r)pse	Wounded Poet	Norge	Will
4 Ruined Mansion	Al Jab'hah	Wounded Lion	Cub	Inspiration
5 Gate of the Ford of the Dead	Sequences for a Tariff	Wounded Wolf	Varg	Melancholy
6 Derelict Monastery	Knightless	Wounded Knight	Sgròb	Acumen
7 Wild Hawthorn Field	Sump	Wounded Travailer	Gypsy	Intuition
8 Old Whaling Station	Meat Spirit	Wounded Demon	Hafoc	Doubt
9 Cave Behind the Waterfall	Taghairm	Wounded Centaur	Donkey	Vision
10 Walled Monastery Garden	Legere	Wounded Angel	Luce	Illumination

The diagram is familiar to me now, but I can't track its logic.
I see that we are all allocated, and that the figures in the room
above are given to each of us and that somehow Kristján con-
nected all this. What did Hafoc mean, when she said we were a
part of him? Allegorical inferences dance across the page. I light
another cigarette and, for a moment, the flame glows through
my fingers. Luce: illumination. Lighting the bonfire, tending
the lighthouse. Luce: illumination. All right. I cross my legs,
pull his overcoat tighter around me.

Hafoc's body vanishes? Obviously a hallucination on my part
– she must have slipped past me, downstairs, left the lighthouse
and is out, wandering.

What about the lack of blood…?

Another tack: the lion's body and the lion figurehead were
still extant after the lion died. All right. So the lion's death did
not affect its figurehead. No. But, Hafoc's injury was affected

by the damaged demon figurehead... ? Or was even *caused* by the severed demon figurehead... The figureheads are where the power lies. Kristján accidentally destroyed his own figurehead... yes. He follows the instructions from Monmhur, (self-reflection) and breaks the chaotic transference from the Sluagh down into tableaux vivants. From there he deduces individual imago agens and pools them to find the central, the defining image...which he then carves. In my case, it is the angel... the burning angel...

I pause in my calculations and relighting the cigarette, find that I cannot perceive my hand reaching for the match. I withdraw it, closing my eyes. Then I reach again and grasp the matchfolder. You must be exhausted, I think, utterly exhausted. So reassured, I open my eyes to strike the flame. The cardboard with its matchstick rows, remains in its place. I attempt this again and now, drawing up the coat sleeve, find my arm begins again to take shape as if reappearing in a fog. Beyond it, I can see my right foot has disappeared. I stand up, discarding Kristján's coat. Rays of sunlight pour in heavy shafts through my left hand. Now the thought is quickening, now it starts to take, licking with flame, and it is this: that two miles along the old coffin road and then another mile into the southern terrain of the island stands an unchained angel, rotted at the base, on a compost bonfire of paperwork and chopped wood in the walled monastery garden and that this angel figurehead must now be beginning to ignite as smoke pearls the tinder, and that my final, fatal, hope is that the snow is thickening; I can see it as the fiery dawn deepens, that the snow is whirling like motes of ash on the sea's horizon and that, if I am swift enough, I might leave now with Varg at my heels and stride out, down that old coffin road, toward the derelict monastery plot to save myself, the wounded angel, from cineration in wind-blown and snow-flecked cerulean flames...

RAVAGE

A FILM

https://vimeo.com/866469158

ACKNOWLEDGEMENTS

My sincerest gratitude to the Fondation Jan Michalski, Switzerland, for a writer residency in 2018, and to Creative Scotland for awarding me an Open Fund to write this book. I am very grateful to the Scottish Poetry Library for housing the Kristján Norge archive, in particular Asif Khan and Jill Mackintosh. My thanks to Dàibhidh Thomàis Ciotach Albannach for his support and advice. I should like to thank publisher and poet Aaron Kent; Nicholas Stone; Rebecca Sharp; Nancy Campbell; cinematographer Anonymous Bosch; photographer Zanne Chaudhry; John and Sue Hemingway; Ginny Fitzroy; Jake Pumphrey; Andy Peters: ships figurehead carver; and poet Steve Ely. My especial thanks to A.R. Thompson and Cairine MacGillivray. Greatest thanks to Nemonie Craven at Jonathan Clowes for her invaluable support and to Tom Josephine Redell for his young flair. Finally my deepest gratitude to Neil Astley, to whom I shall always be indebted.

'Fear Eun Lota' first commissioned by *Modern Poetry in Translation, Our Small Universe: Focus on Languages of the United Kingdom*, Spring Issue 1, 2019.

'Celestial Metre: Wounded Demon Decametre' was published in *How Do We Talk About Knives* (Seahorse Publications, 2023).